THE
SHAH BANO
CONTROVERSY

THE
SHAH BANO
CONTROVERSY

Edited by: Asghar Ali Engineer

Sangam Books

Sangam Books Limited
36 Molyneux Street, London W1H 6DS

By arrangement with
Orient Longman Limited
5-9-41/1 Bashir Bagh, Hyderabad 500 029

© Orient Longman 1987

Published by
Sangam Books Limited 1987

ISBN 0 86131 701 7

Phototypeset in Times by The Typesetters, Bombay
Printed in India by Shantadurga Printers Pvt. Ltd., Bombay

TABLE OF CONTENTS

v

Table of Contents

Interviews

Surveys

Opinions

Controversy over the uniform civil code

DOCUMENTATION

PREFACE

Muslim women in India, like all other Muslim women, have to bear the brunt of the existing social and economic oppression along with the discrimination and injustice — due to Muslim personal law. Of course there is no such thing as a uniform Muslim law and this makes the condition of Muslim women worse than that of women of other communities. It, therefore, has become necessary to think of a codification of Muslim personal law with the necessary changes in keeping with the spirit of human rights and social justice.

The Muslim colleagues in the JWP have often said that a uniform civil code is the only means by which women could be freed from the crippling shackles of personal laws. They were, therefore, very happy with the Supreme Court decision in the Shah Bano case. The JWP congratulated Shah Bano on her bold stand and expressed their solidarity with her.

What followed, in the form of the Muslim Women (Protection of Rights on Divorce) Bill, 1986, shocked everybody and the JWP organized meetings in all its centres to gather the opinion of the common Muslim women and men regarding the implications of the new bill. The popular demand, we understood, was to request the Government not to pass this new piece of legislation which takes away whatever rights a divorced Muslim woman may get under section 125 of the Cr. P. C. These recommendations were sent to the prime minister.

At this stage it became necessary to document the Shah Bano case, and to take note of the opinions and protests from various quarters including both fundamentalist Muslims and human rights' supporters. The Institute of Islamic Studies and, especially Mr Asghar Ali Engineer, were on the lookout for an organization interested in the Shah Bano case and its aftermath. He found, in us, just such a concern. We agreed to collaborate in bringing out this volume of material already published. We hope it will be of use to all those interested in this historic moment in modern India — when justice to discriminated women was at stake.

Jyotsna Chatterji
Associate Director
Joint Women's Programme

ACKNOWLEDGEMENTS

For permission to use copyright material, the editor and publishers are grateful to:

Badr-ud-din Tyabji for *Islam in India today* I & II (10–11 November 1985).

Mr Nikhil Chakravartty for *Secularism segregated in Rajiv's India* (14 March 1986).

Current for the interview with Baharul Islam (8 March 1986); *Surrender to fundamentalists* (8 March 1986).

The Dalit Voice for *The Hindu demand for a common civil code* (16 August 1985).

The Deccan Herald for *Forces behind the agitation* (10 December 1985).

Dr N.Y. Dole for *Constitution of India and the common civil code* (20 February 1986).

Mr Irfan Engineer for *Leadership exploiting masses* (25 December 1985).

The Indian Express for *The government must not capitulate* (7 January 1986); *Waiting for crumbs of relief* (21 April 1986); *Torn between religion & reality* (22 April 1986); *Good in parts bad in motive* (23 April 1986); editorial (8 January 1986); *Goa row over shariat law* (18 February 1986); letters (11 January 1986; 21 January 1986).

Inquilab for the interview: *Mohammad Yunus Salim* (23 March 1986); editorial (12 March 1986); extracts (22 December 1985); *Shah Bano's open letter* (13 November 1985).

Janmabhoomi Pravasi for editorial (23 November 1985).

Kesari for editorial (19 November 1985).

Mr Danial Latifi for *The Muslim Women Bill* (12–13 March 1986). Loksatta for editorial (30 November 1985); interviews (6 December 1985).

The Mainstream for *Don't we have it already?* (6 July 1985).

Manushi for *Pro-Women or anti-Muslim?* (no. 32, 1986).

Mr Kuldip Nayar for *Separate personal laws do not dilute secularism* (15 March 1986).

Mr Saeed Naqvi for *Shah Bano case: the real truth* (4 December 1985).

The Sangam Daily for editorial (26 December 1985).

The Statesman for the *Shah Bano verdict and Muslim law* (23 April 1986); *Most Muslims in U.P. opposed to bill* (7 March 1986); *Why Muslims resist a common civil code* (25 February 1986); editorial (10 March 1986).

The Sunday Observer for *The Supreme Court interpreted Muslim personal law* (8 December 1985); interview: *Dr Tahir Mahmood* (9 March 1986); *Behind demands for a uniform civil code* (23 February 1986)

The Telegraph for *Does the judgement justify agitation?* (1–2 October 1985); *An old woman deprived in the name of God* (22 December 1985); *The bill is a sin against the Quran* (4 March 1986); *Women's rights are far superior under the shariat* (29 April 1986); *Behind the veil* (2 March 1986); interviews: *Rajiv Gandhi* (12 March 1986); *Arif Mohammad Khan* (13 May 1986); *How do Muslims view the divorce bill?* (3 March 1986); editorial (7 March 1986).

The Times of India for *Personal law in Islamic nations* 14–15 March 1986); *Bill evades issues* (8 March 1986); editorial (28 February 1986)

The Urdu Blitz for interview: *Hemwati Nandan Bahuguna* (29 September 1985).

The Urdu Times for *Understand the problems of Muslims with an open heart* (23 May 1986); editorial (7 January 1986).

Every attempt has been made to contact holders of copyright but in some cases there have been no responses. The Publishers would be glad to hear from them to enable them to make acknowledgements in future editions of this book.

For stylistic reasons
certain spellings have been
standardized throughout
the book

INTRODUCTION

The Supreme Court judgement in the *Shah Bano* vs *Mohammad Ahmed Khan* case unleashed a great agitation among the Muslims. The agitation was compared by Maulana Abul Hasan Nadvi, President, Muslim Personal Law Board, to the Khilafat agitation in the second decade of the twentieth century. Truly in proportion and significance, the comparison is valid; but the comparison fails where intent and consequence are concerned. The Khilafat agitation brought about Hindu–Muslim unity and strengthened the movement for Indian freedom. The present agitation arising from the Shah Bano case, on the contrary, has sharpened the Hindu–Muslim cleavage and has weakened the integrity of the country. Secularism, too, is a casualty — almost by default.

Whether the comparison is valid or invalid, one must admit that this agitation is the biggest ever launched by Muslims, post-independence. Another parallel is impossible to find. It is, therefore, very necessary to analyse and understand the real import of this agitation, because it is an important indicator of Muslim thinking in today's India. The meaning and significance of the movement, I emphasize, is more political than religious. However, this does not mean that it is devoid of the religious dimension. Far from it. It has both religious and political aspects. We will first deal with the religious aspect. The political aspect will be dealt with later.

Shariat as divine and immutable

It is argued that the Muslim personal law is based on the shariat and hence is divine and immutable as the shariat itself is. The Muslims in general, and their leadership in particular, show great resentment to any proposal for changing the Muslim personal law (MPL). They justify their resentment by saying that no human agency can tamper with the injunctions and divine commands of the shariat. This debate has been on ever since the Constitution was framed and it is the reason that the idea of the common civil code had to be shifted under the directive principles of the Constitution.

Those who favour change have often pointed out that the MPL is operative in India through an enactment of Parliament and not *by virtue of divine command*. Thus Mulla says in his *Mahomedan Law*[1] that "the power of the courts to apply Mahomedan Law to Mahomedans is derived from and regulated by Statutes of Imperial Parliament *read with Article 225 of the Constitution of India*, but mostly by Indian Legislations." (emphasis in the original).

Fyzee also points out that the MPL are those Islamic civil laws which have been enforced on the Muslims individually in India . . . . There are four sources of the MPL: (1) Shariat or fiqh; (2) Laws made by legislatures; (3) Previous judgements; and (4) Customs.[2] Fyzee also points out that the Britishers in India abolished one Islamic law after the other. Slavery was abolished under the 1843 Act and hence the question of legitimacy of children born of a slave-girl (whether one married her or not) did not arise. Later, a law was promulgated in 1850 according to which the renunciation of Islam (irtidad) no longer meant disinheritance as it had under Islamic law. This law was followed by the enforcement of the Criminal Procedure Code 1860 which replaced Islamic criminal laws. And, in 1872, The Indian Evidence Act was promulgated in place of the Islamic law of evidence. Finally, in 1937, the Shariat Act came into force and the Dissolution of Muslim Marriages Act in 1939.[3]

Is the shariat divine?

The argument against interference in the MPL revolves around the divinity of the shariat. For the Muslims it is a matter of common knowledge and belief that the shariat is divine. In fact, to put the record straight, it is partly divine in as much as it is based on the holy Quran and partly human in as much as it is based on human opinion. The earlier component, based on divine injunctions, is immutable and the latter based on human opinion, mutable. That is why there are four recognized sources for the formulation of the *corpus juris* of Islam: (1) The holy Quran (2) Sunna (the Prophet's sayings and practice) (3) Qiyas (analogy) and (4) Ijma (consensus). Whereas the first two sources are divine (the second being semi-divine according to some) the last two are human. It was mainly on account of the last two sources that many

---

1. cf A. M. Bhattacharjee, *Muslim Law and the Constitution* (Calcutta, 1985) p. 77.
2. Prof. Asaf Fyzee, *Muslim Personal Law* (Urdu) (Delhi, n.d.), p. 11.

schools of Islamic jurisprudence came into existence (among the Sunnis there are five: Hanafi, Maliki, Shafi, Hanbali and Zahiri; among the Shias there are mainly three: Ithna Ashari, Fatimi and Zaidiyah). Had the shariat been totally divine it would not have been divided into so many extant and non-extant schools.

Professor M. Mujeeb goes on to the extent of describing the shariat as an approach to Islam rather than law — thereupon immensely increasing its scope — and goes on to say, "And if it is a matter of approach, why should Muslims confine themselves to texts embodying traditional methods of approach, and not think afresh in the light of present day needs and realities?"[4] It is also interesting to note that the very concept of shariat was absent in Islam up to about the fifth Islamic century. Even its root, sharia, rarely occurs during these centuries. One finds, surprisingly, the absence of the word shariat in the major works of all important jurists and thinkers of the classical period. Whether one scans from the second century hijrah al-Fiqh al-akbar or from the third century of hijrah the works of the Mutazilah or the *Wasiyah* attributed to Abu Hanifah. Whether one goes through the writings of al-Ashari or those of Ibn Battah the Hanbali from the fourth century of hijrah. One would not find this concept in the work of al-Baghdadi (*Kitab usul al-din*) and al-Juwayni (*Kitab al-irshad*) or in the work of al-Ghazali (*al-Iqtisad fi-al-itiqad*) from the fifth century. Even in the sixth century hijrah one does not find it in the works of al-Nasafi and al-Shahrastani.[5]

Cantwell Smith through his diligent research comes to the significant conclusion that in the early centuries of Islam the shari ahkam (injunctions) "are each a divine command morally incumbent and immediately personal, for which men will be answerable on the judgement. Only later does this phrase become depersonalized and eventually de-transcendentalized to the point where it is equivalent to ahkam al-shariah."[6]

Thus we see that the concept of shariat as a congealed body of laws, and binding in the strictly legal and not the moral sense, came into existence much later, in fact later than the seventh Islamic century. By then its growth had also stopped and it was de-transcendentalized, as Professor Smith puts it. Also, in the early Islamic era (until the fourth century) there was no question of strictly following one or another school of law. Taqleed (strict adherence) became the rule much later. The

4. An introductory note to *Changes in Muslim Personal Law* (Organizing Committee of XXVI International Congress of Orientalists, Delhi, 1964) p. 4.
5. For further details see "Shariah and Shar" in Wilfred Cantwell Smith's *On Understanding Islam* (Delhi, 1985) pp. 90-1.
6. Ibid. pp. 99.

four great imams (Shafi, Hanbal, Malik and Abu Hanifa) did not consider their opinion on various matters as *final*. Even as late as the thir-
teenth century, an eminent theologian like Shaykhal Islam Ibn
Taymiyyah refuses to follow any particular school and insists on interpreting the Quran and hadith in his own way. To him there was nothing
like finality for any school of law.

Interestingly, a controversy raged recently in Pakistan on the question of diyat (blood-money) and shahadah (evidence) of women. The
Hanafi school maintains that a woman be paid half the blood-money as
that of a man and that two women's evidence would be equivalent to
that of a man. The government of Pakistan, under its Islamization
scheme, sought to enforce these provisions of the Hanafi school with
respect to women. This touched off a bitter controversy. Maulana
Umar Ahmad Usmani and Justice Aftab Husain (chief justice of the
Federal Shariat Court of Pakistan) maintained that a woman is entitled
to blood-money equivalent to that of a man and that, in court matters,
her evidence is as good as that of a man. They took this position on the
basis of the holy Quran and on the Prophet's sunna. Maulana Umar
Ahmad Usmani published a series of volumes entitled *Fiqh al-Quran*
to prove his point of view on women's rights from the Quran and the
sunna of the Prophet.

Justice Aftab Husain, in his introduction to the sixth volume of
Maulana Usmani's book *Fiqh al-Quran* says that it (diyat: blood-
money) is a matter of ijtihad (proper interpretation) and no one is free
from error in a proper interpretation. There is the difference of heaven
and earth between the women of that time and those of today. No mujtahid (interpreter) can ignore the acceptable notions of time. No one
can ignore the difference between the women of today and those of
yesteryear. In the past women were responsible only for household
affairs and for looking after children. Today a woman, he says, is constrained to work to supplement the family income — something which
only men did in earlier times. He said he knew of families wherein educated girls look after their parents and brothers and sisters and that
there are households in which wives are responsible for meeting the
expenses of their husbands, parents and children. In the Pakistan of
today, he says, higher education is common and among the highly educated there are quite a few women journalists, doctors, advocates,
engineers and professors. Today, women's representative organizations also disagree with the earlier interpretations of the Quran and
sunna and are busy creating an awareness among the women about
their rights. Justice Aftab goes on to say that, in the hadith, equal diyat
is to be paid to the faithful (muminin) and to the dhimmi (protected

non-Muslims) and the faithful include Muslim women as well. How, then, can the diyat of a Muslim woman be half that of a man? It is strange that Imam Jassas who was of the view that women be paid half the amount of diyat, in order to uphold his point of view went to the extent of not accepting Muslim women as mumin, though the Quran addresses both men and women as "O! faithfuls" (Ya ayyohal ladhina amanu). Justice Aftab also refers to the doctrine yataghayyaru al-hukm bi taghayyurizzaman (the rule changes with the change of time).[7]

These arguments make it quite clear that no opinion pronounced by any eminent jurist is final, much less immutable. The whole body of the the shariat consists of opinions of one or the other eminent jurist and these opinions though based on interpretation of the holy Quran and sunna have been influenced by the ethos of their time. That is why these opinions, though they are of eminent jurists thoroughly imbued with Islamic learning, cannot be treated as final. If one studies the actual formulation of the various opinions and debates which went on, one will realize the role human reason has played in these formulations. How can one then deny the role of human reason in today's changed conditions? The holy Prophet encouraged ijtihad (exertion of one's reason to establish a rule) *in his own lifetime* as is clearly shown in his conversation with Madh bin Jabal whom he had appointed governor of Yemen. Ijtihad becomes much more necessary 1400 years after his death.

It is rightly maintained that the shariat is based on the Quran and on the sunna of the Prophet. Its immutability is based on these sources, they being divine. But even the eminent companion of the Prophet like Hazrat Umar was constrained to set aside divine command under the pressure of circumstances. It is widely known that he suspended the punishment of amputating the hand when faced with a famine. He also refused to disburse zakat money to the muallafat al-qulub (incentive money to those whose hearts are to be won) as was laid down in the holy Quran[8] on the grounds that Islam was now dominant and that it was no longer necessary to do so. Ahmad Amin, an eminent Egyptian alim, also points out that Umar sought the intention behind the Quranic judgements and was willing to reverse these judgements when conditions had changed; as when he refused to give a share of the zakat to "those whose hearts are to be composed", even though the Quran stipulates it, on the grounds that Islam had become stronger and no

7. See introduction by Justice Aftab Husain to Maulana Umar Ahmad Usmani's *Fiqh al-Quran* (Karachi, 1985), pp. 30-33.
8. *The Quran*, 9 : 60.

longer needed to buy off its erstwhile enemies in this way.[9]

Ahmad Amin also significantly remarks:

> In twenty-three years the conditions that called forth some judge-
> ments changed, then as the conditions changed some of the judge-
> ments changed. Indeed, a question might require a (positive) com-
> mand, then the circumstance would change and it would require a
> prohibition . . . . So if this happened in twenty-three years in the life
> of the Prophet, what do you think when times have changed and
> more than a thousand years have passed . . .? Does not the observer
> think that if the Prophet were alive and faced these circumstances,
> many verses of abrogation would descend upon him and God the
> Generous and Merciful would not leave the Islamic nation without
> flexible legislation confronting this new life with absolute *ijtihad*?[10]

The Arab customary practices

Another important dimension of the shariat is integration with it of
Arab customary practices. Most of these practices were of the pre-
Islamic period known as the jahiliyyah period. The holy Quran and the
Prophet had improved upon or abrogated many of these practices.
But, in the later period, Arab customs provided the raw material on
which the jurists built. Many of these practices had no Quranic sanction but the jurists, in view of the prevailing conditions, saw no other
recourse and borrowed these concepts and practices to build the *juris
corpus* of Islam. Thus Professor Fyzee points out, " . . . we shall find
many of these customs (Arab customs) adopted wholly or with modifications by the law of Islam. One striking example is the principle of
agnacy or tasib, which is fundamental in the Sunnite law of inheritance."[11]

Fyzee also points out that "the doctrine of consensus draws its
strength from the customs and usages of the ancient Arabs."[12] Fyzee
goes on to say:

> A number of traditions ascribed to the Prophet have come down to
> us in the form of aphorisms or legal maxims. Many of them can be
> demonstrated to be of late origin and cannot be accepted without
> reserve. They are not uniform as to provenance or chronology; but

9. Ahmad Amin, *Hayati*, (Cairo, 1961) pp. 325-26; cf. William Shephard, *The Faith of
   a Modern Muslim Intellectual* (Delhi, 1982).
10. Ahmad Amin, *Duha al-Islam*, vol. III, (Cairo, 1964), p. 11.
11. Asaf A. A. Fyzee, *Outlines of Muhammadan Law*, (Oxford University Press, 1964)
    p. 7.
12. Ibid. p. 28.

as a rule they embody legal usage of early times, and take the form of traditions much later. Familiar examples are "There is no valid marriage without a wali" (guardian), and "My community will not agree on an error."[13]

Thus we see that many Arab customs and usages found acceptance in the form of prophetic traditions. The second source of Islamic law i.e. the sunna of the Prophet should also be treated with due caution. Here it would be interesting to mention the case of triple divorce in one sitting (talaqi thalatha fi Majlis-in wahidin). This is widely practiced in India as it has sanction in the Hanafi school and it is a major source of injustice against Muslim women. It is a most contentious form of divorce denounced even by Hanafites as an innovative and sinful form of divorce. There are cogent arguments for and against it based both on the Quran and Sunna. The Quranic verses and Prophet's traditions have been subjected to different interpretations (which are in direct conflict with each other) supporting or rejecting this form of divorce.

Those supporting the triple divorce in one sitting maintain that the Quran has not laid down any specific method of divorce and, though the Prophet, they maintain, showed his anger against this form of divorce, he did not indicate that such a divorce would not be valid. Some supporters of this talaq al-bida even maintain that the tradition showing anger of the Prophet against it is a weak one. Imam Ibn Hazm (d. 456 A.H.) has given a detailed argument in favour of the triple divorce from the Quran and the sunna. He tries to refute all arguments against the triple divorce in one sitting.[14]

Hafiz Ibn Qayyim, on the other hand has argued, again on the basis of the Quran and Sunna that, even if one pronounces three divorces in one sitting, only one revocable divorce shall take place. Ibn Qayyim, who is a disciple of Ibn Taymiyyah, marshals all his arguments on the basis of the Quran to prove the invalidity of a triple divorce in one sitting. He maintains that the Prophet's companions numbered more than a lakh but can anyone show that even twenty of them ever concurred on the validity of a triple divorce in one sitting?[15] Ibn Qayyim advances many other weighty arguments to disprove the validity of a triple divorce in one sitting.

In the face of all this it would be very difficult to maintain the immutability and divinity of the shariat. If one carefully examines the various

13. Ibid. p. 29.
14. See Dr Tanzilur Rahman (compiled), *Majmuai Qawanin-i-Islam*, vol. II (Islamabad, 1965), pp. 501-3.
15. Ibid. pp. 535-39.

arguments these eminent theologians advanced in favour of their opinions, it becomes quite evident that most of them take *a priori* positions and then prove their point of view with the help of the Quran and Sunna. And it hardly needs to be stated that the *a priori* position has its genesis in the milieu in which one lives. It would not be wrong to hold that it was not the normative theology of the Quran which was responsible for the degradation of women's position in Islam, but that it was the later contextual theology evolved by the jurists working under the medieval milieu.

Controversy about maintenance

The controversy on the question of maintenance started after the Supreme Court delivered its judgement in a criminal appeal No. 103 of 1981. The judgement became highly controversial and created history. The appeal in the Supreme Court was filed by Mohammad Ahmad Khan of Indore against the M.P. High Court judgement granting maintenance to his wife Shah Bano whom he had divorced. The Supreme Court upheld the High Court judgement and felt that the Cr. P.C. 125, which makes it obligatory on husbands to make provision for their divorced wives if they have no other means of sustenance until they remarry or die, would also apply to Muslim husbands. The learned judges say at the outset of the judgement,

> This appeal, arising out of an application filed by a divorced Muslim woman for maintenance under section 125 of the Code of Criminal Procedure, raises a straight-forward issue which is of common interest not only to Muslim women, not only to women generally but, to all those who, aspiring to create an equal society of men and women, lure themselves into the belief that mankind has achieved a remarkable degree of progress in that direction.[16]

The Supreme Court was also charged with the task of deciding whether section 125 of the Cr. P.C. can be applied to the Muslims without interfering in their personal law. The judgement in this respect says:

> The whole of this discussion as to whether the right conferred by section 125 prevails over the personal law of the parties, has proceeded on the assumption that there is a conflict between the provisions of that section and those of the Muslim Personal Law. The argument

16. See the Supreme Court judgement included in this book.

that by reason of section 2 of the Shariat Act, XXVI of 1937 the rule of secession in matters relating, *inter alia* to maintenance 'shall be the Muslim Personal Law' also proceeds upon a similar assumption. We embarked upon the decision of the question of priority between the Code and the Muslim Personal Law on the assumption that there was a conflict between the two because, in so far as it lies in our power, we wanted to set at rest, once for all, the question whether section 125 would prevail over the personal law of the parties, in cases where they are in conflict.[17]

The Supreme Court also consulted the text of the holy Quran. The standard translations and commentaries by well known Muslim authorities such as Allama Abdullah Yusuf Ali, Muhammad Zafarullah Khan, Dr Allamah Khadim Rahmani Nuri and the translation of the holy book published by the Board of Islamic Publications, Delhi, were consulted. The verse 241 of chapter II makes it obligatory on divorcing husbands to make provision for the divorced wives. The verse is as under: "Wa lil mutallaqate mataun bil maruf haqqan al muttaqin," which translated means, "For divorced women maintenance (should be provided) on a reasonable (scale). This is a duty on the righteous."[18]

The Muslim Personal Law Board which was intervener in the case objected to the Supreme Court judgement and described it as gross interference in the MPLB. It also maintained — a refrain taken up by other Muslim leaders as well — that the Supreme Court had no right to interpret the holy Quran. Thus the Supreme Court was held 'guilty' by the Muslim leadership on two counts: firstly it had interfered in the MPL and secondly it had tried to interpret the Muslim holy book and it had no business to do so.

The MPLB and other Muslim leaders launched a countrywide agitation against the judgement and mounted pressure on the Government to undo the judgement by introducing a bill exempting Muslims from the application of section 125 Cr. P.C. The agitation was so intense and it stirred the Muslim sentiments so deeply that the Government was unnerved and agreed to introduce a bill in the Parliament which we will shortly analyse.

It was maintained during the agitation by the Muslim leaders that the Islamic shariat is divine and hence immutable. No human being can ever alter it whatever his eminence and learning. We have shown above that the shariat is not wholly divine; it is partly so. Also that it is

17. Ibid.
18. *The Holy Quran*, (trans. by) Abdullah Yousufali, (Hyderabad, n.d.), p. 63.

alterable in as much as it is based on human reasoning (employing qiyas, ijma, ijtihad) and conditioned by the needs and pressures of time. It is also a well-established doctrine that the amr (injunction) changes with change in time.

The Muslim leaders (theological as well as lay) maintained that in Islam a divorcee can be given maintenance only for the period of iddat (a three-month waiting period before she can re-marry). No more. Some even went to the extent of saying that it is a 'sin' to give beyond this period. Most of the Muslim leaders, whether learned in Islamic lore or not, began to assert these views. In fact if one coolly examines the whole question, rising above partisanship, it would not be difficult to conclude that there is no such theological consensus on the question of maintenance. There have been wide-ranging differences on this issue among Muslim theologians. The contentious word in the Quranic verse quoted above is 'mata' which has been variously rendered in English as 'provision' or 'maintenance' etc.

Imam Malik says in his famous compilation *al-Muwatta* that mata could mean aat mata could mean a pair of clothes at the minimum and a slave boy or girl at the maximum to be given to the divorcee. But he considers this as mustahib (preferable) and not wajib (obligatory). He calls this as mutat al-talaq (gift of divorce).[19]

A Pakistani scholar Professor Rafiullah Shihab says, in his article published in *Pakistan Times*, that, according to the principle laid down by the Hanafite jurist, "if a husband does not maintain his wife properly she can get her maintenance allowance fixed through a court. This fixed maintenance allowance will not only be paid to her as a wife but also after divorce." Then he goes on to quote Allama Najeem (Nujaim?) a famous jurist of the Hanafite school who has discussed this issue in great detail in his famous book *Al-Bahr al-Raiq*. In his book he maintains that there is a difference of opinion among the Hanafite jurists. According to Imam Muhammad, the husband is not required to pay maintenance to his divorced wife while Imam Abu Yusuf felt differently. He is of the opinion that the husband will have to pay this amount even after divorcing her. Imam Ibn Najeem, after quoting these conflicting reports, is of the view that stopping the maintenance allowance of the wife after divorce is weak. He agrees with the consensus of the jurists that a woman, not maintained properly by her husband, can knock at the door of a court and get her maintenance allowance fixed by the court. The husband is bound to pay this fixed amount to the wife regularly. If he refuses to do so, he will be put behind bars. *If it would have been possible for the husband to save his*

19. See Imam Malik, *al-Muwatta* (Saharanpur, 1975), p. 462.

skin by divorcing his wife, he would have preferred to do so. But Islamic law does not allow him to do so. (Emphasis supplied.) He will have to pay this amount even after divorcing her. (*Al-Bahr al-Raiq*, vol. iv, pp. 189–90).[20]

Imam Hasan Basri, a great theologian and a tabi (i.e. follower of the companions of the Prophet) also maintained that "There is no time limit regarding payment of maintenance. It should be paid according to one's capacity." His words are, "laysa fiha shayun muwaqqatun. Yumatte uha ala qadril maysarah" (see *Muhalla*, Ibn Hazm, vol. 10, p. 248). A highly celebrated lexicon of Arabic, written some seven hundred years ago, while defining the word mataa says it is without any time limit as Allah (Mighty and Exalted) has not confined it to any period but commanded to benefit her (i.e. the divorcee). Shaikh Mustafa Assabai who is an eminent theologian of Syria also maintains that, "if the divorced woman is of marriageable age, maintenance should be paid till her remarriage, if she is old, it should be paid till her death.[21]

In Saudi Arabia too, according to Abdul Fattah Ghudah, head, department of Ahadith al-Nabi (prophetic traditions), Riyadh University, if any husband divorces his wife wrongfully, unjustly and if it is so proved, he is liable, in addition to paying maintenance, to be sentenced to six months to ten years imprisonment.[22]

Thus it is seen that, in the matter of maintenance to a divorced wife, there is no unanimity among the theologians. Many of them have maintained that it is payable even after divorce whereas others confine it to the period of iddat only. It is therefore wrong to say that to pay maintenance beyond the period of iddat is un-Islamic. There is no authority even during the classical period who maintained that payment of maintenance would be *un-Islamic* beyond the period of iddat though they may have made it obligatory only for the period of iddat or delivery of child in case the divorcee is pregnant. It would, therefore, not be wrong to maintain that the whole agitation against the Supreme Court judgement was *politically*, and *not religiously*, motivated. We will throw some more light on this aspect.

Politics of the Shah Bano movement

When the Supreme Court judgement came, the leaders of the MPL Board were not sure about the response of Muslims to the protest

20. Rafiullah Shehab, "Islamic Shariat and Shah Bano Case," *Pakistan Times* (Lahore, 9 January 1986).
21. See the memorandum presented to Prime Minister, Rajiv Gandhi by P. V. Shaukat Ali, chairman, Islamic Shariath Board (Kerala, 1 February, 1986).
22. See *Urdu Times* (Bombay, 15 January 1986).

movement against it. They cautiously gave a call for protest on the last Friday of the holy month of Ramadan, a day on which Muslims anyway gather in large numbers. The Muslim leadership was encouraged by the enthusiastic response. It decided to intensify the agitation. The agitation quickly snowballed into a formidable movement. Thousands of Muslim men and women began to join protest rallies and conferences. In Sewan, Bihar, more than four lakh Muslims are reported to have joined a conference convened by the leaders of the Muslim Personal Law Conference (this should not be confused with the Muslim Personal Law Board) in October 1985.[23] Similarly, in Bombay, more than three lakh Muslims joined the protest march organized by a few obscure Urdu journalists on 20 November 1985.[24] Several other such meetings and conferences were held and the whole atmosphere was charged with emotion. It was repeatedly claimed by some Muslim leaders that the Indian Muslims were never united like this before. Why did the Indian Muslims respond so emotionally and with so much vigour?

There are various reasons for this. As some senior journalists such as Kuldip Nayar and others have pointed out, Muslims have been living under a tremendous sense of insecurity for long due to the escalating communal violence in the country. Muslims do feel they are under siege. The emergence of the Vishwa Hindu Parishad (VHP) after the conversion episode in Meenakshipuram in 1981 and its virulent anti-Muslim propaganda greatly heightened this sense of insecurity. Also, the case for banning the holy Quran filed in the Calcutta High Court by some mischievous individuals further convinced the Muslims that their religion is under severe threat. The Supreme Court judgement was perceived by them as yet another attempt to destroy the autonomy of their religion. An agitation was also going on against banning prayers in certain historical mosques by the Department of Archaeology 'for protecting historical monuments'. The virulent campaign by the leaders of the VHP for liberating Ram Janam Bhoomi and some other temples had its own telling effect on the Muslim psyche. All this added up to an equally strong virulent reaction from the Muslims.

However, this was not all. In a democratic set-up, a developing economy, within the capitalistic framework, leads to, as the experience of the third-world countries show, greater and greater religious assertion and sharpening of caste and communal feelings. Fundamentalist movements, in urban areas, become ever more aggressive. The urban areas, with their greater potential for jobs, attract people from villages and even small towns. These people, uprooted from their traditional pattern

23. See *Masail*, Urdu weekly (Patna, 10 November 1985).
24. See *Inquilab*, Urdu daily (Bombay, 21 November 1985).

of life, develop an acute sense of anonymity and alienation in the vast conglomerate of humanity that the modern urban areas are. In such a situation, religious groups as well as religious ceremonies provide, for the common people, a sense of warmth and solidarity so necessary for maintaining psychological integrity. This phenomenon should not be judged and condemned merely from the rationalist point of view, but should also be seen and understood from the psychological viewpoint.

From this it will be seen that religious fundamentalism has a socio-economic root as well and is not merely a religious phenomenon.[25] Religious fundamentalism also draws its strength from an acute sense of insecurity and injustice that is inevitable in a developing capitalist economy. Religious fundamentalism, an urban phenomenon, is cleverly manoeuvred by the secular urban elite for its own political interests, especially in a democracy such as India. Today we see the emergence of fundamentalism among all the religious communities of India and it is being taken advantage of by organizations like the VHP, RSS, Jamat-e-Islami, Muslim League, Akalis and others. Highly emotive religious slogans are used to mobilize the masses for the political interests of a secular urban elite.

The Muslim leadership too used highly emotional words for increasing the appeal of their agitation. Words like farzandane tawheed (children of believers in the unity of godhood), iman afroz bayan (the faith-enhancing statement), valvalae iman (upsurge of faith), millat-e-Islamiya ke shaidai (lovers of the community of Islam) etc., were frequently used. These phrases strike very deep chords among the urban lower middle class Muslims. In fact a content-wise analysis of the words and slogans used in the meetings and in the Urdu newspaper reports would throw a very interesting light on the question of the mobilization of Muslims.

The MPL Board saw, in this agitation, a great opportunity to recover its lost prestige. It succeeded admirably. It convinced Muslims that it, alone, could effectively protect the divine shariat. It was continuously hammered into the Muslim mind that the divine shariat was in danger and it was the sacred duty of every Muslim to protect it. Thus the Rajiv Gandhi government came under severe pressure to undo the Supreme Court judgement by introducing a bill in Parliament to exempt Muslims from the purview of section 125 of the Cr. P.C. The prime minister seems to have panicked specially after the Congress candidate Maulana Asrarul Haque Quasimi, the general secretary of the Jamiatul Ulama-i-Hind, faced a humiliating defeat at the hands of Syed Shahabuddin, a

25. For a detailed analysis, see Asghar Ali Engineer, "Socio-Economic Bases of Religious Revival Among Muslims", in Walter Fernandes (ed.) *Inequality, Its Basis and Search for Solutions* (Delhi, 1986), pp. 248-261.

Janata Party candidate in the Kishanganj (Bihar) by-election for a parliamentary seat in December 1985. Though Mr Shahabuddin claimed that the Shah Bano case was not the issue in the election[26] it was widely believed to be so — a perception shared by the Congress (I) itself. Though, in the Assam election, this was not the main issue, the Muslim voters' alienation from the Congress candidates was also perceived to be due partly to the agitation against the Shah Bano case judgement.

The prime minister seems to have made up his mind for introducing the bill to undo the Supreme Court judgement after the elections in December 1985. It was obvious to anyone who cares to know that the bill was brought about under pressure from the fundamentalist Muslim leadership. The bill seems to have been most hastily drafted and has many flaws, even from the point of view of the shariat. Although the bill has been drafted by the law ministry there is hardly any doubt that it was drafted in consultation with theologians such as Maulana Abul Hasan Nadvi. It is really surprising that these theologians who sneer at the lack of knowledge of shariat among the progressive Muslims, should have themselves betrayed a lack of elementary knowledge of Islamic law. We shall attempt a brief analysis of the contents of this bill which is bad even in Islamic law.

Analysis of the Bill [27]

It is quite ironical that the bill has been named "The Muslim Women (Protection of Rights on Divorce) Bill". In fact this bill takes away whatever rights have been guaranteed Muslim divorcees by the holy Quran. There is no clear provision in the bill for mutatut talaq (i.e. parting gift at the time of the divorce) mentioned by almost all eminent Islamic jurists. It only mentions, vaguely, provision and maintenance together in sub-section 3(1) (a) without defining in any way the word 'provision'. The intention is to deprive the divorced woman of mutatut talaq which could be as high as, according to the standards of those days, a slave or a slave-girl.

26. See Syed Shahabuddin, "Victory", editorial in *Muslim India* (January 1986).
27. The bill was passed by the Lok Sabha on 5 May 1986. An official amendment was incorporated. According to the amendment the divorcing husband and divorced wife can, by mutual consent, opt for application of section 125 of Cr. P.C. provided the option is exercised before filing the suit. The amendment, to say the least, is quite absurd. Which husband would agree to this option and why should he? If he were an ideal husband respecting the rights of his divorced wife he would right away agree to pay reasonable maintenance to her without any need for going to the court. And if he is a difficult husband not agreeable to pay reasonable maintenance how will he agree to opt for Cr. P.C. 125? It seems the law minister did not give this amendment much thought.

Secondly, almost all eminent jurists of Islam have agreed that the mother will haye custody of male children up to the age of 7 or 8 and that of female children until the age of puberty (or marriage according to some other jurists) and the father will pay for the upbringing of the children. There is no difference among Islamic jurists in this respect. And yet the bill provides for children (male or female) for only two years.[28] It is a woeful lack of knowledge of Islamic law on the part of the members of the MPL Board.

The bill requires that after the period of iddat the divorcee would be looked after by her parents or other relatives who are likely to inherit from her. She can claim maintenance from her parents or relatives in a court of law (see sub-section 4 of the bill). The fundamentalists are claiming that this is an Islamic law. Far from it. There is no direct or indirect mention of this in the holy Quran. On the contrary, direct responsibility of provision for the divorced wife has been squarely put on the husband. Is it not a direct defiance of the holy book? The holy Quran has not anywhere made it obligatory that the parents or relatives look after the divorcee after the period of iddat. This is certainly not a matter of principle as far as the Quran is concerned. In fact this was an Arab custom which was sanctified by the jurists drawing inference from a Quranic verse — a section of which says, "wa alal warithi mithlo dhalik" (An heir shall be chargeable in the same way).[29]. In fact, the whole verse has been revealed in the context of suckling children and parents' responsibility. It has nothing to do with a divorced woman.

From the above verse, the Islamic jurists have drawn a general conclusion that any person who is unable to maintain himself or herself would be looked after by those relatives who would have inherited from him or her. This becomes quite clear if one has a look at Allama Abdul Hasan Qadri's work *al-Mukhtasar* when he propounds the general

Such an amendment could have been more useful had it stipulated that, at the time of entering the marital contract, the couple could exercise this option — since the bride has every right to stipulate such conditions. But then it would defeat the very purpose of passing the bill.

Much emphasis has been given in the bill on the settlement of mehr amount at the time of divorce. But there are several Muslim communities like the Bohras wherein the usual amount of mehr is between Rs. 41 to 101. Among ithna Ashari Shias too, the ideal amount of mehr is around Rs. 1000 (the amount of mehr given by the Prophet to his daughter Fatima was 500 dirhams, roughly Rs. 1000 today). What can the divorced woman do with this paltry amount? Even in case of Hanafites, due to every rising percentage of inflation the mehr amount keeps on losing value every year. The much talked about amendment by Syed Shahabuddin about linking mehr to the cost of living index did not materialize after all.

28. Much after the bill was introduced in the Parliament of MPL Board Maulana Abul Hasan Nadvi introduced the amendment that the husband should pay for the upbringing of a male child up to the age of 8 and for a female child until the age of puberty.

29. See *The Quran*, 2 : 233

principle of responsibility of maintenance of those who are unable to maintain themselves.[30]

Surprisingly the bill is quite silent about the maintenance of parents by children whereas it has been greatly emphasized in the Quran and in the shariat. True, the bill is about divorcees but section 125 of Cr.P.C. also talks of maintenance of destitute parents and since apparently after the passage of this bill Muslims would be exempt from the application of section 125, it ought to have been clarified as to whether Muslims would also be exempt from maintaining their destitute parents. In fact, in the case of destitute parents, it is obligatory only on the children to look after them; the qazi cannot order other relatives to do so.[31] Also in the case of a wife the Quran requires her husband to pay even for suckling a child. "Then if they suckle for you, give them their recompense,"[32] says the Quran. Which other scripture gives so many rights to a woman? It is very unfortunate that the Muslim theologians are taking away from women what Allah has given them and still claim to be theologians. They are not even sincere Muslims, let alone knowledgeable theologians.

Which jurist in Islam, one may ask, has made provision in the wakf properties to maintain a divorcee? There is no such precedent in the whole history of Islamic jurisprudence. Such an innovation is being held as a great measure by those who claim to follow Islamic law in all its details without allowing any small change. Is it then ijtihad which the ulama had relegated in favour of taqlid? If it is ijtihad why is ijtihad only in favour of man (divesting a divorcing husband of his responsibility to maintain a divorced wife). Why was something not done in favour of woman? Is this not in the spirit of male-domination? To maintain this domination even the holy book can be defied.

Apart from theological considerations, the bill raises many practical problems as well. Firstly, unlike in the past, there is no joint family system any more. Relatives have scattered all over the country, or even in different parts of the world, to earn their livelihood. Often even two brothers do not live in the same town, these days, to say nothing of other relatives. How, therefore, is the court order going to be enforced? Will it travel from one state to another state and from one country to another country? And how, in the absence of the court's jurisdiction, will the divorcee realize the amount she requires? As far as the responsibility of the wakf boards is concerned, what will happen in those states such as Maharashtra where there are no wakf boards? Who is the

---

30. See Tanzilur Rahman's *Majmuai Qawanin-i-Islam*, vol. II op. cit. 917.
31. Ibid. pp. 915-916.
32. *The Quran*, 65 : 6.

divorcee going to turn to for succour? It has also been pointed out that neither is there any provision in wakf deeds for helping divorcees (each wakf is set up for a specific purpose) nor can the cost of such maintenance be met out of the six per cent levy for administrative expenses; as it is the levy is insufficient even for administrative purposes. Ultimately the central or the state governments may have to make special grants for this purpose. Such a grant would not go unchallenged in court.

The prevalent method of triple divorce (which is sinful and innovative) makes the bill all the more unjust. The husband can pronounce triple divorce any time without any reason, even in a state of inebriation or anger and throw his wife out on the road. How can, in such an eventuality, parents and relatives be made responsible for her maintenance? This amounts to punishing someone for someone else's crime. How can it be justified? The least that the theologians can do is to propose a law for banning this sinful form of divorce and strive towards enforcing talaq based on the Quran and the sunna. Unfortunately, the present bill does not even distinguish between the different forms of talaq. Talaq before consummation of marriage, khula, mubarat (divorce by mutual consent), mughallaza (triple or irrevocable divorce) have all been indistinguishably bracketed together. How can such a bill, so full of various flaws — theological and otherwise — be hailed and claimed a great Islamic measure? This is what the Muslim leaders and the theologians seem to be doing — but sooner or later those who are under their spell will wake up to the fallacy of the claim.

Even the amendment, which Mr Shahabuddin wishes to introduce, that section 125 of Cr. P.C. would apply to a Muslim couple with the mutual consent of husband and wife would not go a long way to provide much relief, as it is not easy for the girls' parents to find a suitable match on their terms. It is invariably the husband who dictates the terms except in the case of a few exceptions. This amendment is, therefore, at best an illusory relief. The bill, in my opinion, can be unhesitantly termed un-Islamic in spirit. By insisting on such a law, the Muslim leadership is trying to restore its flagging prestige. This leadership is so totally bankrupt that it has not won anything which could improve the condition of the poverty-ridden Muslim masses. They have neither striven for the spread of education among Muslims as Sir Syed did; nor have they ever tried to set up cooperatives for Muslim artisans; nor even have they worked for creating better employment opportunities by centralizing and investing zakat funds. They have always based their politics on the most obscurantist issues as it is very easy to arouse religious emotions.

Unfortunately matters have been further complicated by the role played by the Hindu communalists belonging to the VHP, RSS and other similar organizations. They began to vociferously demand an imposition of a common civil code. Whatever the merit of a common civil code (that is a separate, debatable issue) when the demand for it comes from communalist Hindus it arouses deep suspicion even among the Muslim intelligentsia and they begin to perceive it as a Hindu code. In fact, throughout, in the agitation against the Supreme Court judgement, the hands of Muslim fundamentalists were strengthened by Hindu fundamentalists. Had they not demanded an imposition of the common civil code so aggressively, those among the Muslims who are in favour of the Supreme Court judgement would have been able to carry a little more conviction with the Muslim masses. However, one must admit, it is very difficult in a democratic set-up to stop the fundamentalists of other communities from doing this. The Ram Janam Bhoomi controversy also aroused deep apprehensions among the Muslims.

Unfortunately, fundamentalists from both communities have succeeded eminently in swaying the masses and perpetuating the status quo. Highly obscurantist issues have acquired great significance and the real issues confronting the people have been completely pushed to the background. This is what the perpetrators of the status quo really wanted. The ruling group (as well as the ruling classes) are subtly encouraging this game as it helps to shift focus away from the misery of the people and their various unsolved problems.

The secularists, too, have been unable to play a creative and constructive role in this controversy. Either they too demanded a common civil code without taking into account the sensibilities of the minorities or they did not campaign effectively enough for justice to Muslim women minus communal overtones. Usually the fundamentalist Muslims argued, in sum, that the Hindus' concern about maintenance to Muslim divorcees seemed hypocritical for they had shed no tears for Muslim women rendered widows during communal riots. This became a common refrain among Muslim leaders and carried conviction with the Muslim masses. The genuine secularists of the left and democratic convictions could have countered such arguments more effectively as they are quite genuinely opposed to communal violence. A more vigorous campaign by these secularists against communalism and communal violence would have greatly strengthened the hands of the reformists among the Muslims. Unfortunately the left parties' campaign, especially that of the CPM, was more on the political aspect of the issue than on justice to Muslim women. The CPM apparently took up this issue more vigorously because of its differences with the Muslim League in Kerala. The CPI remained, on the whole, rather cool although it did oppose the bill and did support the Supreme Court judgement.

Both these parties have great sympathy with minorities and hence they could have conducted the campaign against the bill more imaginatively so as to win the sympathy of Muslim women in particular, and reasonable Muslims, in general. Where religious sensibilities are involved, especially those of minority communities, one has to tread more cautiously and imaginatively. The genuine grievances the Muslims have could have been combined with an urge for social justice, especially for women. The left parties could also have strongly criticized the oppression of women in general, both Muslim as well as non-Muslim, in our society. The issue should have been made more a women's cause than for or against any community. It could also have been emphasized that religious freedom and diversity should exist, but not at the cost of justice.

However, the campaign of the left parties was not so imaginatively designed. In the eyes of the Muslims, unfortunately, the parties of the left, too, seemed to be against them and their religion. Also, the left parties could have been a little more assertive on the question of unlocking Ram Janam Bhoomi — and thereupon countered the virulent campaign set up by the Vishwa Hindu Parishad. This should have been done not to appease the communal Muslims but to oppose, on secular grounds, the communal designs of the VHP.

This book is a compilation of various articles, editorials, interviews and statements of political leaders, intellectuals, writers, legal luminaries, women's organizations, both Muslim as well as non-Muslim. This is being done with a view to make available to posterity the record of what various people thought and wrote on this important issue. This subject, I am sure, will continue to evoke deep interest for quite some time to come. We have also made available in this book the historic judgement of the Supreme Court as well as the text of the bill. These are very important documents as far as the maintenance of divorced Muslim women is concerned.

Bombay
5.5.1986

Asghar Ali Engineer

PART – I

IN THE SUPREME COURT OF INDIA
CRIMINAL APPELLATE JURISDICTION
CRIMINAL APPEAL NO. 103 OF 1981

Mohd. Ahmed Khan .... Appellant

vs.

Shah Bano Begum & Others .... Respondents

JUDGEMENT

CHANDRACHUD, C. J.

This appeal does not involve any questions of constitutional importance but, that is not to say that it does not involve any question of importance. Some questions which arise under the ordinary civil and criminal law are of a far-reaching significance to large segments of society which have been traditionally subjected to unjust treatment. Women are one such segment. *Na stree swatantramarhati* said Manu, the Law-giver : The woman does not deserve independence. And, it is alleged that the 'fatal point in Islam is the degradation of woman.'[1] To the Prophet is ascribed the statement, hopefully wrongly, that 'Woman was made from a crooked rib, and if you try to bend it straight, it will break; therefore treat your wives kindly.'

This appeal, arising out of an application filed by a divorced Muslim woman for maintenance under section 125 of the Code of Criminal Procedure, raises a straightforward issue which is of common interest not only to Muslim women, not only to women generally but, to all those who, aspiring to create an equal society of men and women, lure themselves into the belief that mankind has achieved a remarkable degree of progress in that direction. The appellant, who is an advocate by profession, was married to the respondent in 1932. Three sons and two daughters were born of that marriage. In 1975, the appellant drove the respondent out of the matrimonial home. In April 1978, the respondent filed a petition against the appellant under section 125 of the Code in the court of the learned Judicial Magistrate (First Class), Indore, asking for maintenance at the rate of Rs. 500/- per month. On November 6, 1978, the appellant divorced the respondent by an irrevocable talaq. His defence to the respondent's petition for maintenance was that she had ceased to be his wife by reason of the divorce granted by him, that he was therefore under no obligation to provide maintenance for her, that he had already paid maintenance to her at the rate of Rs. 200/- per month for about two years and that he had deposited a sum of Rs. 3,000/- in the court by way of dower during the period of iddat. In August 1979, the learned Magistrate directed the appellant to pay a princely sum of Rs. 25/- per month to the respondent by way of maintenance. It may be mentioned that the respondent had alleged that the appellant earns a professional income of about Rs. 60,000/- per year. In July 1980, in a revisional application filed by the respondent, the High Court of Madhya Pradesh enhanced the amount of maintenance to Rs. 179.20 per month. The husband is before us by special leave.

Does the Muslim Personal Law impose no obligation upon the husband to provide for the maintenance of his divorced wife? Undoubtedly, the Muslim husband enjoys the privilege of being able to discard his wife whenever he chooses to do so, for reason good, bad or indifferent. Indeed, for no reason at all. But, is the only price of that privilege the dole of a pittance during the period of iddat? And, is the law so ruthless in its inequality that, no matter how much the husband pays for the maintenance of his divorced wife during the period of iddat, the mere fact that he has paid something, no matter how little, absolves him forever from the duty of paying adequately so as to enable her to keep her body and soul together? Then again, is there any provision in the Muslim Personal Law under which a sum is payable to the wife 'on divorce'? These are some of the important, though agonizing, questions which arise for our decision.

The question as to whether section 125 of the Code applies to Muslims also is concluded by two decisions of this Court which are reported in *Bai Tahira* v. *Ali Hussain Fidaalli Chothia* [2] and *Fazlunbi* v. *K. Khader Vali* [3]. Those decisions took the view that the divorced Muslim wife is entitled to apply for maintenance under section 125. But, a Bench consisting of our learned Brethren, Murtaza Fazal Ali and A. Varadarajan, J. J., were inclined to the view that those cases are not correctly decided. Therefore, they referred this appeal to a larger Bench by an order dated February 3, 1981, which reads thus:

As this case involves substantial questions of law of far-reaching consequences, we feel that the decisions of this Court in Bai Tahira *v.* Ali Hussain Fidaalli Chothia & Anr. and Fazlunbi *v.* K. Khader Vali & Anr. require reconsideration because, in our opinion, they are not only in direct contravention of the plain and unambiguous language of s. 127(3) (b) of the Code of Criminal Procedure, 1973, which far from overriding the Muslim Law on the subject, protects and applies the same in case where a wife has been divorced by the husband and the dower specified has been paid and the period of iddat has been observed. The decision also appears to us to be against the fundamental concept of divorce by the husband and its consequences under the Muslim Law which has been expressly protected by s. 2 of the Muslim Personal Law (Shariat) Application Act, 1937 — an Act which was not noticed by the aforesaid decisions. We, therefore, direct that the matter may be placed before the Hon'ble Chief Justice for being heard by a larger Bench consisting of more than three judges.

Section 125 of the Code of Criminal Procedure which deals with the right of maintenance reads thus:

Order for maintenance of wives, children and parents
    125. (1) If any person having sufficient means neglects or refuses to maintain —
(*a*) his wife unable to maintain herself,
(*b*) ....
(*c*) ....
(*d*) ....
a Magistrate of the first class may, upon proof of such neglect or refusal, order such person to make a monthly allowance for the maintenance of his wife..........................,
at such monthly rate not exceeding five hundred rupees in the whole, as such Magistrate thinks fit........

    Explanation — For the purpose of this chapter,
(*a*) ....
(*b*) "Wife" includes a woman who has been divorced by, or has obtained a divorce from, her husband and has not remarried.
(2) ....
(3) If any person so ordered fails without sufficient cause to comply with the order, any such Magistrate may, for every breach of the order, issue a warrant for levying the amount in the manner provided for levying fines, and may sentence such person, for the whole or any part of each month's allowance remaining unpaid after the execution of the warrant, to imprisonment for a term which may extend to one month or until payment if sooner made:

provided . . . .
provided further if such person offers to maintain his wife on condition of her living with him, and she refuses to live with him, such Magistrate may consider any grounds of refusal stated by her, and may make an order under this section notwithstanding such offer, if he is satisfied that there is just ground for so doing.

Explanation — If a husband has contracted marriage with another woman or keeps a mistress, it shall be considered to be just ground for his wife's refusal to live with him.

Section 127 (3) (*b*), on which the appellant has build up the edifice of his defence reads thus:

Alteration in allowance
127. (1) . . . .
      (2) . . . .
      (3) Where any order has been under section 125 in favour of a woman who has been divorced by, or has obtained a divorce from, her husband, the Magistrate shall, if he is satisfied that —
      (*a*) . . . .
      (*b*) the woman has been divorced by her husband and that she has received, whether before or after the date of the said order, the whole of the sum which, under any customary or personal law applicable to the parties, was payable on such divorce, cancel such order —
      (*i*) in the case where such sum was paid before such order, from the date on which such order was made.
      (*ii*) in any other case, from the date of expiry of the period, if any, for which maintenance has been actually paid by the husband to the woman.

Under section 125 (1) (*a*), a person who, having sufficient means, neglects or refuses to maintain his wife who is unable to maintain herself, can be asked by the Court to pay a monthly maintenance to her at a rate not exceeding five hundred rupees.

By clause (b) of the Explanation to section 125(1), 'wife' includes a divorced woman who has not remarried. These provisions are too clear and precise to admit of any doubt or refinement. The religion professed by a spouse or by the spouses has no place in the scheme of these provisions. Whether the spouses are Hindus or Muslims, Christians or Parsis, pagans or heathens, is wholly irrelevant in the application of these provisions. The reason for this is axiomatic, in the sense that section 125 is a part of the Code of Criminal Procedure, not of the civil laws which define and govern the rights and obligations of the parties belonging to particular religions, like the Hindu Adoptions and Maintenance Act, the Shariat, or the Parsi Matrimonial Act. Section 125 was enacted in order to provide a quick and summary remedy to a class of persons who are unable to maintain themselves. What difference would it then make as to what is the religion professed by the neglected wife, child or parent? Neglect by a person of sufficient means to maintain these and the inability of these persons to maintain themselves are the objective criteria which determine the applicability of section 125. Such provisions, which are essentially of a prophylactic nature, cut across the barriers of religion. True, they do not supplant the personal law of the parties but, equally, the religion professed by the parties or the state of the personal law by which they are governed, cannot have any repercussion on the applicability of such laws unless, within the framework of the Constitution, their application is restricted to a defined category of religious groups or classes. The liability imposed by section 125 to maintain close relatives who are indigent is founded upon the individual's obligation to the society to prevent vagrancy and destitution. That is the moral edict of the law and morality cannot be clubbed with religion. Clause (*b*) of the Explanation to section 125(1) which defines 'wife' as including a divorced wife, contains no words of limitations to justify the exclusion of Muslim women from its scope. Section 125 is truly secular in character.

Sir James Fitz-James Stephen who piloted the Code of Criminal Procedure, 1872 as a Legal Member of the Viceroy's Council described the precursor of Chapter IX of the Code in which section 125 occurs as 'a mode of preventing vagrancy or at least of preventing its consequences'. In *Jagir Kaur* v. *Jaswant Singh*,[4] Subba Rao, J. speaking for the Court said that Chapter XXXVI of the Code of 1898 which contained section 488, corresponding to section 125, "intends to serve a social purpose". In *Nanak Chand* v. *Shri Chandra Kishore Agarwala*, Sikri, J., while pointing out that the scope of the Hindu Adoptions and Maintenance Act, 1956 and that of section 488 was different, said that section 488 was "applicable to all religions and has no relationship with the personal law of the parties."

Under section 488 of the Code of 1898, the wife's right to maintenance depended upon the continuance of her married status. Therefore, that right could be defeated by the husband by divorcing her unilaterally as under the Muslim Personal Law, or by obtaining a decree of divorce against her under the other systems of law. It was in order to remove this hardship that the Joint Committee recommended that the benefit of the provision regarding maintenance should be extended to a divorced woman, so long as she has not remarried after the divorce. That is the genesis of clause (*b*) of the Explanation to section 125(1), which provides that 'wife' includes a woman who has been divorced by, or has obtained a divorce from her husband and has not remarried. Even in the absence of this provision, the Court has held under the Code 1898 that the provisions regarding maintenance were independent of the personal law governing the parties. The induction of the definition of 'wife' so as to include a divorced woman lends even greater weight to that conclusion. 'Wife' means a wife as defined, irrespective of the religion professed by her or by her husband. Therefore, a divorced Muslim woman, so long as she has not remarried, is a 'wife' for the purpose of section 125. The statutory right available to her under that section is unaffected by the provisions of the personal law applicable to her.

The conclusion that the right conferred by section 125 can be exercised irrespective of the personal law of the parties, is fortified, especially in regard to Muslims, by the provision contained in the Explanation to the second proviso to section 125(3) of the Code. That proviso says that if the husband offers to maintain his wife on condition that she should live with him, and she refuses to live with him, the Magistrate may consider any grounds of refusal stated by her and may make an order of maintenance notwithstanding the offer of the husband, if he is satisfied that there is a just ground for passing such an order. According to the Explanation to the proviso:

> If a husband has contracted marriage with another woman or keeps a mistress, it shall be considered to be just ground for his wife's refusal to live with him.

It is too well known that "A Mahomedan may have as many as four wives at the same time but not more. If he marries a fifth wife when he has already four, the marriage is not void, but merely irregular." (See Mulla's *Mahomedan Law*, 18th Edition, paragraph 255, page 285, quoting Baillie's *Digest of Mohummudan Law*; and, Ameer Ali's *Mahomedan Law*, 5th Edition, vol. II, page 280). The explanation confers upon the wife the right to refuse to live with her husband if he contracts another marriage, leave alone 3 or 4 other marriages. It shows, unmistakably, that section 125 overrides the personal law, if there is any conflict between the two.

The whole of this discussion as to whether the right conferred by section 125 prevails over the personal law of the parties, has proceeded on the assumption that there is a conflict between the provisions of that section and those of the Muslim Personal Law. The argument that by reason of section 2 of the Shariat Act, XXVI of 1937 the rule of decision in matters relating, *inter alia*, to maintenance "shall be the Muslim Personal Law" also proceeds upon a similar assumption. We embarked upon the decision of the question of priority between the Code and the Muslim Personal Law on the assumption that there was a conflict between the two because, in so far as it lies in our power, we wanted to set at rest, once for all, the question whether section 125 would prevail over the personal law of the parties, in cases where they are in conflict.

The next logical step to take is to examine the question, on which considerable argument has been advanced before us, whether there is any conflict between the provisions of section 125 and those of the Muslim Personal Law on the liability of the Muslim husband to provide for the maintenance of his divorced wife.

The contention of the husband and of the interveners who support him is that, under the Muslim Personal Law, the liability of the husband to maintain a divorced wife is limited to the period of iddat. In support of this proposition, they rely upon the statement of law on the point contained in certain textbooks. In Mulla's *Mahomedan Law* (18th Edition, para 279, page 301), there is a statement to the effect that, "After divorce, the wife is entitled to maintenance during the period of iddat".

At page 302, the learned author says:

Where an order is made for the maintenance of a wife under section 488 of the Criminal Procedure Code and the wife is afterwards divorced, the order ceases to operate on the expiration of the period of iddat. The result is that a Mahomedan may defeat an order made against him under section 488 by divorcing his wife immediately after the order is made. His obligation to maintain his wife will cease in that case on the completion of her iddat.

Tyabji's *Muslim Law* (4th Edition, para 304, pages 268-269), contains the statement that:

On the expiration of the iddat after talaq, the wife's right to maintenance ceases whether based on the Muslim Law, or on an order under the Criminal Procedure Code.

According to Dr Paras Diwan:

When a marriage is dissolved by divorce the wife is entitled to maintenance during the period of iddat .... On the expiration of the period of iddat, the wife is not entitled to any maintenance under any circumstances. Muslim law does not recognise any obligation on the part of a man to maintain a wife whom he had divorced.
(*Muslim Law in Modern India*, 1982 Edition, page 130).

These statements in the textbooks are inadequate to establish the proposition that the Muslim husband is not under an obligation to provide for the maintenance of his divorced wife, *who is unable to maintain herself*. One must have regard to the entire conspectus of the Muslim Personal Law in order to determine the extent, both in quantum and in duration, of the husband's liability to provide for the maintenance of an indigent wife who has been divorced by him. Under that law, the husband is bound to pay mehr to the wife as a mark of respect to her. True, that he may settle any amount he likes by way of dower upon his wife, which cannot be less than 10 dirhams, which is equivalent to three or four rupees (Mulla's *Mahomedan Law*, 18th Edition, para 286, p. 308). But, one must have regard to the realities of life. mehr is a mark of respect to the wife. The sum settled by way of mehr is generally expected to take care of the ordinary requirements of the wife, during the marriage and after. But these provisions of the Muslim Personal Law do not countenance cases in which the wife is unable to maintain herself after the divorce. We consider it not only incorrect but unjust, to extend the scope of the statements extracted above to cases in which a divorced wife is unable to maintain herself. We are of the opinion that the application of those statements of law must be restricted to that class of cases, in which there is no possibility of vagrancy or destitution arising out of the indigence of the divorced wife. We are not concerned here with the broad and general question whether a husband is liable to maintain his wife, which includes a divorced wife, in all circumstances and at all events. That is not the subject matter of section 125. That section deals with cases in which, a person who is possessed of sufficient means neglects or refuses to maintain, amongst others, his wife who is unable to maintain herself. Since the Muslim Personal Law, which limits the husband's liability to provide for the maintenance of the divorced wife to the period of iddat, does not contemplate or countenance the situation envisaged by section 125, it would be wrong to hold that the Muslim husband, according to his personal law, is not under an obligation to provide maintenance, beyond the period of iddat, to his divorced wife who is unable to maintain herself. The argument of the appellant that, according to the Muslim Personal Law, his liability to provide for the maintenance of his divorced wife is limited to the period of iddat, despite the fact that she is unable to maintain herself, has therefore to be rejected. The true position is that, if the divorced wife is able to maintain herself, the husband's liability to provide maintenance for her ceases with the expiration of the period of iddat. If she is unable to maintain herself, she is entitled to take recourse to section 125 of the Code. The outcome of this discussion is that there is no conflict between the provisions of section 125 and those of the Muslim Personal Law on the question of the Muslim husband's obligation to provide maintenance for a divorced wife who is unable to maintain herself.

There can be no greater authority on this question than the holy Quran, "The Quran, the Sacred Book of Islam, comprises in its 114 Suras or chapters, the total of revelations believed to have been communicated to Prophet Muhammed, as a final expression of God's will." (*The Quran Interpreted* by Arthur J. Arberry). Verses (Aiyats) 241 and 242 of the Quran show that according to the Prophet, there is an obligation on Muslim husbands to provide for their divorced wives. The Arabic version of those Aiyats and their English translations are reproduced below:

Arabic version	*English version*
Aiyat No. 241	For divorced women
WA LIL MOTALLAQATAY	Maintenance (should be
MATA UN	provided)
BILL MAAROOFAY	On a reasonable (scale)
HAQQAN	This is a duty
ALAL MUTTAQEENA	on the righteous.

Arabic version	English version
Aiyat No. 242	
KAZALEKA YUBAIYYANULLAHO	Thus both God
	Make clear His Signs
L'AHUM AYATEHEE LAW	To you : in order that
ALLAKUM TAQELOON	ye may understand.

(See *The Holy Quran* by Yusuf Ali, page 96)

The correctness of the translation of these Aiyats is not in dispute except that, the contention of the appellant is that the word 'Mata' in Aiyat No. 241 means 'provisions' and not 'maintenance'. That is a distinction without a difference. Nor are we impressed by the shuffling plea of the All India Muslim Personal Law Board that, in Aiyat 241, the exhortation is to the 'Mutta Queena' that is, to the more pious and the more God-fearing, not to the general run of the Muslims, the 'Muslimin'. In Aiyat 242, the Quran says: "It is expected that you will use your commonsense."

The English version of the two Aiyats in Muhammed Zafrullah Khan's *The Quran* (page 38) reads thus:

For divorced women also there shall be provision according to what is fair. This is an obligation binding on the righteous. Thus does Allah make His commandments clear to you that you may understand.

The translation of Aiyats 240 to 242 in *The Meaning of the Quran* (vol. 1, published by the Board of Islamic Publications, Delhi) reads thus :

240-241.
Those of you, who shall die and leave wives behind them, should make a will to the effect that they should be provided with a year's maintenance and should not be turned out of their homes. But if they leave their homes of their own accord, you shall not be answerable for whatever they choose for themselves in a fair way; Allah is All-Powerful, All-wise. Likewise, the divorced women should also be given something in accordance with the known fair standard. This is an obligation upon the God-fearing people.

242
Thus Allah makes clear His commandments for you: It is expected that you will use your commonsense.

In *The Running Commentary of the Holy Quran* (1964 edition) by Dr Allamah Khadim Rahmani Nuri, Aiyat 241 is translated thus:

241
And for the divorced woman (also) a provision (should be made) with fairness (in addition to her dower); (This is) a duty (incumbent) on the reverent.

In *The Meaning of the Glorious Quran, Taxt and Explanatory Translation*, by Marmaduke Pickhall, (Taj Company Ltd., Karachi) Aiyat 241 is translated thus:

241
For divorced women a provision in kindness: A duty for those who ward off (evil).

Finally, in *The Quran Interpreted* by Arthur J. Arberry, Aiyat 241 is translated thus :

241

There shall be for divorced women provision honourable — an obligation on the godfearing. So God makes clear His signs for you Happily you will understand.

Dr K.R. Nuri in his book quoted above: *The Running Commentary of The Holy Quran* says in the preface:

"Belief in Islam does not mean mere confession of the existence of something. It really means the translation of the faith into action. Words without deeds carry no meaning in Islam. Therefore the term "believe and do good" has been used like a phrase all over the Quran. Belief in something means that man should inculcate the qualities or carry out the promptings or guidance of that thing in this action. Belief in Allah means that besides acknowledging the existence of the Author of the Universe, we are to show obedience to His commandments. . . .

These Aiyats leave no doubt that the Quran imposes an obligation on the Muslim husband to make provision for or to provide maintenance to the divorced wife. The contrary argument does less than justice to the teachings of the Quran. As observed by Mr M. Hidayatullah in his introduction in Mulla's *Mahomedan Law*, the Quran is Al-furqan, that is, one showing truth from falsehood and right from wrong.

The second plank of the appellant's argument is that the respondent's application under section 125 is liable to be dismissed because of the provision contained in section 127(3)(b). That section provides, to the extent material, that the Magistrate shall cancel the order of maintenance, if the wife is divorced by the husband and, she has received "the whole of the sum which, under any customary or personal law applicable to the parties, was payable on such divorce". That raises the question as to whether, under the Muslim Personal Law, any sum is payable to the wife 'on divorce'. We do not have to grope in the dark and speculate as to which kind of a sum this can be because, the only argument advanced before us on behalf of the appellant and by the interveners supporting him, is that mehr is the amount payable by the husband to the wife on divorce. We find it impossible to accept this argument.

In Mulla's *Principles of Mahomedan Law* (18th Edition, Page 308), mehr or dower is defined in paragraph 285 as "a sum of money or other property which the wife is entitled to receive from the husband in consideration of the marriage". Dr Paras Diwan in his book, *Muslim Law in Modern India* (1982 edition, page 60), criticises this definition on the ground that mehr is not payable "in consideration of marriage" but is an obligation imposed by law on the husband as a mark of respect for the wife, as is evident from the fact that non-specification of mehr at the time of marriage does not affect the validity of the marriage. We need not enter into this controversy and indeed, Mulla's book itself contains the further statement at page 308 that the word 'consideration' is not used in the sense in which it is used in the Contract Act and that under the Mohammedan law, dower is an obligation imposed upon the husband as a mark of respect for the wife. We are concerned to find whether mehr is an amount payable by the husband to the wife on divorce. Some confusion is caused by the fact that under the MPL, the amount of mehr is usually split into two parts, one of which is called "prompt", which is payable on demand, and the other is called "deferred", which is payable on the dissolution of the marriage by death or by divorce. But, the fact that deferred mehr is payable at the time of the dissolution of marriage, cannot justify the conclusion that it is payable 'on divorce'. Even assuming that, in a given case the entire amount of mehr is of the deferred variety payable on the dissolution of marriage by divorce, it cannot be said that it is an amount which is payable on divorce. Divorce may be a convenient or identifiable point of time at which the deferred amount has to be paid by the husband to the wife. But, the payment of the amount is not occasioned by the divorce, which is what is meant by the expression 'on divorce', which occurs in section 127(3)(b) of the Code. If mehr is an amount which the wife is entitled to receive from the husband in consideration of the marriage, that is the very opposite of the amount being payable in consideration of divorce. Divorce dissolves the marriage. Therefore, no amount which is payable in consideration of the marriage can possibly be described as an amount payable in consideration of divorce. The alternative premise that mehr is an obligation imposed upon the husband as a mark of respect for the wife, is wholly detrimental to the stance that it is an amount payable to the wife on divorce. A man may marry a women for love, looks, learning or nothing at all. And he may settle the sum upon her as a mark of respect. Therefore, a sum payable to the wife out of respect cannot be a sum payable 'on divorce'.

In an appeal from a Full Bench decision of the Allahabad High Court, the Privy Council in *Hamira Bibi* v. *Zubaide Bibi* [6] summed up the nature and character of mehr in these words:

"Dower is an essential incident under the Mussulman law to the status of marriage; to such an extent is it so that when it is unspecified at the time the marriage is contracted, the law declares that it must be adjudged on definite principles. Regarded as a consideration for the marriage, it is, in theory, payable before consummation; but the law allows its division into two parts, one of which is called "prompt", payable before the wife can be called upon to enter the conjugal domicile; the other "deferred", payable on the dissolution of the contract by the death of either of the parties or by divorce. (pp. 300–1).

This statement of law was adopted in another decision of the Privy Council in *Syed Sabir Husan* v. *Farzand Hasana*.[7] It is not quite appropriate and seems invidious to describe any particular bench of a court as "strong" but, we cannot resist the temptation of mentioning that Mr Syed Ameer Ali was a party to the decision in *Mamira Bibi* while Sir Shadi Lal was a party to the decisions in *Syed Sabir Husain*. These decisions show that the payment of dower may be deferred to a future date as, for example, death or divorce. But, that does not mean that the payment of the deferred dower is occasioned by these events.

It is contended on behalf of the appellant that the proceedings of the Rajya Sabha dated December 18, 1973 (volume 86, column 186), when the bill which led to the Code of 1973 was on the anvil, would show that the intention of the Parliament was to leave the provisions of the Muslim Personal Law untouched. In this behalf, reliance is placed on the following statement made by Shri Ram Niwas Mirdha, the then Minister of State, Home Affairs:

Dr Vyas very learnedly made certain observations that a divorced wife under the Muslim law deserves to be treated justly and she should get what is her equitable or legal due. Well, I will not go into this, but say that we would not like to interfere with the customary law of the Muslims through the Criminal Procedure Code. If there is a demand for change in the Muslim Personal Law, it should actually come from the Muslim community itself and we should wait for the Muslim public opinion on these matters to crystallise before we try to change this customary right or make changes in their personal law. Above all, this is hardly the place where we could do so. But as I tried to explain, the provision in the Bill is an advance over the previous situation. Divorced woman have been included and brought within the ambit of clause 125, but a limitation is being imposed by this amendment to clause 127, namely, that the maintenance orders would cease to operate after the amounts due to her under the personal law are paid to her. This is a healthy compromise between what has been termed a conservative interpretation of law or a concession to conservative public opinion and liberal approach to the problem. We have made an advance and not tried to transgress what are the personal rights of Muslim women. So this, I think, should satisfy honourable Members that whatever advance we have made is in the right direction and it should be welcomed.

It does appear from this speech that the Government did not desire to interfere with the personal law of the Muslims through the Criminal Procedure Code. It wanted the Muslim community to take the lead and the Muslim public opinion to crystallise on the reforms in their personal law. However, we are not concerned with the question whether the Government did or did not desire to bring about changes in the Muslim Personal Law by enacting sections 125 and 127 of the Code. As we have said earlier and, as admitted by the Minister, the Government did introduce such a change by defining the expression 'wife' to include a divorced wife. It also introduced another significant change by providing that the fact that the husband has contracted marriage with another woman is a just ground for the wife's refusal to live with him. The provision contained in section 127(3)(b) may have been introduced because of the misconception that dower is an amount payable "on divorce". But, that cannot convert an amount payable as a mark of respect for the wife into an amount payable on divorce.

It must follow from this discussion, unavoidably a little too long, that the judgements of this Court in *Bai Tahira*[2] (Krishnan Iyer J., Tulzapurkar J. and Pathak J.) and *Fazlunbi*[3] (Krishna Iyer J., one of us, Chinnappa Reddy J. and A.P. Sen J.) are correct. Justice Krishna Iyer who spoke for the Court in both these cases, relied greatly on the teleological and schematic method of interpretation so as to advance the purpose of the law. These constructional techniques have their own importance in the interpretation of statutes meant to ameliorate the conditions of suffering sections of the society. We have attempted to show that taking the language of the statute as one finds it, there is no escape from the conclusion that a divorced Muslim wife is entitled to apply for maintenance under section 125 and that, mehr is not a sum which, under the Muslim Personal Law, is payable on divorce.

Though *Bai Tahira*[2] was correctly decided, we would like, respectfully, to draw attention to an error which has crept in the judgement. There is a statement at page 80 of the Report, in the context of section 127 (3) (b), that "payment of mehr money, as a customary discharge, is within the cognizance of that provision". We have taken the view that mehr, not being payable on divorce, does not fall within the meaning of that provision.

It is a matter of deep regret that some of the interveners who supported the appellant, took up an extreme position by displaying an unwarranted zeal to defeat the right to maintenance of women who are unable to maintain themselves. The written submissions of the All India Personal Law Board have gone to the length of asserting that it is irrelevant to inquire as to how a Muslim divorcee should maintain herself. The facile answer of the Board is that the Personal Law has devised the system of mehr to meet the requirements of women and if a woman is indigent, she must look at her relations, including nephews and cousins, to support her. This is a most unreasonable view of law as well as life. We appreciate that Begum Temür Jehan, a social worker who has been working in association with the Delhi City Women's Association for the uplift of Muslim women, intervened to support Mr Danial Latifi who appeared on behalf of the wife.

It is also a matter of regret that Article 44 of our Constitution has remained a dead letter. It provides that "The State shall endeavour to secure for the citizens a uniform civil code throughout the territory of India". There is, no evidence of any official activity for framing a common civil code for the country. A belief seems to have gained ground that it is for the Muslim community to take a lead in the matter of reforms of their personal law. A common civil code will help the cause of national integration by removing disparate loyalties to laws which have conflicting ideologies. No community is likely to bell the cat by making gratuitous concessions on this issue. It is the state which is charged with the duty of securing a uniform civil code for the citizens of the country and, unquestionably, it has the legislative competence to do so. A counsel in the case whispered, somewhat audibly, that legislative competence is one thing, the political courage to use that competence is quite another. We understand the difficulties involved in bringing persons of different faiths and persuasions on a common platform. But, a beginning has to be made if the Constitution is to have any meaning. Inevitably, the role of the reformed has to be assumed by the courts because, it is beyond the endurance of sensitive minds to allow injustice to be suffered when it is so palpable. But piecemeal attempts of courts to bridge the gap between personal laws cannot take the place of a common civil code. Justice to all is a far more satisfactory way of dispensing justice than justice from case to case.

Dr Tahir Mahmood in his book *Muslim Personal Law* (1977 edition, pages 200–2), has made a powerful plea for framing a uniform civil code for all citizens of India. He says: "In pursuance of the goal of secularism, the State must stop administering religion-based personal laws." He wants the lead to come from the majority community but, we should have thought that, lead or no lead, the State must act. It would be useful to quote the appeal made by the author to the Muslim community:

> Instead of wasting their energies in exerting theological and political pressure in order to secure an "immunity" for their traditional personal law from the state's legislative jurisdiction, the Muslim will do well to begin exploring and demonstrating how the true Islamic laws, purged of their time-worn and anachronistic interpretations, can enrich the common civil code of India.

At a seminar held on October 18, 1980, under the auspices of the Department of Islamic and Comparative Law, Indian Institute of Islamic Studies, New Delhi, he also made an appeal to the Muslim community to display by their conduct a correct understanding of Islamic concepts on marriage and divorce (See *Islam and Comparative Law* Quarterly, April–June, 1981, page 146).

Before we conclude, we would like to draw attention to the *Report of the Commission on Marriage and Family Laws*, which was appointed by the Government of Pakistan by a Resolution dated August 4, 1955. The answer of the Commission to Question No. 5 (page 1215 of the Report) is that

> A large number of middle-aged women who are being divorced without rhyme or reason should not be thrown on the streets without a roof over their heads and without any means of sustaining themselves and their children.

The Report concludes thus:

> In the words of Allama Iqbal, "the question which is likely to confront Muslim countries in the near future, is whether the law of Islam is capable of evolution — a question which will require great intellectual effort, and is sure to be answered in the affirmative.

For these reasons, we dismiss the appeal and confirm the judgement of the High Court. The appellant will pay the costs of the appeal to respondent 1, which we quantify at rupees ten thousand. It is needless to add that it would be open to the respondent to make an application under section 127 (1) of the Code for increasing the allowance of maintenance granted to her on proof of a change in the circumstances as envisaged by that section.

.... C.J.

.... J.
(D.A. DESAI)

.... J.
(O. CHINNAPPA REDDY)

.... J.
(E.S. VENKATARAMIAH)

.... J.
(RANGANATH MISRA)

New Delhi
23 April 1985

References

1. Edward William Lane, *Selection from Kuran*; 1843;
   Reprint 1982; XC (Introduction)
2. 1979 (2) SCR 75.
3. 1980 (3) SCR 1127
4. 1964 (2) SCR 73, 84
5. 1970 (1) SCR 565
6. 43 I.A. 294.
7. 65 I.A. 119, 127.

S.C. Judgement on Maintenance

FORCES BEHIND THE AGITATION

Asghar Ali Engineer

The Supreme Court judgement on the applicability of section 125(2) of the Criminal Procedure Code to Muslim divorcees has created a great stir throughout India. In the *Mohammad Ahmed Khan* v. *Shah Bano* case, the Court decided that the section 125(2), according to which a destitute divorced wife is entitled to maintenance after divorce, would also be applicable to Indian Muslims. The highest court in the country was seized of the seriousness of the problem it was dealing with and with the serious implications of its judgement.

Muslims in India, like Parsis and Christians, have a separate personal law of their own covering matters pertaining to marriage, divorce, inheritance, and custody of children. The British legislature enacted the Shariat Act in 1937 covering these matters and it is known as the Muslim personal law in common parlance. Unlike the personal law, there is no separate criminal law for Muslims in India and hence the important question before the Supreme Court was whether section 125 of the Criminal Procedure Code as regards the provision of maintenance to a divorced wife would apply to Muslims or not. The dilemma was that there is a common criminal code and any of its provisions should be uniformly applicable to all the communities, but also that the application of section 125 (2) would have a bearing on Muslim personal law.

Ultimately the court decided to apply section 125 of the Cr. P.C. to Shah Bano and awarded maintenance to her. In the opinion of a noted Muslim lawyer of Calcutta, M.A. Latif,

The court in rejecting Ahmed's ... defence laid down the true relation between civil and criminal law in general and in particular between the personal law and the provisions of criminal law on the point of maintenance for a wife, including a divorced "wife" who cannot support herself. Choosing its words carefully, it aptly said that while the provisions of Section 125 Cr. P.C. do not "supplant" the personal law, personal law has no "repercussion" on the applicability of section 125 Cr. P.C. unless applicability is restricted under some Constitutional provision.

However, the Supreme Court was well aware of the possible strong reaction of the Muslim leaders and Ulama to its judgement. Hence the judges decided to support their judgement from the Quran as well. It was the only way to convince the ordinary Muslims. The learned judges consulted various authoritative translations of the scripture. Of the three translations consulted they accepted that of Abdullah Yousuf Ali. The relevant verse in this respect is 241 of chapter 2. He translates this verse as: "For divorced women maintenance (should be provided) on a reasonable (scale). This is a duty on the righteous."

However, the learned judges unknowingly ran the risk of trying to interpret the holy scripture — a right exclusively claimed by the Ulama. It became one of the issues in the agitation launched by the Muslim Personal Law Board. The judges were strongly denounced not only for their judgement but also for daring to interpret the holy scripture. Little did the poor Muslims know that the judges had only consulted the authoritative translations generally accepted by the Muslims everywhere. The key word under dispute used in the verse quoted above is mataa, which has been rendered differently by different translators and commentators, introducing a human element into it.

The agitation launched by the Ulama, members of the Muslim Personal Law Board and other Muslim leaders has shaken the entire Muslim community. Maulana Abul Hasan Ali Nadvi, the president of the Personal Law Board, has described it as most momentous since the Khilafat movement in the late twenties. The Muslim leaders are also claiming in their speeches that the judgement is a blessing in disguise in as much as it has united all Muslims of different sects and opinions to oppose it.

Is this claim true? The truth is more complex than what is claimed by ideologues, orators and rabble-rousers. It is true that a large number of meetings are being organized everyday throughout India to oppose the judgement. In some meetings, if one goes by the Urdu newspaper reports, women, too, came to protest in their thousands. Many educated women, teachers and lecturers, it is reported, have addressed exclusive meetings for women and affirmed that their religion is dearer to them than the pittance they are likely to get by way of maintenance. They also declared, eloquently, that it is against their dignity to claim maintenance from those who have divorced them.

It is also true that every Muslim leader or alim has been rushing to address meetings in protest against the judgement. In these meetings, Shias and Sunnis, Wahabis and Deobandis have been pledging their loyalty to the Islamic shariat from the same platform.

However, there is a sizable section of Muslims, both men and women, which has welcomed the Supreme Court judgement. This section, it is true, has not been bold enough to publicly articulate its views and, even if willing to do so, does not succeed in getting its views published in the Urdu press. It can only use either the English or other language papers.

Powerful vested interests among the Muslims often raise a hue and cry against those who desire justice for Muslim women. The case of Prof. Abida Samiuddin of Aligarh Muslim University may be cited here. Prof. Abida, a teacher in political science, wrote two articles in *Quami Awaz*, an Urdu daily from Delhi, supporting the Supreme Court judgement. Her brave posture elicited a strong reaction from an Urdu daily *Al-Mashriq* from Calcutta which editorially demanded her dismissal from the AMU.

A Hindustani Muslim Forum was formed in Bombay on October 19 to support the Supreme Court judgement in particular and to work for the rights of Muslim women in general. The forum has been joined by many prominent Muslim women and men and its activists have launched a signature campaign in favour of the judgement. A Muslim college teacher from Bhopal has written vigorously campaigning for the judgement and against the amendment of the section. She has pointed out in one of her articles that section 125 of the Cr. P.C. also makes it obligatory on children to take care of their destitute parents. If section 125 is amended so as not to apply to Muslims, would it not mean that Muslims would be exempt from maintaining their destitute parents as well? Will this conform to the Islamic shariat?

It is also important to note that an increasing number of Muslim women are going to court to claim maintenance from their former husbands. According to an enquiry in a district court in Dahod (a middle-sized town in the Panch Mahals district of Gujarat), as many as 85 cases are pending pertaining to maintenance by Muslim divorcees. This large number of cases is causing the community to mount increasing pressure on the divorcees — to force them not to seek legal redress.

With a greater degree of urbanization, changing socio-economic conditions and the consequent stresses and strains, the number of divorces is increasing. Among Muslims, divorce being easier, Muslim women face greater hazards. But they are becoming more conscious and the courts are also taking a liberal view of maintenance claims. Earlier a magistrate in the lower court could not award a maintenance decree. Now the Supreme Court holds that even a magistrate can pass an interim order for maintenance. The Cr. P.C. provides a quick remedy to protect the woman against starvation.

Muslims sometimes resort to an easy divorce against the specific injunctions of the holy Quran. Shah Bano, too, the judgement in whose case, by the Supreme Court, has aroused the ire of Muslim leaders and the Ulama, was thrown out by her husband after four decades of marriage and, when she claimed maintenance, was instantly divorced. What is most shocking is that not a single alim or leader has any word of sympathy for Shah Bano or other similarly suffering Muslim women. On the contrary a deputation of Ulama from Madhya Pradesh led by Maulana Inamur Rahman Khan of Jamat-e-Islami has in its investigative report lavished praise on Shah Bano's husband and subjected her to taunts. To our utter shock, Mohammad Ahmed Khan has been praised as a modern Muslim with a great sense of justice and fair play and the report has even justified his taking a second wife "irked by Shah Bano's behaviour".

For Shah Bano, the maulana opines that she does not deserve maintenance as she has three young sons who are earning and they are not oblivious of her needs. The maulana does not refer to the inconvenient fact that Shah Bano was instantly divorced (using the un-Islamic formula of three divorces in one sitting) when she claimed maintenance from her "justice-loving husband" and that, in the Islamic shariat, custody of children after a particular age rests with the father.

From what has been said above it is not difficult to conclude that the whole agitation against the Supreme Court judgement launched by the Ulama and Muslim leaders is not motivated by religious concern, much less by religious fervour. It is, in fact, motivated by a curious mixture of male chauvinism and political interests. Had it been motivated by religious concern, as is claimed by them, they would have launched a vigorous movement against the gross abuses of three divorces in one sitting known in the shariat as talaq al-bida. All Hanafi Ulama agree that three divorces in one sitting is against the holy Quran and the sunnah (practice) of the Prophet and is a later innovation, and yet it is a most widely practised form of divorce without any protest from the Ulama.

I would like to throw some light here on this issue from the point of view of the Islamic shariat since the whole agitation is being conducted in its name. It is being maintained that maintenance to a divorced woman can be given only for the period of iddat (which is three months if the woman is not pregnant, and if she is pregnant, until she lays down her child) and not thereafter, according to the Quran and sunnah (of course the Quran does not lay down any such period for maintenance of a divorce except in the case of a pregnant woman). The founders of all the four major Sunni schools agree on this.

But as far as maintenance to a divorced woman is concerned, the matter is not that simple. In Islamic jurisprudence there is another form of divorce known as talaq al-farr, which, rendered in English, would roughly mean divorce to run away (from responsibility). This form of divorce is generally resorted to by a husband dying of illness to deprive his wife of her share in his property. Such a form of divorce has been disallowed by the jurists in Islam. The Islamic jurists have also defined clearly the dying illnesses. Divorce does take place in such instances but, according to the jurists, a wife so divorced does not lose her share in her husband's property. And according to Imam Malik, she would be entitled to this share even if she has remarried.

The apparent logic of Imam Malik's ruling is that since the husband's real intention was to deprive his wife of her share in his property and this is injustice, we would also become a party to this injustice if we do not get her her share of her former husband's property even after she remarries. If we apply this analogy it is not difficult to see that any divorce used to get rid of one's responsibility to pay maintenance should not allow the erring husband to be rid of such responsibility. This is precisely what happened in the case of Shah Bano. When she claimed maintenance from her husband (she was separated from him for quite some time as he had married again), he resorted to divorce to escape the payment of maintenance.

Some Islamic countries such as Syria have insured against precisely this. In Syria any divorce without reasonable grounds is treated on a par with talaq al-farr and the divorcee is given maintenance in such cases for a period of one year. Dr Mustafa al-Sayai, a Syrian jurist, in fact feels that, taking Imam Malik's logic as sound, the divorcee in such cases should be allowed to claim maintenance till such time as she remarries or dies.

It would thus be seen that the agitation launched by the Ulama and Muslim leaders is not quite in keeping with the religious spirit and has ulterior motives. There is also another ground to believe this. Every year hundreds of Muslims are killed in major and minor communal riots in India. Only recently in the communal violence which rocked the state of Gujarat for more than four months, more than 200 Muslims were killed. In Nellie, Assam, more than 3,000 Muslims lost their lives in February 1983. But the conscience of our Ulama and Muslim leaders was not shaken. They thought it sufficient to issue a mere formal statement. No serious agitation was ever launched.

Had the tremendous energy expended on the Supreme Court judgement been spent on agitating to arouse the conscience of the nation against communal butchery, it could have paid great dividends. But that would mean risking one's political career rather than promoting it. We must take cognizance of other factors as well in understanding the mechanism of this agitation. Apart from the Ulama, secular leaders are also showing a great deal of militancy on purely religious issues. It was not so earlier. Even the Muslim League leaders before Partition did not promote religious frenzy (communal, sectarian politics on secular issues apart). Jinnah kept his distance from the Ulama during the Khilafat agitation.

But in post-Independence India the Ulama came to completely dominate the scene. One important reason for this was that the Ulama had participated in the freedom struggle on the side of the Indian National Congress and had acquired a lot of prestige in independent India. For this reason they did not prefer to migrate to Pakistan. Moreover, because of their good relations with the Congress which was ruling the country, they could protect the interests of the Muslims who remained in India. Thus the Ulama came to dominate the leadership of Indian Muslims. Most secular Muslims migrated to Pakistan in search of better pastures. The few like Dr Zakir Hussain, who remained behind, slowly vanished from the scene, leaving a vacuum. The present secular leadership among the Muslims, which has appeared recently on the scene, is weak and vacillating and enjoys no prestige among the masses.

The secular leadership tries to snatch at any opportunity in order to strike roots among the Muslims. The Muslims in India have an acute minority complex and a heightened sense of danger to their religio-cultural identity. The secular Muslim leadership thus plays up any issue which has a bearing on the religio-cultural identity of Muslims. The wave of religious fundamentalism has further enhanced the importance of such issues. It is unfortunate that though Indian Muslims are facing acute problems, no leadership of great vision and integrity has emerged, a leadership which is modern and yet not indifferent to religion, a leadership which is moderate and yet not oblivious of the acute crisis, a leadership which is not conservative and yet not ignorant of the importance of a religio-cultural identity. Without filling this bill the Indian Muslims cannot cope with the acute crisis they are faced with.

It is equally unfortunate that the Urdu press plays a very opportunistic role on such matters. It also plays up emotional issues in order to increase its circulation. One seldom finds well-argued or investigated articles on the number of issues confronting Muslims in India. It has played an equally negative role on the Supreme Court judgement. One hardly finds any analytical, humanistic and progressive article on this issue. It is amusing to see that the papers which wax eloquent in defence of the shariat are full of semi-naked pictures of film heroines in the form of film advertisements. One finds the contrast really obscene and sickening. But even the conservative readers do not mind this as long as these papers cry themselves hoarse over protecting the shariat.

There is no doubt that the Supreme Court judgement on maintenance has deeply shaken the Indian Muslims and has stirred them deeply. But they are, by no means, united on the issue. As pointed out above there are gross misuses of the shariat, especially by men, as they are socially in command. A wise leadership, moved deeply by religious concern, would have used this opportunity to start a reform movement. However, that is not to be. Political opportunism is so rampant that it overwhelms all other concerns. Indian Muslims are not unique in facing this tragedy.

Extract from the *Deccan Herald*
10 December 1985

SHAH BANO VERDICT AND MUSLIM LAW
P. Jaganmohan Reddy

A lively and earnest debate for and against divorced Muslim women being given maintenance by the husband after the period of iddat is now going on. Apparently, irrespective of public opinion among both Muslims and others, particularly women, the prime minister is treating the issue as a matter of personal prestige. Thus, all Congress (I) MPs who are opposed to the bill now before Parliament (to make sections 125 and 127 of the Code of Criminal Procedure inapplicable to Muslim women and ensure that the Shah Bano judgement does not apply to them), are being persuaded to change their attitude so as to uphold the prime minister's prestige regardless of how such a move affects the country's unity and integrity.

Sections 125 to 127 are the successors to section 488 of the Code of Criminal Procedure (Act V of 1898) which, in turn, was the successor to the 1872 Act piloted by Sir James Fitz-James. The erstwhile Hyderabad State, which a renowned orientalist, Wilfred Blunt, described in 1880 as an Islamic state, had a Criminal Procedure Code in Urdu similar to the Indian Criminal Procedure Code and called "Khanoon Zabte Foujdari Sirkara Aali" 1313 Fasli (1903). It succeeded the earlier law of 1308 Fasli (1898–99). Section 411 of the 1313 Fasli Act was analogous to Section 488 of the British Indian Criminal Procedure Code of 1898.

Both codes — of "the Islamic State of Hyderabad" and British India — provided for maintenance to wives and children irrespective of the religion to which they belonged. The purpose of these respective provisions, as stated by Sir James Fitz-James when piloting the 1872 bill, was to make them a "mode for preventing vagrancy or at least of preventing its consequences". The late K. Subba Rao, chief justice of India, characterized these provisions, in the *Jagir Kaur* v. *Jaswant Singh* case, as being intended "to serve a social purpose", and Sikri, J. (as he then was) observed in *Nanakchand* v. *Chandra Kishor Agrawal* that they were "applicable to all persons belonging to all religions and (have) no relationship with the personal law of the parties".

A law based without reference to any religion, and meant for universal application to wives who are destitute, has thus been in force in India for over a century. Even in its changed form from 1974, it has been, without any controversy, complied with and its validity has been upheld by several judgements of the Supreme Court for nearly 12 years. Such a law is being sought to be made inapplicable to Muslims on the ground that sections 125 and 127 as interpreted by the court in Shah Bano's case, offends Muslim personal law, because a divorced woman can be given maintenance even after the period of iddat.

A minister of the Union Government has used language unbecoming to his stature as minister and MP merely because non-Muslim judges had drawn a conclusion on shariat law which is contrary to his views and because they had even purported to show knowledge of the holy Quran. The Supreme Court held on the interpretation of sections 125 and 127, by repealing the argument based on the shariat, (namely that it did not authorize payment of maintenance after dower was paid to the divorced wife) that a divorcee could be granted maintenance beyond the iddat period. Because of this, the chief justice and four other judges constituting that Bench were deemed to have argued against Islamic personal law, according to the union minister. However, the fact is that this judgement is nothing new as it follows earlier decisions of the same court.

A short history of the new provisions of section 125 and 127 of the 1974 Code would help to explain the real issue. When the comprehensive Criminal Procedure Code of 1973 was on the anvil, Section 488 was sought to be re-enacted conferring a right on the courts to grant maintenance to a divorced wife also. Orthodox Muslims vehemently opposed this provision as it enabled the court to award maintenance beyond the three-month iddat period. In the face of this opposition and the prevailing political situation the Government capitulated and the discussion on the bill, which had terminated was reopened, setting a precedent in legislative history. The provision as it finally emerged was that if post-divorce entitlement under personal law was realized by the divorced wife, this should be taken into account, and if maintenance had been granted earlier, it could be cancelled. This appears to have satisfied orthodox Muslim opinion.

Thereafter, in 1979, the Allahabad High Court held that under section 125(3), a divorced woman gets an additional right to receive maintenance beyond the period of iddat and this additional right does not, in fact, conflict with the right which already accrues to her under Muslim law. Judgements in the *Bai Tahira* v. *Ali Husain Fidalli Chothia* and *Faizul Nabi* v. *Khader Vali* cases also held that a divorced wife was entitled to apply for maintenance. Murtaza Fazal Ali and Varadarajan, J.J., wanted these decisions to be reconsidered by a Bench of more than three judges and hence Shah Bano's case was referred to five judges who confirmed the view taken by the earlier judgements of the court.

Before the decision of the Supreme Court in Shah Bano's case Mr Banatwala, general secretary of the Indian Union Muslim League, introduced a bill on March 15, 1985, to undo the Supreme Court's earlier decisions. In the light of this, the Ministry of Home Affairs prepared a comprehensive note on July 24, 1985, opposing the Banatwala bill, particularly after the decision in Shah Bano's case on April 23, 1985. Mr Arif Mohammad Khan, minister of state for Home Affairs also supported this position. The background note on the maintenance of divorced Muslim women and generally on the status of women in Islamic countries (which was to have been circulated among MPs and on whose basis all parties were to be consulted) was not, however, circulated. It would have fully supported the Shah Bano judgement and would have shown that Islamic countries which are Darul Harab had effected reforms in personal law giving a better deal to Muslim women.

The Legal Adviser's note of May 25, 1985 shows that the Supreme Court correctly interpreted the law, that the "provisions of maintenance for divorced wife do not conflict with the Mohammedan law" and that in fact, the court "has simply interpreted the relevant provisions of the Criminal Procedure Code without any interference with the Muslim law as such". The Law Secretary also noted that the Court's decision was on

the true scope of sub-section (3) of section 127 vis-a-vis the right to claim maintenance by a divorced woman under section 125. The decision of the court cannot be regarded as an encroachment on Muslim personal law, which is of a civil nature whereas section 125 is a provision contained in the Criminal Procedure Code. In view of the foregoing, the bill to amend sections 125 and 127 of Criminal Procedure Code should be opposed.

This view was accepted and endorsed by the minister of state for Law on June 1, 1985 and by Mr Asoke Sen, union law minister, on June 2, 1985. The Home Ministry also expressed a similar opinion. The opinions were in respect of the earlier decisions of the Supreme Court ought to be set aside by Mr Banatwala's bill. Then the Congress (I) lost some crucial seats in by-elections. Immediately therenister to the surprise of all, completely changed course and decided upon the controversial bill.

Meanwhile, a minister of state in Mr Gandhi's Cabinet initiated a new debate when he questioned the Supreme Court's right to discuss the Quran and shariat law. Despite the unparliamentary language used, the prime minister defended his colleague's right to criticize the judgement which, in fact, was a diatribe against the judiciary itself. How unreasonable this criticism is becomes evident if the circumstances in which the Quran and the shariat came to be referred by the Supreme Court are ascertained.

The court would have confined itself, as indeed it did, to the interpretation of sections 125 and 127 in the light of its own earlier judgements, and those of the Privy Council, on the nature and implications of mehr. But when the counsel for the Muslim Personal Law Board, which intervened in the Shah Bano case, invited the court to consider the verses of the Quran it did so and was bound to do so.

A perusal of the translations of Aiyat 241 and 242 of the Quran which were produced by the learned counsel, whether as translated by Yousuf Ali or by Dr Allamah Khadum Rahman Nuri or by the late Mohammed Zafrullah Khan, a former judge of the undivided Federal Court of India, or by the Board of Islamic Publications, Delhi, or by Marmaduke Pickhall — all adherents of the Islamic faith and all well versed in Arabic — would lead to only one conclusion: Prophet Mohammad was enjoined by Allah as a matter of duty on the righteous to make provision for the maintenance of divorced women.

Yousuf Ali's translation reads: "For divorced women, maintenance (should be provided) on a reasonable (scale). This is a duty on the righteous (Aiyat 241). Thus doth God make clear His signs to you in order that you may understand." It appears that some dispute was raised by counsel as to the meaning of the word "mataa" in Aiyat 241 as meaning "provision" and not "maintenance". This, the chief justice said, was a distinction without a difference.

Again, the All-India Muslim Personal Law Board seems to have contended that in Aiyat 241 the exhortation to the "Mutta Queena" refers more to the pious and godfearing and not to the general run of Muslims, the "Muslimin". It was contended by the same Muslim Personal Law Board that Aiyat 241 of the Quran says, "It is expected that you will use your common sense" instead of Yousuf Ali's translation that "God makes clear his signs to you in order that you may understand". Here again the Chief Justice said he was not impressed by the aforesaid shuffling plea.

Dr Nuri translated Aiyat 241 to read: "And for the divorced women (also) a provision (should be made) with fairness (in addition to her dower). (This is) a duty (incumbent) on the reverent." Marmuduke

Pickhall's translation of Aiyat 241 is: "For divorced women a provision in kindness. A duty for those who ward off (evil)." The English version of the two Aiyats by Zafrullah Khan is: "For divorced women also there shall be a provision according to what is fair. This is an obligation binding on the righteous. Thus does Allah make his Commandments clear to you that you may understand."

The translation of Aiyats 240 to 242 by the Board of Islamic Publications, Delhi, reads thus: "Those of you who shall die and leave wives behind them, should make a will to the effect that they shall be provided with a year's maintenance and should not be turned out of their homes. But if they leave their home of their own accord, you shall not be answerable for whatever they choose for themselves in a fair way; Allah is all powerful, all wise. Likewise, the divorced women should also be given something in accordance with the known fair standards. This is an obligation upon the God-fearing people."

Arthur J. Arberry's translation of Aiyat 241 was also brought to the Court's notice and referred to but is not different in purport. I am not discussing it because Arberry is not a Muslim and therefore, in the eyes of the union minister of state whose criticism of the Supreme Court I have referred to, his rendering would amount to a "tamboli doing the work of a teli, or of a carpenter doing the job of an engineer."

Extract from *The Statesman*
23 April 1986

ISLAMIC SHARIAT AND THE SHAH BANO CASE

Prof. Rafiullah Shehab

The Shah Bano case is being heatedly discussed in the Indian press nowadays and glimpses of this discussion are reported in our press off and on.

This case relates to a divorced Muslim woman who requested the Indian Supreme Court to compel her husband to pay the maintenance allowance to her. The court in the light of section 125 of the Cr. P.C. of the Indian Constitution granted her request.

However the husband did not accept this decision and managed to get a fatwa from the Ulama that this court decision was against the teachings of Islam and an undue interference in the family laws of the Muslim community. This fatwa was given wide publicity and Muslims in various parts of the country have started an agitation against the decision of the court. They are demanding the repeal of this decision of the court. They are demanding the repeal of this decision and their exemption from section 125 of the Indian Constitution. Some of the Ulama have requested the Indian prime minister for a personal meeting to discuss the issue.

On the other hand, the Association of Indian Lawyers and Judges have condemned the attitude of the Muslims in this respect. They have treated the agitation of the Muslim masses as a challenge to the sanctity of the courts. This situation has provided a chance for the opponents of Islam to pass derogatory remarks about the faith. Shah Bano was divorced after passing a major part of her life with her husband. They maintain that a religion which opposes the provision of maintenance allowance to an old helpless divorced woman cannot be a true religion and in this respect the Indian Constitution is better for it makes such provisions. Such a state of affairs demands that a thorough study of the issue be made in the light of the teachings of Islam.

It seems that the verdict (fatwa) against the decision of the Indian Supreme Court was issued in haste. Had the relevant parties studied the details of Islamic law in this respect, their attitude would have been different. Actually this verdict is based on the views of those jurists who believe that divorce ends the relations between the husband and wife. Resultantly she is not entitled to any maintenance allowance after divorce, the reason being that they treat maintenance allowance as a sort of compensation for enjoying the company of the wife. However, the verdict of the Hanafite jurists in this respect is totally different. According to the principles laid down by them in various similar cases a woman after divorce is entitled to claim maintenance allowances.

The basic principle in this respect is that maintenance allowance is not a compensation for conjugal rights. It is actually a sort of a reward or a present. (*Al-Bahr al-Ra'ik* by Al-lama Ibne Najeem vol. IV p. 186). It is unfortunate that in the Shah Bano case the difference between compensation (muawaza) and reward (silla) was ignored. This made it an intricate problem. This difference can be better illustrated by the concrete example of the emoluments of a government servant. The pay drawn by him is compensation for the work done by him during his service while at the end of his service he is rewarded with a pension for which he performs no work.

This principle of the Hanafite is based on the following verse of the holy Quran: "And for the divorced women provision (must be made) in kindness. This is incumbent on those who have regard for duty" (Al-Baqrah-241).

According to a number of Muslim jurists including of course the Hanafite, this provision is made in addition to the dower money due to the wife and its payment is compulsory. (Tafsir Kabir, vol. VI, pp. 148 & 172).

There is a difference of opinion about the details of this provision. The word 'mataa' used for this purpose has been defined differently by different authorities. According to Hazrat Abdullah bin Umar a payment of thirty dirhams to the divorced woman is sufficient for this purpose, while Hazrat Ibne Abbas considered that the best form of mataa is the provision of a paid servant to the divorced wife who should serve her during her remaining life. Usually the husbands paid handsome amounts to their divorced wives so that these may help them in contracting a second marriage. Hazrat Hassan bin Ali provided twenty thousand dirhams or dinars and a water-skin full of honey to his divorced wife for their purpose. (*Al-Jama al-Ahkam al-Quran*, vol.III, p. 201).

In the light of this tradition, good Muslims in the early periods of Islam always paid a handsome amount to their divorced wives so that someone may contract marriage with them for the sake of this money. Servants were provided to those divorced women who had passed the limit of marriageable age. The expenses of this servant were always borne by the divorcing husband. If the husband is expected to pay the expenses of a servant, he can do so in respect of payment of maintenance allowance to her.

No doubt, according to a number of Muslim jurists, the relations between the husband and wife end after divorce. On the basis of this, they prevent the divorced woman in her waiting period to participate in the mourning of her husband if he dies during this period. But some other jurists including Imam Abu Hanifa, Imam Abu Yousaf, Imam Mohammad, Imam Sauri, Imam Hassan bin Haye and Imam Abu Sour maintain that in spite of divorce a relationship still remains between them and the divorced woman must participate in the mournings of her husband. (*Al-Jama al-Ahkam al-Quran*, vol. III, p. 182). In the light of this example, payment of maintenance allowance to a divorced woman can be made after divorce and it will not be tantamount to a violation of the teachings of Islam in any way.

The third principle followed by the Hanafite jurists in similar issues is more clear. According to this principle, if a husband does not maintain his wife properly, she can get her maintenance allowance fixed through a court. This fixed maintenance will not only be paid to her as a wife but also after divorce. Al-lama Ibne Najeem, a famous jurist of the Hanafite school, has discussed this issue in great detail in his famous book *Al-Bahr al-Raik*.

In this book he maintains that there is a difference of opinion among the Hanafite jurists. While according to Imam Mohammad, the husband is not required to pay maintenance allowance to his divorced wife, Imam Abu Yousaf differed with him in this respect. He is of the opinion that the husband will have to pay this amount even after divorcing her. Imam Ibne Najeem after quoting these conflicting reports gives his verdict maintaining that the view about stopping the maintenance allowance of the wife after divorce is weak. In this respect he argues that there is a consensus among the jurists that a woman whom a husband does not maintain properly can knock at the door of a court and get her maintenance allowance fixed by the court. The husband is bound to pay his fixed amount to the wife regularly. If he refuses to do so, he will be put behind bars. If it would have been possible for the husband to save his skin by divorcing his wife, he would have preferred to do so. But Islamic law does not allow him to do so. He will have to pay this amount even after divorcing her. (*Al-Bahr al-Raik*, vol. IV, pp. 189–190).

In the light of these details it is suggested that the Ulama should study this issue in the light of the teachings of the Quran and sunnah.

Extract from the *Pakistan Times*
9 January 1986

REVIVAL OF ISLAMIC FUNDAMENTALISM?

Dr Nusrat Bano Ruhi

The private member bill introduced by G. M. Banatwala to exempt the Muslims from the purview of section 125 of the Code of Criminal Procedure and also to amend Article 44 of the Indian Constitution is a very obnoxious move. The demand, apparently religious, is irrational, anti-Islamic and anti-constitutional. It is also anti-democratic, anti-liberal and represents a fascist trend.

If the demand is conceded, it will create two contradictory parallel legal authorities in the country — one, a democratic, secular, political authority and the other, an antiquated, orthodox, obscurantist, separatist and so-called religious authority which will be above the secular law of the land.

This will create a state within the state and will take us back to medieval Europe where the main controversy was between the popes and emperors over the boundaries of the secular and ecclesiastical authorities.

Indian Muslim women are first and foremost Indian citizens. By birth they are citizens of a secular, democratic republic and, in that capacity, are entitled to all legal rights and privileges granted to the citizens of India by the Constitution or by any other law of the land.

An amendment in section 125 of Cr. P. C. will be an open discrimination against them. They will also be deprived of their national identity. No temporal power on earth will be able to protect them. They will remain only Muslim, and not Indian, women, who will be left completely at the mercy of a cruel society which promises them nothing except rude exploitation and oppression. They will become second grade citizens inferior to other women in the national and international community as even their sisters in the Muslim countries are comparatively better off in social status.

Article 14 of the Constitution of India says that the State shall not deny to any person equality before the law or the equal protection of the laws within the territories of India. Equality before the law means the absence of any special privilege in favour of any individual. There is also Article 15 which prohibits any discrimination on grounds of religion, race, caste, sex and place of birth. The State has been allowed to make special provisions for women and children and for the advancement of any socially and educationally backward classes of citizens or for scheduled castes and scheduled tribes.

The right by this article is conferred on a citizen as an individual and is guarantee against any discrimination by the state in the matter of rights, privileges and immunities pertaining to him/her as a citizen generally. One is surprised to note that the bill introduced by Mr G. M. Banatwala is fundamentally against the very spirit of the Indian Constitution and will deface its basic character, leading to the formation of a theocratic, fascist dictatorship in place of a secular, democratic republic.

If the proposed amendment is carried, either it will be *ultra vires*, or, if we accept the Banatwala philosophy, amendment of Article 14 and 15 (maybe of many more) will become a precondition for it. It will also set a bad precedent to other minorities.

Contrarily, Article 25 which confers freedom of religion is not an absolute right. It is subject to 'public order', 'morality' and 'health' and to other "provisions of the Part III (Fundamental Rights) that all persons are equally entitled to freedom of conscience and the right freely to profess, practise and propagate religion".

However, the Article goes on: "nothing in this Article shall affect the operation of any existing law or prevent the State from making any law regulating or restricting any economic, financial, political or other secular activity which may be associated with religious practice, etc." Thus in comparison to other fundamental rights, the right to freedom of religion is more restricted.

Let us have a look into the nature and scope of section 125 Cr. P. C. also. The section under reference comes under Chapter IX of the Code and is entitled, "Order for Maintenance of Wives, Children and Parents". It was enacted about a century back with the object of enabling discarded wives, helpless and deserted children and destitute parents to secure much-needed relief. Provisions of this chapter apply whatever may be the personal law by which the parties are governed. Section 125 runs as follows:

> If any person having sufficient means neglects or refuses to maintain (*a*) his wife, unable to maintain herself, or (*b*) his legitimate or illegitimate minor child whether married or not, unable to maintain itself, or (*c*) his legitimate or illegitimate child (not being a married daughter) who has attained majority, where such child is, by reason of any physical or mental abnormality or injury unable to maintain itself, or (*d*) his father or mother, unable to maintain himself or herself...

> A magistrate of the first class may, upon proof of such neglect or refusal, order such person to make a monthly allowance for the maintenance of his wife or such child, father or mother, at such monthly rate not exceeding five hundred rupees in the whole, as such magistrate thinks fit, and to pay the same to such person as the magistrate may from time to time direct.

For the purpose of this chapter 'wife' includes a woman who has been divorced by, or has obtained a divorce from her husband and has not remarried. It also means a legitimate wife, i.e., the marriage must be a legitimate one under the personal law applicable to the parties. According to the Calcutta High Court, this section applies to a wife who is duly wedded to a person and is abandoned by him. (1882-8 Cal. 736.)

There are various provisions to this section. If such person offers to maintain his wife on condition of her living with him, and she refuses to live with him, the magistrate may consider any grounds of refusal stated by her and may make an order under this section notwithstanding such offer, if he is satisfied that there is just ground for so doing. If a husband has contracted another marriage it shall be considered a just ground for his wife to refuse to live with him.

However, no wife shall be entitled to receive an allowance from her husband under this section if she is living in adultery, or if they are living separately by mutual consent. The magistrate is also authorized to cancel the order if any of the above conditions is proved.

It looks very disgraceful in any civilized society to demand exemption from such a just and benevolent law. I believe that the bill proposed by

Mr Banatwala could not have demanded the exemption for Muslims from their responsibilities towards their parents and children. Only the unfortunate Muslim wife is denied every right in the name of Islam.

There is sufficient proof in the history of Islamic jurisprudence to prove that the Banatwala bill is wholly and substantially anti-Islamic. Maulana Abdul-Salam Nadvi has pointed out in *Tareekh Fiqh Islami* that Islam has commanded Muslims to be benevolent to their women even during the period of iddat (p. 114). It prohibits them to be cruel to them (p. 116). He further writes that the system of divorce laid down by the shariat is the best one. If it is followed it will yield good.

In case the bitterness created between husband and wife reaches a point of no return, there is no compulsion to live together. But, at the same time, separation is not so easy without providing security and maintenance (p. 123). The author has produced various illustrations in support of his statement: "Hazrat Abdul Rehman Bin Auf (may God bless him) divorced his wife during illness. Hazrat Osman (Caliph III, may God bless him) gave her share of inheritance from his property even after Iddat." (p. 175).

Yet another illustration given by Maulana A. Salam Nadvi may be found on page 178. Hazrat Omar (Caliph II, may God bless him) delivered a fatwa to give right of maintenance and residence to a woman who was divorced thrice (*Tareekh Fiqh Islami*, second ed. Urdu; Azamgarh: Darul-Musanifin; S. no. 30). It may be noted here that the book under reference is an Urdu translation of the *History of Fiqh Islami* compiled by Allama Mohd. Khizri, a world renowned scholar and historian of Egypt.

The demand of Mr Banatwala to deprive the Indian Muslim women from their legal and constitutional rights, reminds us of the apartheid regime of South Africa which is brutally suppressing the people of God. They are doing it in the name of racism while we are facing oppression in the name of religious fanaticism. Alas, the religion which removed all human distinctions and differences, and established human equality and dignity, today must see its followers cast everything into creating differences among the people of God. They are not playing fair in changing the law of the land.

One should be quite clear in one's mind that the Banatwala bill has nothing to do with Islam — rather it has earned dishonour for it. The bill is politically motivated. In fact the anti-democratic and obscurantist forces, bent upon failing the Indian political system, are blackmailing the Government of India by pressurizing them into accepting an anti-democratic and anti-constitutional demand and thus creating a permanent threat to democracy and secularism. The way they have aroused the religious feelings of the Indian Muslims throughout the length and breadth of the country, may lead to terrible consequences.

Hence, it is an urgent need that the innocent Indian Muslim masses be kept away from the evil influence of the so-called religious leaders. They should be informed that once again some unscrupulous and ambitious people want to expropriate them in the name of Islam only to get some titles and benefits from the Government.

Excerpt from *Clarity*
1 December 1985

PRO-WOMEN OR ANTI-MUSLIM?

The Furore over Muslim Personal Law

Madhu Kishwar

The position under the Criminal Procedure Code and the Muslim personal law is stated by Danial Latifi in his written arguments for an intervention in the *Shah Bano* v. *Mohammed Ahmed Khan* case.

Section 125 Cr. P. C. provides for maintenance up to a maximum amount of Rs 500 a month for a needy wife, child or parent. Section 127(3)(b) provides that a maintenance order under section 125 shall be cancelled where "The woman has been divorced by her husband and... she has received, whether before or after the date of the said order, the whole of the sum which, under any customary or personal law, applicable to the parties, was payable on such divorce".

Mr Justice Krishna Iyer had interpreted this clause to mean that if the amount paid under personal law was sufficient to save the woman from destitution, the maintenance order under section 125 would be cancelled, but in case the amount paid under personal law was not sufficient to save her from destitution, then the order under section 125 would stand. He argued that section 125 exists to protect people from destitution, and to see that the State is not burdened with their upkeep if they have close relatives who should look after them.

However, Mohammed Ahmed Khan challenged this interpretation, pointing out that section 127 clearly states that if "the whole" amount payable under personal law has been paid, the woman is not entitled to relief under section 125. Therefore, the Supreme Court had to decide whether Shah Bano had in fact received the whole amount payable to her under Muslim personal law.

Mohammed Ahmed Khan had paid the mehr of Rs 3,000 and also

the maintenance during iddat. He claimed that under Muslim personal law these are the only two payments due to a woman on divorce.

Shah Bano's counsel argued that apart from these two payments, another payment known as mataa is also due to a woman on divorce, under Aiyat 241 of Sura II (Sura-al-Baqr) of the holy Quran:

"Wa lil motallaqatay mataa un bil maroofay haqqan allai muttaqeena" which translates as "And for divorced women let there be a fair provision. This is an obligation on those who are mindful of God." (trans. Dr Syed Abdul Latif, 1969).

Shah Bano had not been paid mataa. Her husband's counsel argued that this provision is not obligatory on all Muslims but only on the "muttaqeena" or those who are specially pious, which he does not claim to be. Shah Bano's counsel replied that the Quran is addressed, right in its beginning, to the "muttaqeena" so if all Muslims believe it is addressed to them, then all Muslims are "muttaqeena" and this verse applies to all of them.

Shah Bano's counsel also cited several respected authorities' interpretations of this verse:

"Two reputed authorities who have dealt with this matter are Maulana Baizawi and Ibn Kather.... These commentators have declared that the obligation upon the husband of paying mataa-un-bil-maaroof (reasonable provision) to his divorced wife is imperative and binding and not merely optional. It may be noted that the opinion of Imam Shafei particularly is acceptable to all the schools of Sunni, including the Hanafi jurisprudence.... The same view has been expressed perhaps with even greater force, by Imam Jafar-al-Sadiq, the highest authority among all schools of Shia jurisprudence. Prof. Fyzee states: 'Imam Jafar-al-Sadiq held it (mataa-un-bil maaroof) to be obligatory (farida wajiba) and always decreed its payment.' He further states: 'The mataa should be a generous payment.'"

Thus according to several respected authorities, Muslim personal law is in favour of a generous payment to a woman at the time of divorce apart from mehr and maintenance during iddat. Shah Bano's counsel appealed to the court to uphold the law in this matter, which they did. The interpretation of Aiyat 241 relied upon by the Supreme Court judges was that of jurists like Imam Shafei and not the judges' own.

Maintenance law in India is far from satisfactory, whether under the Cr. P.C., Hindu law or Muslim law. The issue of maintenance and alimony needs to be re-examined and made more equitable in law.

Maintenance is available to Hindu women under the Hindu Adoption and Maintenance Act, 1955. A woman can claim a maximum of one-third of the joint incomes of her husband and herself. That means that if, for example, she is earning Rs 500 and her husband Rs 1,000, she cannot claim anything because she already has one-third of the joint income which is Rs 1,500.

In practice, however, it is extremely difficult for a woman to claim and get her right under Hindu personal law, just as it is extremely difficult to get the "generous payment" under Muslim personal law. The case is a civil one which means that the husband can employ all sorts of dilatory tactics to drag the case out for years. What a woman may finally get is a pittance, like the Rs 179 that Shah Bano got from the High Court and which the Supreme Court confirmed. She will have spent much more on court expenses, by that time. And there is no way of ensuring that the husband will regularly make payments. If he stops paying, the woman has no redress but to go to court again. She cannot approach the police to compel the husband to pay her.

Therefore, most women prefer to plead under 125 Cr. P.C. which is not really the relevant provision for maintenance of a divorced wife. Maintenance is the right of a divorced woman whereas 125 Cr. P.C. exists to safeguard all destitute women, children and old parents. Yet most divorced women have to sue for maintenance under this clause because it is a criminal case and they can get relief somewhat more quickly. But under this clause they can get a maximum of only Rs 500 which is much less than the amount many of them would be entitled to as maintenance after divorce. Also, the sum of Rs 500 is a fixed one and bears no relation to the income of the husband. Even if he is earning lakhs she can claim a maximum of only Rs 500. Under the personal law, she may be able to claim more, but the procedures under the civil law are so cumbersome that it is hardly worth fighting for maintenance under those clauses. Thus, women are caught in a dilemma created by a biased system.

Thus, in practice, all the laws of maintenance are highly inadequate. It is not enough to state that a woman should get a "fair" or "generous" payment because the definition of generosity varies widely. Women have been too long dependent on the generosity of men. What is needed is an assertion that maintenance is a woman's right. She does not have to be a destitute to claim maintenance.

The procedures for claiming maintenance have to be such that a woman can quickly get relief, and the sum payable has to be in proportion to the husband's income. The society and State too have a responsibility in this regard, not merely to safeguard women from dying of destitution, but to ensure a decent standard of living to a woman who is maltreated or abandoned by her husband.

Shah Bano's case is only one instance of the way most Indian women have to struggle for maintenance. She had to spend ten years knocking at the doors of the secular legal system before she got a pitiful amount of maintenance — Rs 179 per month, which is less than half the statutory minimum wage in most parts of the country. Earlier she had been granted a sum of around Rs 25 by the lower courts, which is more of an insult than an award.

Can an ordinary woman, without the support of fairly well-off male family members (in this case, Shah Bano's sons) afford to carry on such a prolonged battle after she has been abandoned by her husband, and to get so little in return?

Yet, the media completely and deliberately ignored this aspect of the plight of women, whether Muslims, Hindus, Christians or Sikhs. Instead of sounding embarrassed or ashamed at this example of the failure of the legal system to offer any meaningful relief to a woman in distress, the judges made it seem as if they were bestowing a great boon on Shah Bano and, by implication, on all Muslim women. The media too has been mindlessly projecting the judgement as a great "victory" for Muslim women.

Powerful members of any community, whether the majority or a minority, ought not to have the right to oppress vulnerable sections of the community in the name of religion or any other ism. But Muslim men are certainly not unique in using religion as a shield for the purpose of exploiting women.

Most of the non-Muslims who are vigorously demanding the scrapping of Muslim law seem to be under the erroneous impression that only minorities are governed by personal laws. Most Hindus seem to believe that their law is "secular and Indian" and not "religious" at all. But the fact is that Hindus continue to be governed by Hindu personal law in such matters as marriage, divorce and succession.

It is true that Hindu personal law has undergone some reform, and shed some of its blatantly discriminatory aspects. However, it continues to be heavily biased against women in many important ways. Let me give some notable examples.

A daughter's inheritance rights are severely circumscribed in comparison to a son's. A son, from the moment of his birth, is considered a coparcener, that is, an equal owner of the family's joint property, with other male members. A daughter cannot be a coparcener in a Hindu undivided family. She can only get a portion of what her father inherits if and when the property is divided. An unmarried daughter has a right to maintenance from the family property. But once she marries, she has no right to maintenance from her natal family's property, not even if she is divorced, abandoned or widowed.

In the father's self-acquired property, a Hindu daughter is supposed to have an equal share if he dies without making a will. However, most Hindu fathers are averse to giving property rights to daughters so they usually make a will disinheriting their daughters. Even when a father dies without making a will, daughters are usually pressured into signing away rights in favour of their brothers.

Under the Hindu Minority and Guardianship Act, 1955 (read in conjunction with the Guardians and Wards Act), a Hindu father is the "natural guardian" of his legitimate child over the age of five. This means that if there is a conflict over child custody between separated spouses, the primary right over the child belongs to the father. The mother can get custody only by proving in court that he is unsuitable to be the child's guardian. This law is an important weapon in the hands of men who can keep blackmailing their wives into continuing a bad marriage, by refusing to relinquish custody over the children.

Under the Hindu Adoption and Maintenance Act, 1955, a Hindu man or woman who is single can adopt a child in his or her name. But a married Hindu woman cannot adopt a child in her name. The child has to be adopted by her husband.

Further, there are many religious elements in the Hindu personal law which can and do cause serious problems for women. For instance, under the Hindu Marriage Act, 1955, a Hindu marriage is valid even if it is registered. It is normally considered complete only if certain ceremonies like saptapadi are performed. Many men undergo a second marriage and deliberately omit certain parts of the ceremony. Since the second marriage takes place in public with pomp and show, it is recognized by society, but since a certain religious ceremony required by the law was not performed, the court will not consider the marriage a valid Hindu marriage. This is one reason why it is almost impossible for a Hindu wife to get a husband punished for bigamy. So even though bigamy is prohibited for Hindus, in practice it continues to take place.

Of equal if not greater importance, is that, though there are some differences between Hindu and Muslim law, there is very little difference between the practice of the two communities.

Most Hindus do not follow the codified Hindu law as represented by the Acts passed in 1955. Instead, they follow the customary laws prevalent in their own kinship group and region. For instance, a very large number of Hindu girls are still married and their marriages consummated before the girls attain the age of 18, despite laws to the contrary.

In some respects, reformed Hindu law is worse than unreformed Muslim law. For instance, a Muslim daughter cannot be disinherited by her father making a will. But a Hindu daughter can be and often is deliberately excluded by her father making a will exclusively in favour of his sons.

Even where Hindu law is better in words, it is usually not worth much more in practice. For instance, the committee on the status of Women in India stated in its 1975 report that a Census of India survey had revealed that the incidence of polygamy was 5.8 per cent among Hindu men and 5.7 per cent among Muslim men. That is, there is no meaningful difference in the incidence of polygamy amongst Hindus as compared to Muslims even though polygamy is legal for Muslims and illegal for Hindus.

In practice, the law can be evaded or ignored by men, by virtue of their dominant position in society, the family, and the community. A woman, whether Hindu or Muslim, can very often be compelled to accept her husband's bigamy if she is economically and socially dependent on him, or has no security against violence or threats of violence.

Much has been made of the injustice done to a Muslim woman by the provision which allows a man to divorce his wife by pronouncing the word talaq or "I divorce you" three times. But, when a man walks out on an unemployed woman and refuses to maintain her or their children, it makes very little difference whether he says to her "I divorce you" or whether he omits to say this.

Extract from *Manushi*
No. 32; 1986

(Please see Appendix for postscript)

DOES THE JUDGEMENT JUSTIFY AGITATION?

M. A. Latif

The recent judgement of the Supreme Court, by a bench of five judges presided over by the then chief justice Mr Y. V. Chandrachud in *Md. Ahmed Khan* v *Shah Bano Begum and Others* (popularly known as the Shah Bano case) has raised a storm of protest among a section of Muslims. An all-India protest day, ominously termed "Shariat day" has already been observed with street meetings and demonstrations. Four Muslim organizations, including a Muslim students' body, have called a Bangla bandh on October 4. Even further programmes of action cannot be ruled out.

Conceding that agitation, regardless of the issue to be highlighted, the aim to be achieved or the form to be adopted, is the order of the day, and further conceding that in a democratic set-up a judicial pronouncement is not immune from public criticism, the scale and form of the attack mounted on the judgement, with a potential for communal mischief, cannot but raise the question of whether the agitation is justified.

A justification of sorts was sought to be provided by Syed Shahabuddin, a general secretary of the Janata Party. Speaking at a symposium in Calcutta on the "Status of Women in Islam", he is reported to have given a list of grievances of Muslims over the judgement. Mr Shahabuddin is said to have claimed that the judgement had "injured" the sentiments of Muslims because (1) the Supreme Court had tried to interpret the holy Quran, in doing which (2) it had "usurped" the role of a social reformer and (3) violated the basic rules of the shariat.

A fourth grievance of Mr Shahabuddin is on the score of the advice in the judgement as to a common civil code mentioned in Article 44 of the Constitution. His overall reaction to the judgement was reported to be that it had delayed reforms in Muslim society by a decade. It is an irony that a judgement rendered in discharge of ordinary judicial duty, conceived broadly — given the nature of the case — in a legitimate concern for social advance, should be assailed as a factor delaying social reform. Is the judgement, then, an unfortunate instance of the path to hell being paved with good intentions? Let us first look at the issues and the decision.

Ahmed, the appellant before the Supreme Court, had married respondent Shah Bano in 1932 and, after 43 years of living together and begetting three sons and two daughters, drove away Shah Bano from the matrimonial home in 1975. After payment of maintenance for two years at the rate of Rs 200 per month it was stopped. In April 1978 Shah Bano filed an application before the Judicial Magistrate, 1st Class, Indore, under section 125 of the Code of Criminal Procedure, 1973, for maintenance at the rate of Rs 500 per month, stating that Ahmed, who is an advocate, had an annual professional income of Rs 60,000. In November 1978 during the pendency of Shah Bano's application for maintenance, Ahmed divorced Shah Bano and deposited in court Rs 3,000 in payment of her dower. Ahmed then claimed that under his personal law he had no responsibility for Shah Bano's maintenance. The magistrate negatived Ahmed's claim, but ordered maintenance at the sum of Rs 25 per month. Shah Bano went to the High Court of Madhya Pradesh, which raised the rate of maintenance to Rs 179.20.

Ahmed then appealed to the Supreme Court, raising a two-fold defence. His first defence was that under the Muslim personal law he had no responsibility for the maintenance of Shah Bano, whom he had divorced and, as such, the provisions of the Criminal Procedure Code providing for maintenance for a divorced "wife" were not applicable to him. Ahmed's defence, therefore, put the Muslim personal law, which is part of the civil law of the country, in conflict with the criminal law of the country, which includes the Criminal Procedure Code containing the provisions for maintenance to a divorced "wife".

The two laws, civil and criminal, being in conflict, according to Ahmed's defence, and Ahmed claiming primacy of his personal law over the criminal law of the country, the Supreme Court had to decide the first issue as to whether an applicable personal law will prevail over the criminal law where there is a conflict between the two. Thus, the first issue is entirely a secular one, and involves application of a purely relevant principle of jurisprudence. The Supreme Court having assumed that the Muslim personal law on the point of issue was what Ahmed had claimed it to be, no scriptural interpretation was called for, nor resorted to.

Ahmed's second defence was that, he having paid and Shah Bano having received all that was due to her under her personal law, he was entitled to the benefit of section 127(3)(b) of the Code of Criminal Procedure. This provision directs a magistrate to cancel an order for maintenance in favour of a woman if the woman has been divorced by her husband and she has received the whole of the sum payable to her under her customary or personal law "on divorce". The material words "on divorce" fell for interpretation to determine if Ahmed's payment of dower was a payment "on divorce".

Ahmed's claim that his personal law prevailed over the criminal law of the country was untenable both on legal principles and on practical considerations. The practical implication of Ahmed's theory is that society will be an idle spectator of evils and abuses, however offending or debasing, if only a peg to hang them on can be found or claimed in an applicable personal law. On this view, sati and human sacrifices, not without a sort of sanction in the relevant personal law would have still been flourishing with full fury. Nothing is better suited to making the present a permanent prisoner of the past.

But as far as section 125 Cr.P.C. is concerned, it is an instance of the criminal law of the country providing an alternative compartment of legal redress to a wife, including a divorced "wife". Civil law, which includes different personal laws is not thereby displaced, but remains — no doubt in competition with the remedy provided by the criminal law. The wife in distress is given a choice of forum to proceed either under the civil, that is her personal law, or under criminal law. But a defence rooted in civil, that is personal law, cannot defeat an action by a wife for maintenance under the criminal law, because that would be allowing personal law to displace criminal law.

The court in rejecting Ahmed's first defence laid down the true relation between civil and criminal law in general and in particular between the person's personal law and the provisions of criminal law on the point of maintenance for a wife, including a divorced "wife" who cannot support herself. Choosing its words carefully, it aptly said that while the provisions of section 125 Cr. P.C. do not "supplant" the personal law, personal law has no "repercussion" on the applicability of section 125 Cr. P.C. unless applicability is restricted under some Constitutional provision.

Thus, the Supreme Court's judgement gives full recognition to shariat law, which, as the court reiterates, is not displaced — but with the legally sound and commonsense rider that while personal law is supreme in its own sphere it cannot trespass into the domain of criminal law. The charge that the judgement attacks the shariat law is thus without foundation.

An analogy in support of the principle applied in the judgement is readily provided by section 18 of the Hindu Adoption and Maintenance Act, 1955, which is an enacted piece of Hindu personal law. That section by silence necessarily implies that a Hindu husband has no responsibility for maintenance of a "wife" whom he has divorced. But a Hindu husband cannot plead this position of his under his personal law to defeat an action by his divorced "wife" under section 125 Cr. P.C. The point made in the judgement is also illustrated by the fact that a Muslim cannot disown his liability to pay income-tax on the ground that his personal law contains provisions for "zakat".

Ahmed's second defence was negatived on the ground that the two words "on divorce" occurring in clause (b) of sub-section (3) of section 127 Cr. P.C. referred to payment occasioned by divorce, and not made on the occasion of divorce. Having regard to the nature of dower as well as the basic purpose of preventing vagrancy for which section 125 Cr.P.C. has been enacted, the distinction is vital and, with due respect, rightly drawn by the court.

Thus, the judgement of the Supreme Court, rendered on nothing but general juristic principles and involving no interpretation of the Quran, is legally unassailable.

The Supreme Court's findings of Ahmed's two-fold defence were sufficient to dispose of his appeal. And they were arrived at, be it noted again, by the application of general legal principles and involved no interpretation of the Quran. Therefore, the criticism that the court tried to interpret the Quran and in the process "usurped the role of a social reformer and violated the basic rule of shariat", is farfetched and unwar-

Incidentally, the claim that civil courts, including the highest, cannot go to the scriptural sources before extending to a rule of shariat, and must docilely and deferentially accept commentaries made centuries ago, is a proposition which will perhaps require serious scrutiny. But in this case no such examination was involved, because the court was basically concerned with the applicability of a provision in the criminal law of the country, and the questions raised could be and were answered without such examination.

The court, having decided the appeal on the basis of what was claimed by Ahmed to be the Muslim personal law on the point at issue, was however invited to "see", and not determine, what provision, if any, there was in the Quran on the point of a Muslim husband's responsibility for maintenance of a divorced wife. Not being essential to its decision, the exercise was essentially in the nature of an "obiter". The point will arise directly for decision only when a Muslim divorced "wife" lodges a claim for maintenance under her personal law, and not under the provisions of criminal law, as Shah Bano did.

Two verses of the Quran, 241 and 242, were cited before the court and several renderings in English of the two verses by eminent authors, Indian, Pakistani and English, were placed before the court. There was no dispute that those two verses did require a Muslim to provide for his divorced "wife"; there was, however, a difference as to the quantum and duration of the provision. It was contended on Ahmed's behalf that the word "mataa" in verse 241 meant "provision" and not "maintenance", implying that the Quran required a Muslim to give at the time of divorce "something", i.e. a one-time lump-sum payment and not maintenance at a reasonable scale till remarriage or death. This contention made the Quranic injunction as being inspired only by a desire to delay and not prevent, vagrancy; and the court rightly rejected it. The submission made on behalf of the All India Muslim Personal Law Board that the verses 241 and 242 were meant for more pious and godfearing Muslims and not the general run was, as the court put it, too shuffling a plea to impress the court.

What, then, is the net result of the decision in Shah Bano's case? It is nothing more than that the Muslim citizen of the country, just as his fellow Hindu, Christian, Parsi citizens, has a duty to society to see to it that the woman with whom he had once shared many a joy and sorrow is not thrown out as a vagrant. A Muslim husband enjoying a far easier divorce law certainly needs to be reminded of this duty to society all the more. And that is all that the "guilty" Supreme Court judgement does. The duty is not the court's creation, but is prescribed by the criminal law of the country.

Towards the end of the judgement, reference is made to a common civil code as enjoined in Article 44 of the Constitution. The reference seems to have annoyed Mr Shahabuddin most, although at the Calcutta symposium, he claimed that Muslim women in Islam enjoyed a very high position, which, according to him, was at times even equal to that of men. A uniform civil code will no doubt have a much wider scope, but the status of women will constantly be an important chapter in it inasmuch as it is a sphere where the ghost of the past, aided and abetted by present socio-economic constraints, is, if anything, more active. With his high evaluation of the status of Muslim women, Mr Shahabuddin could have been expected to be less hostile to a common code, because whatever is salutary in Muslim personal law can find its place there.

The Hindu mind, though shackled on the social plane through the centuries, has shown a capacity to absorb ideas and concepts from other sources, as is to be seen in the adoption in its modern personal law such novelties as women's right to inheritance, divorce, etc. Both afraid and angry, Mr Shahabuddin has been less than just to the Supreme Court on the score of its anxiety for a uniform common code, and, in the process, has perhaps unconsciously shown more concern to protect such dark practices as polygamy, divorce as a male whim, etc.

The political leadership of the country, increasingly preoccupied with the facade to the neglect of the inner structure, appears to rest on its laurels on begetting a brand of secularism which is nothing more than a multi-theocracy with a predilection for Hindu rites and rituals, and which, in relation to the secular interests of the minorities, is capable of breeding only a flock of show-boys and sycophants. The majority – minority relation in all its aspects is fast becoming an exigent problem of grave dimensions. If the judicial conscience of the highest tribunal is stirred in this situation, is the initiative to be deprecated? Unfortunately, that is what Mr Shahabuddin does.

Muslims stand at the crossroads of history, as they once did at the time of the emergence of the British in India. The wrong choice of exclusiveness they made then has left them with a legacy which, notwithstanding the later mitigating endeavours of Sir Syed Ahmed and others, exacts its toll to this day. The yawning cultural gap between the Hindu and Muslim segments of any mixed village is too pronounced to be missed by even the most casual observer.

Muslims can now hardly avoid a choice of the road they will take. Will they opt for permanent habitation on an isolated island of minority privileges and permanent minority status, or move towards the abolition, step by step, of the majority–minority distinction in secular matters? The latter road, however rough and difficult initially, holds for the

Muslims the prospect of permanent gain in a much-needed social renaissance which will equip them to face the severest competition on merit.

Spoon-feeding, necessarily limited in extent, is more injurious to the fed because it makes a cripple of him who is unable to realize his full potentiality. Remembering the wise words of Aldous Huxley that experience is not what happens to a man but what he does with what happens to him, Muslims must not allow undue play of what may be painted as past "experience" in making their choice for the future.

Heirs to a revolutionary religion, Muslims have a great heritage to renew. Will they do it willingly or will fate drag them to do it?

Extracts from *The Telegraph*
1-2 October 1985

AN OLD WOMAN DEPRIVED IN THE NAME OF GOD
Seema Mustafa

It should have been expected but, unfortunately, the so-called progressives were so caught up in intellectual debates on the Supreme Court judgement awarding maintenance rights to divorced Muslim women, that everyone forgot about 75-year old Shah Bano Begum. Everyone who should have been with her to give her the support she needed in the face of increasing pressures from the communal leaders and parties were in Delhi trying to get the maximum publicity for themselves out of the issue. The fundamentalists, upset at losing the argument on the intellectual and legal plane, worked hard on the old woman to force her to come out against the very judgement that had sought to give her some economic dignity in life. She held a press conference, actually others held it for her, where she put her thumb impression on a statement demanding that the Supreme Court withdraw its verdict as it amounted to interference in the Muslim personal law (MPL).

The mullahs, and in this category one includes Muslim League leaders like MP Ebrahim Suleiman Sait and Mr G. M. Banatwalla and Janata leader Syed Shahabuddin along with other like-minded politicians, refuse to allow the community to progress. Instead of preaching a progressive doctrine, they work overtime to push Muslim youths into religious schools and keep Muslim girls in purdah. They raise the bogey of annihilation and any attempt at progress is immediately attacked by these bearded pinnacles of Islam as an attack against the religion. The tragedy is that the middle class, steeped as it is in superstitions and religious beliefs, swallow their arguments in toto, thereby ensuring that the community at large is unable to pull itself out of the ghetto of illiteracy and economic deprivation. Although it is not within the scope of this article, one must add for the record here that the fundamentalists amongst the Hindus only help to strengthen the argument of the Muslim clergy and ensure that the minorities remain backward. Otherwise, why would the RSS leadership come out with statements supporting the viewpoint of their Muslims counterparts?

Muslim women today are under more pressure than others. The MPL in which reforms are being stoutly resisted by Muslim men and surprisingly, even women leaders (Mrs Najma Heptullah and Begum Abida Ahmed) ensures this discrimination. The lower-middle and middle-class women are the ones most adversely affected. They are denied education, kept in purdah and are meant to be neither seen nor heard. After marriage, in numerous cases they are discarded by their husbands for second wives, are not paid maintenance or even 'mehr' and are left with a brood of children to look after. Being illiterate and without any resources, they are unable to approach the court, and even if they want to, it is unlikely that their families will agree.

Their life is a tale of unbearable suffering which, the Muslim clergy ensures, is never alleviated.

But this discrimination is not confined to the middle class. Women of the upper and rich classes are equally victimized, the only difference being that the poorer women suffer in silence with a fatalistic attitude towards their life while the educated and economically richer women are unable to reconcile themselves to their existence. But neither class is able to do much about it — and Shah Bano's withdrawal from the fray has dealt a further blow to their morale.

The following examples should suffice to portray the plight of these women who must remain anonymous.

A beautiful young girl, educated in the US, returned to India in the early 1960s. She was smart, independent and wanted to live her own life. Marriage was far from her thoughts but not from her father's. He insisted that she get married and that, too, only to an IAS officer. Her protests went unheeded and her father lost no time in accepting a proposal of marriage from an IAS officer in a southern state. He was from a very conservative southern Indian family with nothing in common with the girl — neither culture, lifestyle, language nor ideals, principles and values. They were married and her independence, which perhaps attracted him earlier, became an embarrassment immediately after marriage when he took her home to his family. Within a few weeks it became a positive irritant. The girl returned to her parents in Delhi, miserable — and pregnant. Before she could go back to her in-laws, she received a letter from her husband, divorcing her without a hearing.

Under the MPL, she can get no relief as he was fully within his rights, or so the clergy would claim. She gave birth a few months later to a son and the husband hearing this, regained interest, not in her but in his heir. Then followed a long-drawn battle for the custody of the child (under the MPL, a child can live with the mother only until the age of seven years, after which he goes to the father, regardless of whether the father is a debauch or a criminal) which ended with the child, by now a young boy far too serious for his age, having to make appearances in court. She might still not have been able to keep her son but for the fact that her ex-husband remarried and lost interest in the matter. Is this justice?

Or, take the case of a Muslim woman married for 15 years, again from the upper strata of society. One day her husband decided he needed a change and left her for another man's wife. He did not give her a divorce, he did not need to as he can, under the law, keep four wives — and who cares about that prohibiting moral clause 'only if he can give them all equal treatment'? Anxious to get maintenance for herself and her son she had to fight at length in the courts just to get a divorce. The tension was unbearable but she was determined to get her dues. The man, thanks again to the mullahs, is living somewhere with his second wife without being accountable to any court of law.

A third case is of a young woman married and settled with her husband in the US. She came home to visit her parents for a few months. Her husband, unknown to her, flew to India, obtained a divorce document in her absence from an obliging qazi, and, after posting it to her here, flew back to the US. It was as simple as that. She was left wondering whether there was any point in approaching the court. And for what? Her marriage was over at her husband's whim.

There are hundreds, more likely thousands of such cases. There is not a single Muslim family in India today whose members are not acquainted with some woman — a relative or a friend — who has been so victimized. If educated men can treat their womenfolk so shabbily, one dreads to imagine the mostly unpublicized cases of harassment prevailing in the illiterate sections which are more prone to religious dogmas — one of which propounds the "male is superior" theory.

It is difficult to believe that Shah Bano Begum's recent press statement demanding that the Supreme Court withdraw its verdict was voluntary. It is not, and it cannot be, for why would she have fought a long-drawn battle for maintenance if she had to withdraw at the end? The Supreme

Court, after examining all aspects of the case, has made it clear that in its opinion Shah Bano Begum is completely unable to maintain herself and hence the ruling that "Muslim women unable to maintain themselves are entitled to maintenance from their husbands after divorce".

One shudders to think of the kind of men who have exerted such pressure on an old destitute woman just so that they are not required to pay maintenance to divorced women. Shah Bano Begum, who was earlier heralded as a champion of the Muslim women's cause and made to attend numerous receptions in her honour, has been compelled to let them down by retracting from her stand.

The Supreme Court judgement of course stands and it will doubtless benefit women in the future. It is just that Shah Bano Begum who had made Muslim women speak out against the oppression to which they are subjected, has dealt a grave blow to their morale without of course realizing that she is just a pawn in a devious power game. One cannot blame her because in Muslim society today, it is difficult for an old woman or any woman for that matter, to face the threat of social ostracism which must have definitely been brought to bear upon her.

After being unable to fight the progressives within and outside the community verbally, the communalists resorted to underhand tactics by using oppressive methods against Shah Bano Begum. Her statement was followed by similar utterances from the expelled Congress (I) MP F. M. Khan who, finding himself without a berth, has jumped onto the communal bandwagon, and Mr Suleiman Sait who was unable to counter Union Minister of State for Power Arif Mohammad Khan's arguments in Parliament. They have deprived the old, illiterate woman of her rights and of the little money that would have helped to make her last few years on earth a little comfortable — all in the name of God.

Extract from *The Telegraph*
22 December 1985

SHAH BANO CASE : THE REAL TRUTH
by Saeed Naqvi

A sordid family quarrel between stepbrothers and sisters, and warring Muslim divines looking for an issue, are at the bottom of the controversy surrounding the Shah Bano case. Before we visit Shah Bano, her husband Mohammad Ahmed Khan and other *dramatis personae* in their habitat in Indore, Juna Risala, a rundown, predominantly Muslim enclave of this former capital of Holkar state, let us get a few facts straightened out:

Shah Bano happens to be Mohammad Ahmed Khan's first cousin from the mother's side. His second wife, Halima Begum, is also his first cousin. In other words, Shah Bano and Halima Begum are cousins as well. Shah Bano is totally illiterate; Halima Begum is only slightly better. From Shah Bano, Ahmed Khan has three sons and two daughters; from Halima Begum, one son and six daughters.

The sons from Shah Bano, Hamid Ahmed Khan, 52, Saeed Ahmed Khan, 45, and Jamil Ahmed Khan, 40, are technical assistant in a textile mill, manager in a transport company and branch manager in the Citizen Urban Cooperative Bank respectively. The son from Halima Begum, Zafar Ahmed Khan, 35, shares his father's thriving legal practice. Both, father and son, are among the city's most prominent lawyers.

For years, this enormous triangular family lived in a medium-sized haveli, a 500 sq. ft. quadrangle enclosed on all sides by a 10-feet high whitewashed wall. While three sides of this haveli are surrounded by narrow and stinking lanes, the front opens onto the main road.

The entrance door has on either side nameplates of the two lawyers, rather like epaulettes. The door opens into a long, narrow room, lined with legal books, files. There is a table and chairs at one end of the room and a large, garish painting of the Taj Mahal resting on a table at the other. This is the office.

Adjacent to it is the living room followed by an open verandah and a courtyard, all of the same length and width. At the two narrow ends of these spaces are other smaller rooms. When Mohammad Ahmed Khan's parents were alive there were at times a total of 16 adults and their children living in the haveli, even though some of the sons and daughters got married and moved out.

Imagine the bedlam, the explosive raw material for a riotous routine. You do not need the testimony of one part of the family or the other to establish a scenario of daily bickerings, fights, violence. A recipe for a separation was inherent in the congestion.

At the rear of the haveli are a set of small apartments, with two to three rooms and a pock-marked facade with peeling plaster and an uneven stone slab as a foothold to cross the gutter into a living room the size of a kitchen. In 1975 Shah Bano and her brood moved out of the haveli. After a brief stay in her village of Kantaphod, Shah Bano started living with her younger son, Jamil Ahmed Khan, in one of these apartments, virtually attached to the haveli.

Largely inspired by the sons, Shah Bano began a series of disputes on the ownership of certain properties and, of course, maintenance. The maintenance suit was won by Shah Bano in all the courts including the famous victory at the Supreme Court. The Supreme Court in its historic judgement directed Mohammad Ahmed Khan to pay Shah Bano a monthly maintenance allowance of Rs 179.20 and the costs of the appeal which was quantified at Rs 10,000.

Since Mohammad Ahmed Khan had appealed under the Muslim personal law and lost, he became an instant hero among the more conservative maulvi elements. Some Muslims in Indore maintain that, given the history of bitterness between the two wings of the family, Mohammad Ahmed Khan would have resorted even to pagan law if it helped him win the case. He went in appeal not to uphold the Muslim personal law but to win — not so much against Shah Bano as against his sons who, he alleged, have insulted him times without number on the plea of supporting their mother.

But then there was another section of opinion, particularly among women, for whom Shah Bano was becoming the symbol of the evolution of women's rights within the Islamic framework.

So the divines started working overtime. How to neutralize Shah Bano? Community pressure began to mount on her and her sons. They would be ostracized by the one and a half lakh Muslims of Indore if they did not recant. Muslim divines from far and near began to descend on Indore in the pious pursuit of obtaining Shah Bano's retraction.

Prominent among the maulanas who visited Shah Bano was Maulvi Abdul Karim Parekh of Nagpur and representatives of Maulana Azad Madani of Jamiat e Ulema-i-Hind. The arrival of "alien" maulvis led to a sub-sectarian upheaval in the city.

The local maulvi, Mufti Malwa Mohammad Halid Yar Khan, a man of medium build, possibly in his thirties, wearing an embroidered cap, was up in arms. "If Shah Bano hands over a written retraction to Maulana Parekh then Shah Bano's family would be dubbed Wahabis or number 24," he thundered. ("Number 24" according to local Muslims, is a term used by the Sunni Muslims against those who, in their perception, have joined a renegade sect.)

According to Zafar Ahmed Khan, the lawyer and Mohammad Khan's son by his second wife, "Maulvi Parekh and others belong to the Deoband school of thought, while the local mufti and, indeed, the entire Sunni Muslim community of Indore belongs to the Bareli school." If Deobandis get away with Shah Bano's signed retraction, "then the entire credit will go to them." The local mufti was determined that this should not happen, says Zafar.

"They tried everything," says the mufti, squatting on the floor in his modest room attached to the local Jama Masjid. "They even promised Shah Bano's sons lucrative jobs in Oman," he says. "But they have not succeeded," adds the mufti triumphantly.

The Supreme Court judgement directs Ahmed Khan to pay Shah Bano two separate sums: Rs 10,000 as costs and Rs 179.20 per month as monthly maintenance. By rejecting the judgement as an afterthought will Shah Bano forfeit both these claims? I ask the mufti.

"Rs 10,000 is the cost she incurred in fighting the case and Mohammad Ahmed Khan should pay that sum," says the mufti.

But that directive is part of the judgement. Does the mufti imply that he accepts half the judgement even though it is outside the pale of Muslim personal law? The mufti throws up his hands. "We shall see; we shall see!"

Seated on inexpensive cane furniture in her small living room, decorated with a photograph of the Kaba and green and blue curtains, Shah Bano runs a bony finger across her wrinkled face. "Most of us read the Quran but do not understand it," she says, without any expression in her shining, light-coloured eyes. "I was ignorant when I fought the case all these years. The maulvis have now told us that it would be un-Islamic if I accepted the judgement."

But she has already collected a total of Rs 24,000 since 1975 by way of maintenance even prior to the Supreme Court judgement. Will she return this "haram" money?

"If someone has been drinking alcohol all his life and repents in the end, does it mean he has to vomit out all the alcohol he has consumed?" she replies smartly.

Mohammad Ahmed Khan is a well-built man of medium height, impeccably clad in pinstripe trousers, black jacket, tabs in his collars and a lawyer's gown on his left shouder. He looks infinitely younger than Shah Bano which could only partly be attributed to his dyed hair. He has an important case in court and suggests that I discuss the subject with his lawyer son.

"Shah Bano wishes to have the best of both the worlds," says Zafar Ahmed Khan. "She has made a public statement that she does not accept the Supreme Court judgement but her lawyers have filed claims in the court of the first class judicial magistrate Miss Premlata Pradhan for Rs 10,000 and in the court of Miss Baghel for Rs 179.20 per month." The cases are listed for hearing on December 7 and 12 respectively.

When I mention this to the mufti he says the claim for Rs 179.20 per month will be withdrawn. He is silent on the Rs 10,000. "In fact Mohammad Ahmed Khan has yet to pay Shah Bano Rs 120,000 by way of mehr (dower)." This figure has been computed in the following way: the mehr agreed to in 1932 was 3,000 kaldars or silver coins. "All that Khan has paid Shah Bano is Rs 3,000." Each silver coin weighed one tola which is worth Rs 40 at current rates. "Therefore, the total works out to Rs 120,000."

Then the mufti turns upon the father-and-son team. "They only pretend to have fought for the protection of the Muslim personal law," he says. "Do you know that they themselves have fought cases for the maintenance of Muslim women?" He then cites the case of one Shafiqur Rehman whose son has divorced his wife. "Do you know who is fighting the case for the woman's maintenance?" he asks meaningfully. "Mr Zafar Ahmed Khan," he says, thumping a book lying by his side.

But in his office, Zafar is thumping the table on another issue. "A few days ago the mufti came to us and requested us to pay the compensation to Shah Bano privately, without any fanfare, and allow Shah Bano to make her retraction publicly," he says, looking very angry. "The mufti thinks we are a pair of asses!"

Extract from the *Indian Express*
4 December 1985

LEADERSHIP EXPLOITING MASSES

Irfan Engineer

The communal leadership of the Muslims are crying themselves hoarse on awarding life-long maintenance to a 75-year-old poor Muslim divorced woman Shah Bano under section 125 of the Criminal Procedure Code. Mohammad Ahmed Khan, a prominent lawyer in Indore whose monthly income is more than Rs 5,000 will have to pay Rs 179.20 per month as maintenance life-long.

The Ulamas utilized the traditional Moharram Vaaz all over the country to condemn the judgement as an interference in their personal law, and roused the sentiments of the Muslim masses, proclaiming Islam to be in danger. In the week following Moharram, meetings were addressed by Muslim political leaders of different parties.

However, this is not the first time that the slogan of 'Islam in danger' has been raised. The Muslim leadership has mainly exploited highly emotional issues to retain their leadership. These issues are the Muslim personal law, character of the Aligarh Muslim University (AMU) and unfair treatment to the Urdu language.

A number of conventions have been frequently held by various Muslim parties and groups to pass resolutions opposing any change in the Muslim personal law. In October 1977, two such conventions were organized — one at Delhi and the other at Ranchi. The former was convened to discuss various problems confronting Indian Muslims. But six out of the seven resolutions passed, however, were for the social, educational and economic upliftment of the poor Muslims. No solutions were discussed for the needy handloom weavers and the artisans who are on the verge of starvation.

This was particularly surprising as there was no move either by the Government or by any other section to force any change in the personal law. The Majlis-e-Mushwarat was to sponsor a national convention of Muslim legislators on July 27–28 1985, to discuss the problems of the Muslims. The 1,000-odd legislators and ex-legislators who were to participate were from different political parties. They tried to get Rajiv Gandhi to inaugurate it but were discouraged and the convention was postponed indefinitely. However, its draft statement issued on 28 February 1986, was a 'curious mix of sentimentality and warped ambiguity'. The draft agenda evaded any direct reference to concrete issues, even the then serious controversy around the proposal to give Urdu the status of a second official language in UP. The concern of the leadership with the personal law which has rightly or wrongly become a symbol of their religious identity is understandable but their obsession with it to the exclusion of all other problems is inexplicable.

The problems of the Muslim community are not just religio-cultural. The basic issues that concern the masses of Muslims are of a general nature which they share with other citizens of India. These problems are the result of backwardness of the productive forces of our country and, to aggravate it, unequal distribution of the resources. These problems are — poverty, illiteracy, unemployment etc. One has just to go round the areas where Muslims stay to believe in what miserable conditions the majority of Muslim masses live. With other citizens, they share the drudgery of the chawl system, the hutments and footpaths, without proper water and sanitary facilities.

Has any Ulama or Muslim leader visited Dharavi where the Muslims stay? Have they seen the condition of the Muslims in Deonar? Anybody would hang his head in shame that Christian organizations are working in these Muslim majority bastis (though they have their own vested interest) whereas the Muslim leaders are busy counting their votes and manipulating electoral politics. When the slums along the railway tracks in Mahim and Mahim Causeway were being demolished and many Muslims were rendered homeless, none of the Muslim leaders came to their rescue. The organizations of other minorities such as the Dalit

Panthers are organizing the masses to face the threat of slum demolitions. Many Muslims will be de-housed but not a single Muslim leader has so much as even condemned demolitions! What has the Muslim League done for civic facilities in the areas from where their candidates are elected and which are obviously Muslim majority areas? On the contrary, in Bombay, the League joined hands with the Shiv Sena in the Municipal Corporation after exploiting the emotionally charged issue *Vande Mataram* in 1973 to get a few seats on the Standing Committee.

The Muslim women are worst hit by the backwardness of the community as well as by the Ulamas' interpretation of the holy Quran with the prejudices of a male-dominated society. They are victims of the worst feudal values.

Very few are allowed to obtain education besides in the madrasahs where religious training is imparted. They are confined, most of the time, within the four walls of the house. Poverty drives them to resort to prostitution. It is a fact that the proportion of Muslim women taking to prostitution is higher — a shameful fact which does not stir the pious Ulamas and the leaders. Islam is a revolutionary religion which came as a liberator of women from the clutches of the then prevailing traditions. Islam gives them full right to own property. The concept of dower (mehr) is to make the women property-owners. The male-dominated society makes a mockery of dower by giving just Rs 10 or Rs 7. The interpretation by the Ulamas of the holy Quran is according to their prejudices. However, the Mutazila theologians point out that polygamy was an Arab practice and the Quran permitted it only in the context of orphan girls, whose properties were often misappropriated, so that justice be done to them. Similarly, divorce in one sitting is not according to prophetic traditions but is a later practice.

Why don't the Ulamas and the Muslim leaders who raise a big hue and cry about the divinity of the shariat say a word against its misuse? Many Muslim women whose husbands take a second wife are neglected. Often, even the maintenance of such women is neglected. Why don't these protectors of Islam fight for the maintenance of such women as prescribed by the Quran? Do they ensure the Quranic condition of equal treatment to all wives? Isn't the shariat violated then?

The exploitation by Arabs of Indian Muslim women is a well-known fact. Their marriage is nothing but legal prostitution. Many parents out of sheer poverty sell their daughters for a handsome amount to these Arabs under the garb of marriage, though they are fully aware of it. Many such girls have committed suicide. But the Ulamas are tight-lipped about such misuse of religion. When the aggrieved women knock on the door of justice, they are turned out by the Kazis, but the Ulamas suddenly wake up and call people to shed their blood to 'save' Islam.

The Muslim workers employed in small industries by their own co-religionists are exploited by them to the best of their ability. These employers are also the fund-raisers for the Muslim communal parties. These workers sweat and toil for 12 hours a day for a pittance of Rs 300 to Rs 400 per month. At times, their work is semi-skilled or even skilled. The Bhiwandi powerlooms are just an example of this. About 70 per cent of Muslims live below the poverty line.

Though unemployment is a general phenomenon, the level of unemployment is higher among the Muslims. Education is often pointed out as the reason but it is the other way round. The religious bias against Muslims results in a much higher percentage of the educated unemployed. It is unwritten policy — both in the private as well as in the public sector — not to employ Muslims, unless, of course, they hold some exceptional qualifications. In rural areas, the Muslims are mostly landless or small peasants. In urban areas, they are mostly artisans, petty traders, hawkers, mechanics, coolies, rickshaw-pullers, taxi-drivers, tongawallas, fishermen, beedi workers, butchers, masons, weavers, dyers, ironsmiths etc. The Muslim artisans are among the best Indian artisans. The carpet weavers of Kashmir, handloom weavers of Malegaon and Bhiwandi, sari weavers of Banaras, bangle workers of Moradabad, etc., have been keeping alive and enriching the best traditions of Indian craftsmanship. They however work on starvation wages and are exploited by their financiers or middlemen.

The Muslim leaders by and large cannot be bothered to organize these starving artisans into cooperatives and pressurize the state and Central Government for special credit facilities to such artisans. The fast-expanding modern industrial sector has driven many petty artisans out of business. These are swelling the ranks of the unemployed.

Instead of forming a Muslim Personal Law Board, had these leaders and Ulamas been sincere, they would have formed a kind of all India Zakat Board or a similar financial organization to pool all such charitable resources in order to finance these cooperatives or small-scale industries either on low interest or no interest at all. None of them has made any serious efforts to persuade the Arab countries to finance cooperative projects amongst Muslims or to finance modern educational institutions.

The communal leadership of the Muslims have made much noise

about the minority character of the AMU. Though barely 10 per cent of Muslim students admitted to the university in July 1978 were from outside Aligarh, yet the issue has been converted into an all-India problem. For the Muslim leaders (as with other minorities), minority character means nothing more than a pawn to be used in the game for more political power and greater representation on the university court. With their feudal outlook, none of them is capable of transforming AMU into a dynamic centre for scientific learning. The agitation against the world-famous historian Prof. Irfan Habib by the fundamentalists opposing his scientific approach is a case in point. Under their leadership, the university will very likely degenerate into a stagnant institution.

The backward-looking leadership has singularly failed in promoting education among the Muslims, in sharp contrast to the Christian missions. If anything, they have impeded the efforts of some other devoted Muslim organizations. In Kerala, the Muslim League started a verification campaign against the Muslim Education Society members which was, fortunately, unsuccessful.

According to a rough estimate, the Muslims have wakf properties and accumulated funds running into Rs 1,500 million which fetches an annual income running into crores of rupees. Today all the money is spent on madrasahs or pocketed by corrupt mutawallis.

The Muslim leaders have always found an easy way up the ladder by appealing to the religious sentiments of their co-religionists. Proper education and an economic uplift of the Muslims would destroy the religious hold these leaders have.

Even in the pre-partition days, the Muslim leadership could not be bothered much about the more mundane problems of existence facing the Muslims. The whole charter of fourteen demands drawn up by the Muslim League did not include a single demand pertaining to the poor Muslim peasants or toiling Muslim workers and artisans. The Muslim League was the party representing feudal and upper class interests. It always fought for the number of seats to be reserved for the Muslims in the central and provincial legislatures and for reservation of jobs in the top echelons of the administration. These demands mainly served the interest of the upper-class Muslims and hardly reflected the aspirations of the Muslim masses.

Most of these leaders joined the Congress when it was the ruling party. None of them resigned from the Congress ministry even after the mass killings in Ahmedabad in 1969 or in Bhiwandi in 1970. Those Muslim leaders who joined hands with the Janata Party were no different. The massacre of Muslims in Varanasi, Aligarh, Jamshedpur etc., barely stirred them. The frequent flare-up of riots in old Hyderabad is another example of the role of communal leadership of the Muslims' Majlis-e-It-tehadul Muslemeen ruse to lose the assembly seats though the old city is predominated by Muslims. But with the RSS–BJP appealing to Hindu sentiments, the Majlis were able to mobilize votes to get their four candidates elected. While Hyderabad city drowned in communal riots, the Majlis president S. S. Owaisi was busy vying for the position of Speaker in the Andhra Pradesh Assembly when NTR was thrown out of power.

It must be pointed out that many prominent intellectuals who studied the Hyderabad riots blamed NBR for fuelling the riots to de-stabilize the NTR government. It didn't matter how many Muslims were killed; the Majlis supported NBR so that Owaisi could become Speaker. In the recent riots in Ahmedabad hundreds of Muslims were victims of the communal wrath of the RSS–BJP, Congress dissidents and the police — without any provocation from their side whatsoever. None of the parties, Muslim League, the Majlis etc., went beyond giving an occasional statement to the press. None of them organized the Muslims to defend themselves. This is too painstaking a work for them when easy means such as the Muslim personal law are available. Besides, doing concrete work on this front would embarrass the Government and hence jeopardize their electoral prospects. Those who talk of shedding even the last drop of blood to defend their personal law hide themselves while the people suffer. Even the Urdu press which fills it pages with the speeches of these leaders rousing the Muslims on emotional issues such as Muslim personal law, could not find much space for the riots and its analysis. Communal riots suit the political designs of these leaders in the sense that they give them greater political leverage vis-à-vis the ruling party.

All this clearly shows that the Ulamas and the Muslim leadership are not interested in the genuine and burning problems of the Muslim masses but appeal to them on emotional issues by raising a cry of Islam and the divine shariat in danger and thus utilize them as vote banks. Muslim personal law as practised in India was codified by the British by the Shariat Act of 1937 and the Dissolution of Muslim Marriages Act, 1939, to suit their purposes. Muslim women accordingly have a right to go for divorce on eight grounds. These leaders who claim that no human agency can tamper with the divine law, have already accepted the law as codified and amended by the Britishers. Muslim personal law as practised in India is properly called the Anglo-Mohammadan law.

The Minority Commission is conducting a survey to find out the opinion of various sections of Muslims as regards the changes desirable within the personal law. Why are the Ulamas asking the people to boycott this survey? After all, various sections of the Muslims are being consulted and not the non-Muslims. Are they afraid that these sections would opt for a correct interpretation of the divine law in the true spirit of the holy Quran? Are they afraid of being exposed?

Excerpt from *The Daily*
25 December 1985

PERSONAL LAW IN ISLAMIC NATIONS
W. M. Shaikh

Mr Rajiv Gandhi conceded recently that some changes in Muslim personal law are necessary but should be evolved by consensus among the religious leaders concerned rather than by unilateral enforcement. Perhaps the best way to begin is to prepare a background paper analysing all the issues raised by the Shah Bano judgement and detailing the law and practices in other Islamic countries. It may even become the basis of a consensus acceptable to all. This is all the more necessary in view of the raging controversy over the so-called Muslim Women Bill now pending before Parliament.

The status of Muslim personal law overseas relating to polygamous marriages and dissolution of marriages alone is pertinent in this context but it affects the rights of all Muslim women. We, therefore, will deal in these articles exclusively with this and not with the Muslim laws of inheritance, parentage, legitimacy and guardianship which, although important, do not affect the rights of women. Nor are they of a controversial nature.

Before the advent of Islam, unlimited polygamy was a general practice in the Arabian tribes. Mohammad restricted the right of polygamy to four concurrent wives. (Incidentally, in lay circles at least, the Prophet is wrongly misjudged as the originator of this system). In the Quranic text, the law is laid down in Sura 4, verse 3.

> If ye fear that ye shall not
> Be able to deal justly
> with the orphans,
> Marry women of your choice,
> Two, or three or four,
> But if ye fear that ye shall not
> Be able to deal justly (with them),
> Then only one, or (a captive)
> That your right hands possess.
> That will be more suitable,

To prevent you
From doing injustice.

All schools are agreed that a Muslim man does not require permission to contract a second marriage or subsequent marriages up to a maximum of four. Many liberated groups of women, particularly those affected by Western education and culture, regard the man's right to take a second wife and a third wife and a fourth wife as severely hindering progress towards the emancipation of Muslim women. On the other hand, the conservative sections of the Muslim community have been challenged into issuing a continuous stream of apologistic or polemical explanations to counter the criticism of many Western orientalists. As a matter of fact polygamy is decreasing as Western ideas of marriage and romantic love spread in the Muslim community.

Now let us examine the law relating to polygamy in Islamic countries. In Jordan, there is provision that a woman, at the time of marriage, can stipulate that she will have the right to divorce in specified circumstances or to live in a specified place. Indeed, she can even stipulate that the husband should not saddle her with a co-wife. But such a stipulation can be enforced only if it is incorporated in the registered marriage deed and also in the certificate by the qazi. In Iran, marriage with more than one wife is not allowed except with the permission of the qazi and the grant of such permission is usually based on the condition that the husband's financial position is sound enough to take care of more than one wife. Likewise, in Iraq, marriage with more than one wife is not permitted except with the permission of the qazi who grants such permission if the husband's financial position is sound and where injustice between the wives is not feared. All those who enter into a contract of marriage with more than one woman in contravention of the above conditions are liable to imprisonment for a period not exceeding one year, or a fine not exceeding hundred dinars, or both.

In Tunisia, on the other hand, plurality of wives is positively prohibited. Any person who, being already married and, before the marriage is lawfully dissolved, marries again, shall be liable to imprisonment for one year or a fine of 2,40,000 francs, or both. In Syria, the qazi can refuse a married man permission to marry another woman if it is proved that he is not capable of maintaining two wives.

In Pakistan the position is similar to that of other Muslim countries, except that there the competent authority is an administrative body which is clothed with limited judicial powers. Earlier, the task was performed by union committees but these were abolished in 1972 and the functions of their chairman have been taken over by civil judges. If a second marriage is solemnized, the man faces the possibility of criminal proceedings being instituted against him but the second marriage is maintained as valid. The second marriage, however, cannot be registered; and the absence of registration would make it extremely difficult to prove the existence of a valid marriage.

In India there has been no legislative reform at all of the Muslim personal law on polygamy. The only protection that is available is a stipulation in the contract that the husband shall not take a second wife.

It can thus be seen from the above that, unlike in India, certain external checks in most of the Islamic countries act as a brake upon second or third marriages. In Tunisia, of course, polygamy has been completely abolished by law.

Let us now consider the reforms achieved in some of the important Islamic countries in the matter of dissolution of marriages or repudiation of marriages which, in simple and common terms, has come to be known as talaq.

Talaq has taken different forms. First, there is talaq as-sunna (ahsan) where the husband pronounces talaq during the tuhr period, that is when the wife is free from her menstrual flow. He then refrains from sexual intercourse during the iddat period of three menstrual cycles (or if she be beyond the age of menstruation, three lunar months). At the end of the iddat period, the marriage is terminated.

The other form is talaq as-sunna (hasan). In this the husband repudiates his wife three times; the first talaq takes place during a tuhr period. Then he pronounces the third talaq and the talaq becomes irrevocable. These two forms of talaq are the most approved methods of repudiation although ahsan in better than hasan.

Now there is a third method of talaq and this is called the talaq al-bida. The most common method of talaq al-bida is for the triple pronouncement of talaq hasan to be brought together in a single sitting. Such a divorce creates an irrevocable termination of the status of marriage. This is the most common method of repudiation of the marriage although it has been disapproved of by classical jurisprudence.

There are two other forms of repudiation: the ila and the zihar. Under ila, the husband swears on oath to abstain from marital relations for four months. If the husband keeps his oath, it is equivalent to one irrevocable pronouncement of divorce. The zihar is an impious declaration as much as saying to the wife "you are for me as the back of my mother". Zihar by itself is not a divorce. Neither ila nor zihar are of any particular importance today.

In Egypt what has been adopted is the hasan and ahsan methods by abolishing the talaq al-bida. In Syria, the position is a little different in the sense that the matter is brought before a qazi and, where the qazi considers that a husband has repudiated his wife without reasonable cause, he may ask the husband to pay his wife compensation limited to one year's maintenance and support. This follows from the Quranic statement in Sura II, verse 241: 'for divorced women maintenance on a reasonable scale.'

Tunisia has done one better and the provision of the law states that extra-judicial divorces are no longer to be effective. Any divorce outside a court of law is without legal effect. In Iran, too, the right of the husband to repudiate his wife without any judicial intervention has been abolished. The husband has to apply to the court for arbitrators to be appointed on one or a number of grounds based primarily on the culpability of the other party. The arbitrators attempt reconciliation and, in the event of failure, submit a report to the court, which will then issue what is referred to as a 'certificate of impossibility of reconciliation'. The certificate remains valid for a three-month period.

In Pakistan, a husband is required to issue to the chairman of the union council a notice in writing of the talaq immediately after the pronouncement. The effect of the notice is to freeze the talaq for 90 days during which time the union council appoints an arbitration council for purposes of reconciliation. After the expiry of 90 days, talaq takes effect unless a reconciliation is effected.

However unsatisfactory the law might be in Pakistan, there is at least an opportunity that the hasty impetuous repudiation will be thought over once again and the marriage will not be dissolved. No such reform has taken place in India so far.

Not all the countries where changes have been brought about in personal law are really Islamic in substance though they have retained an outward Islamic form. Most of these countries carry a socialistic stamp and the changes they have made in Muslim personal law are governed mostly by their secular attitudes. Tunisia offers a vivid example.

But one has to admit that, over the years, Tunisia has made mincemeat of the shariat. Therefore, it cannot be relied upon to provide any effective guidelines in the Indian situation. It is said that Islam having risen from Arabia in the 6th century has now finally settled in India because India has provided the necessary focus and wherewithal for its development on truly traditional lines. Yet some changes appear to be necessary especially those affecting the rights of women. For example, polygamous marriages will have to be rigorously controlled by a system of checks and balances and by bringing the practice within the purview of civil judges. Similarly, in the matter of dissolution of marriages, we shall have to adopt the ahsan and the hasan methods by abolishing the talaq-al-bida.

Excerpt from *The Times of India*
14-15 March 1986

THE SUPREME COURT INTERPRETED MUSLIM PERSONAL LAW, IT DIDN'T INTERFERE IN IT

Ajoy Bose interviews Y. V. Chandrachud

AB: Your judgement in the Shah Bano case has attracted a lot of criticism from influential sections of the Muslim community, particularly after Shah Bano herself recently opposed the judgement. Any comment?
YVC: The unfavourable reaction to the judgement in the Shah Bano case is sentimental rather than rational, political rather than sociological. It may perhaps be that the minorities have a sense of insecurity which is reflected in their resistance to any departure from the status quo. The judgement interprets the personal law of the Muslims in so far as the nature of mehr or dower debt is concerned. The Supreme Court need not have gone into the question for the purpose of applying section 125 of the Criminal Procedure Code; it was unnecessary to go into the personal law of the Muslims. But it was the husband's counsel and the counsel of the Muslim Personal Law Board who contended that section 125 cannot be made applicable to Muslims because of the provisions contained in section 127.

Now the relevant provision in section 127 says that if the personal law of the parties provided for the payment of a sum in consideration of divorce and the sum has been paid, then section 125 will not apply. The husband's plea was that mehr was paid in consideration of divorce and therefore section 125 should not apply to him.

We, on the other hand, relying on decisions and authentic textbooks, interpreted that mehr is a payment which the husband has to make in consideration of marriage and not divorce. Therefore section 127 had no application in the case. What the Supreme Court did was to interpret the Muslim personal law and not interfere in it. Interpretation of law, personal or otherwise, is not only the function but the obligation of the court.
AB: Muslim fundamentalist leaders however charge that you in your judgement had made a plea for the abolition of Muslim personal law.
YVC: We have only drawn attention to Article 44 of the Constitution which is a principle of directive policy. Article 44 says that the state shall endeavour to secure for citizens a uniform civil code throughout the territory of India. This does not mean interference in the personal law of Muslims. Suppose a Muslim commits murder: what is the law which applies to him? It is the Indian Penal Code and the Criminal Procedure Code. You don't try and punish him according to Muslim personal law, do you?

AB: You had however gone beyond this in the judgement and made several observations about the anti-woman aspects of Muslim personal law which seems to have upset a lot of members of the community.

YVC: Observations made by the Supreme Court on the state of personal law were not confined to Muslim personal law. The thesis of the court was that women are generally treated with discrimination under personal laws, be it Hindu personal law or Muslim personal law. In fact, we quoted Manu, the law-giver who said women do not deserve to be independent.

AB: And yet, a large number of Muslims felt that your observations were a direct affront to their religion?

YVC: It is distressing that a judgement which brings about some social reform should produce a hostile reaction which pleads for an express pronouncement exempting Muslims from the purview of section 125. It would be a sad day when women of any community, be they Hindu, Muslim, Sikh, Christian or Parsi will be denied the paltry benefits which flow out of section 125. That section is in the nature of a stop-gap arrangement designed to ameliorate the misery of destitute women. It does not displace the rights and obligations of the parties, whatever they may be, under the law.

AB: Personally, was it a great disappointment for you that Shah Bano herself went against the Supreme Court judgement in her favour?

YVC: I do not believe that she has gone back. I am not prepared to believe that Shah Bano repents for having succeeded before us. Any right-thinking person can infer why it is propagated that the successful appellant wants to disown her success. The fear of social ostracism is a powerful thing which compels people to act in a manner which is contrary to their interests and to the larger interests of society.

AB: Is it legally possible for Shah Bano to get the judgement reviewed and changed?

YVC: Review of a judgement is a remedy which an unsuccessful litigant may seek. Shah Bano, having succeeded in her appeal, would not be justified in asking for a review of the judgement.

AB: Is this the first time a successful appellant is seeking a review of a judgement?

YVC: I have never known of a successful party asking for a review of a judgement in her own favour.

AB: One of the ominous developments in the wake of Shah Bano's *volte face* is the increasing clamour by Muslim fundamentalists for exemption for the community from civil law. It is also disturbing that senior political leaders, including Prime Minister Rajiv Gandhi, have promised to look into the matter. With no help from the government can the courts resist such pressure?

YVC: Courts must, as in fact they do, resist the pressure of these reactionary lobbies. The support of the government in such resistance will indeed strengthen the hands of the court. On the other hand, a lack of governmental support also ought not to distract the courts from their obligations under the Constitution.

AB: After the strange twist to the Shah Bano case, do you feel that the courts by themselves can be an instrument of social change? Don't you feel that a social movement is necessary to implement true justice?

YVC: Courts can activate social reforms by removing obstacles which hamper social injustice. But ultimately it is for society to implement the court's decisions in the spirit in which they were conceived.

AB: Do you feel that courts have lost their credibility over the past few decades?

YVC: Society at large still appears to repose great faith in the judicial process. Occasionally, there are aberrations which give a jolt to the people's faith in the courts. But such stray occasions apart, there is not enough evidence to justify the contention that courts are losing their credibility. In fact, a large number of Muslim women and women belonging to other communities approach the courts either formally or through correspondence praying for relief from destitution. Courts are the fortress of people's freedom and the foundations of this fortress must remain unshaken for the effective functioning of our democracy.

AB: But don't you feel that the courts are more and more giving into pressures, particularly from the government? Can you honestly say that courts in this country are completely independent?

YVC: Those who believe that courts are not independent from government pressures are being unfair both to the government and the courts; more to the courts. There is an unfortunate tendency of regarding every judgement in favour of the government as a favour done to the government for ulterior reasons or as a result of political pressure. So many judgements which go against the government are conveniently overlooked by these critics.

Excerpt from *The Sunday Observer*
8 December 1985

PART – II

THE MUSLIM WOMEN (PROTECTION OF RIGHTS ON DIVORCE) BILL, 1986

A

BILL

to protect the rights of Muslim women who have been divorced by, or have obtained divorce from, their husbands and to provide for matters connected therewith or incidental thereto.

Be it enacted by Parliament in the Thirty-seventh Year of the Republic of India as follows:–

1. (1) This Act may be called the Muslim Women (Protection of Rights on Divorce) Act, 1986.

   (2) It extends to the whole of India except the State of Jammu and Kashmir.

2. In this Act, unless the context otherwise requires,

   (a) "divorced woman" means a Muslim woman who was married according to Muslim law, and has been divorced by, or had obtained divorce from, her husband in accordance with Muslim law;

   (b) "iddat period" means, in the case of a divorced woman,

      (i) three menstrual courses after the date of divorce, if she is subject to menstruation;

      (ii) three lunar months after her divorce, if she is not subject to menstruation; and

      (iii) if she is enceinte at the time of her divorce, the period between the divorce and the delivery of her child or the termination of her pregnancy, whichever is earlier;

   (c) "Magistrate" means a Magistrate of the First class exercising jurisdiction under the Code of Criminal Procedure 1973, in the area where the divorced woman resides.

3. (1) Notwithstanding anything contained in any other law for the time being in force, a divorced woman shall be entitled to—

   (a) a reasonable and fair provision and maintenance to be made and paid to her within the iddat period by her former husband;

   (b) where she herself maintains the children born to her before or after her divorce, a reasonable and fair provision and maintenance to be made and paid by her former husband for a period of two years from the respective dates of birth of such children;

   (c) an amount equal to the sum of mehr or dower agreed to be paid to her at the time of her marriage according to Muslim law; and

   (d) all the properties given to her before or at the time of her marriage by her relatives or friends or the husband or any relatives of the husband or his friends.

   (2) Where a reasonable and fair provision and maintenance or the amount of mehr or dower due has not been made or paid or the properties referred to in clause (d) of sub-section (1) have not been delivered to a divorced woman on her divorce, she or anyone duly authorised by her may, on her behalf, make an application to a Magistrate for an order for payment of such provision and maintenance, mehr or dower or the delivery of properties, as the case may be.

(3) Where an application has been made under sub-section (2) by a divorced woman, the Magistrate may, if he is satisfied that —

(a) her husband having sufficient means, has failed or neglected to make or pay her within the iddat period a reasonable and fair provision and maintenance for her and the children; or

(b) the amount equal to the sum of mehr or dower has not been paid or that the properties referred to in clause (d) of sub-section (1) have not been delivered to her,

make an order, within one month of the date of the filing of the application, directing her former husband to pay such reasonable and fair provision and maintenance to the divorced woman as he may determine as fit and proper having regard to the needs of the divorced woman, the standard of life enjoyed by her during her marriage and the means of her former husband or, as the case may be, for the payment of such mehr or dower or the delivery of such properties referred to in clause (d) of sub-section (1) to the divorced woman.

Provided that if the Magistrate finds it impracticable to dispose of the application within the said period, he may, for reasons to be recorded by him, dispose of the application after the said period.

(4) If any person against whom an order has been made under sub-section (3) fails without sufficient cause to comply with the order, the Magistrate may issue a warrant for levying the amount of maintenance or mehr or dower due in the manner provided for levying fines under the Code of Criminal Procedure, 1973, and may sentence such person, for the whole or part of any amount remaining unpaid after the execution of the warrant to imprisonment for a term which may extend to one year or until payment if sooner made, subject to such person being heard in defence and the said sentence being imposed according to the provisions of the said Code.

4. (1) Notwithstanding anything contained in the foregoing provisions of this Act or in any other law for the time being in force; where a Magistrate is satisfied that a divorced woman has not remarried and is not able to maintain herself after the iddat period, he may make an order directing such of her relatives as would be entitled to inherit her property on her death according to Muslim law to pay such reasonable and fair maintenance to her as he may determine fit and proper, having regard to the needs of the divorced woman, the standard of life enjoyed by her during her marriage and the means of such relatives and such maintenance shall be payable by such relatives in the proportions in which they would inherit her property and at such periods as he may specify in his order:

Provided that if any such relative is unable to pay his or her share of the maintenance ordered by the Magistrate on the ground of his or her not having the means to pay the same, the Magistrate may, on proof of such inability being furnished to him, order that the share of such relatives in the maintenance ordered by him be paid by such of the other relatives as may appear to the Magistrate to have the means of paying the same in such proportions as the Magistrate may think fit to order.

(2) Where a divorced woman is unable to maintain herself and she has no relatives as mentioned in sub-section (1) or such relatives or any one of them have not enough means to pay the maintenance ordered by the Magistrate or the other relatives have not the means to pay the shares of those relatives whose shares have been ordered by the Magistrate to be paid by such other relatives under

the proviso to sub-section (1), the Magistrate may, by order, direct the State Wakf Board established under section 9 of the Wakf Act, 1954, or under any other law for the time being in force in a State, functioning in the area in which the woman resides, to pay such maintenance as determined by him under sub-section (1) or, as the case may be, to pay the shares of such of the relatives who are unable to pay, at such periods as he may specify in his order.

5. (1) The Central Government may, by notification in the Official Gazette, make rules for carrying out the purposes of this Act.

(2) Every rule made under this Act shall be laid, as soon as may be after it is made, before each House of Parliament, while it is in session, for a total period of thirty days which may be comprised in one session or in two or more successive sessions, and if, before the expiry of the session immediately following the session or the successive sessions aforesaid, both Houses agree in making any modification in the rule or both Houses agree that the rule should not be made, the rule shall thereafter have effect only in such modified form or be of no effect, as the case may be; so, however, that any such modification or annulment shall be without prejudice to the validity of anything previously done under that rule.

STATEMENT OF OBJECTS AND REASONS

1. The Supreme Court, in *Mohd. Ahmed Khan* v *Shah Bano Begum and others* (A.I.R. 1985 S.C. 945), has held that although the Muslim law limits the husband's liability to provide for maintenance of the divorced wife to the period of iddat, it does not contemplate or countenance the situation envisaged by section 125 of the Code of Criminal Procedure, 1973. The Court held that it would be incorrect and unjust to extend the above principle of Muslim law to cases in which the divorced wife is unable to maintain herself. The Court, therefore, came to the conclusion that if the divorced wife is able to maintain herself, the husband's liability ceases with the expiration of the period of iddat, but if she is unable to maintain herself after the period of iddat, she is entitled to have recourse to section 125 of the Code of Criminal Procedure.

2. This decision has led to some controversy as to the obligation of the Muslim husband to pay maintenance to the divorced wife. Opportunity has, therefore, been taken to specify the rights which a Muslim divorced woman is entitled to at the time of divorce and to protect her interests. The Bill accordingly provides for the following, among other things, namely:–

(a) a Muslim divorced woman shall be entitled to a reasonable and fair provision and maintenance within the period of iddat by her former husband and in case she maintains the children born to her before or after her divorce, such reasonable provision and maintenance would be extended to a period of two years from the dates of birth of the children. She will also be entitled to mehr or dower and all the properties given to her by her relatives, friends, husband and the husband's relatives. If the above benefits are not given to her at the time of divorce, she is entitled to apply to the Magistrate for an order directing her former husband to provide for such maintenance, the payment of mehr or dower or the delivery of the properties;

(b) where a Muslim divorced woman is unable to maintain herself after the period of iddat, the Magistrate is empowered to make an order for the payment of maintenance by her relatives who would be entitled to inherit her property on her death according to Muslim law in the proportions in which they would inherit her property. If any one of such relatives is unable to pay his or her share on the ground of his or her not having the means to pay, the Magistrate would direct the other relatives who have sufficient means to pay the shares of these relatives also. But where a divorced woman has no relatives or such relatives or any one of them has not enough means to pay the maintenance or the other relatives who have been asked to pay the shares of the defaulting relatives also do not have the means to pay the shares of the defaulting relatives, the Magistrate would ask the State Wakf Board to pay the maintenance ordered by him or the shares of the relatives who are unable to pay.

3. The Bill seeks to achieve the above objects.

A. K. SEN
NEW DELHI
19th February '86

4A. If, on the date of the first hearing of the application under sub-section (2) of section 3, a divorced woman and her former husband declare by affidavit or any other declaration in writing in such form as may be prescribed, either jointly or separately, that they would prefer to be governed by the provisions of sections 125 to 128 of the Code of Criminal Procedure 1973, and file such affidavit or declaration in the court hearing the application, the magistrate shall dispose of such application accordingly.

5. (2) In particular and without prejudice to the foregoing power, such rules may provide for—

    (A) The form of the affidavit or other declaration in writing to be filed under section 4A;

    (B) The procedure to be followed by the magistrate in disposing of applications under this Act, including the serving of notices to the parties to such applications, dates of hearing of such applications and other matters.

    (C) Any other matter which is required to be or may be prescribed.

5. (3) (1) The Central Government may, by notification in the official gazette, make rules for carrying out the purposes of this Act.

    Every rule made under this Act shall be laid as soon as may be after it is made before each House of Parliament, while it is in session. For a total period of 30 days which may be comprised in one session or in two or more successive sessions, and if, before the expiry of the session immediately following the session or the successive sessions aforesaid, both Houses agree in making any modification in the rule or both Houses agree that the rule should not be made, the rule shall thereafter have effect only in such modified form or be of no effect, as the case may be. So, however, that any such modification or annulment shall be without prejudice to the validity of anything previously done under that rule.

6. Every application by a divorced woman under section 125 or under section 127 of the Code of Criminal Procedure, 1973, pending before a magistrate on the commencement of this Act shall, notwithstanding anything contained in that code and subject to the provisions of section 4A of this Act, be disposed of by such magistrate in accordance with the provisions of this Act.

Amendment an excerpt from the
Indian Express
7 May 1986

THE BILL IS A SIN AGAINST THE QURAN

V. R. Krishna Iyer's letter to Prime Minister Rajiv Gandhi
on the Muslim Divorce Bill

February 28, 1986

Dear Shri Prime Minister,

I am reluctant to write this unpalatable letter to you, knowing that your mind is perhaps dead set on the 'amendatory' solution to the Shah Bano syndrome. But beholding vividly the macabre portents of the legislative bill now being hurriedly piloted through Parliament, I cannot remain silent. You are our prime minister and it behoves me, as a citizen, to do my duty by my country and speak publicly when dangerous mistakes are unwittingly made by the highest political echelons. Criticism is a duty when public power goes awry. And men in authority have a patent responsibility to keep themselves fully informed of others' viewpoints. Prof. Whitehead put it best:

> Duty arises from our potential control over the course of events. Where attainable knowledge could have changed the issue, ignorance has the guilt of vice.

I plead with you, dear Prime Minister, to remember Cromwell's historic words:

> I beseech you, in the bowels of Christ, think it possible you may be mistaken.

All of us are fallible, after all. I want you to win the battle for gender justice but wish you did abandon what mayhems their right to equal justice.

I need not remind you that not only are secularism and equality non-negotiable constitutional-fundamentals but gender justice is a pregnant facet of social justice which too is a guarantee of the *Supreme lex*. No prime minister, no parliament should defeat or diminish these hallowed values. The Preambular pledge of equality of status and the fundamental right to equal protection of the laws, with special provision for women and children, make legal discrimination on the ground of religious denomination (attempted by the dubious bill) anathema and invalid. To keep harrowing Muslim women out of the benign ambit of section 125 when traumatically talaqed by heartless husbands, and to promise them the illusory prospect of being free-fed from a bizzare basket is blatantly unconstitutional and litigatively treacherous: and even if three readings and an assent, together with 'the mysterious virtue of wax and parchment' get the bill into the statute book the final verdict belongs to the Constitution and the Court and, ultimately, to the people. Will this law meet with its Waterloo at the next polls with Hindu fundamentalists and Muslim fundamentalists, both inflamed by this indiscreet amendment, struggling for the victory of numbers? Secularists will be a sore minority at the elections, and should the sleeping Hindu giant be provoked into communal frenzy? Every measure to buy the ayatollahs' pleasure alienates the 'Viswa Hindu' incendiaries. That is the tragic price. The impact on the stability of the state is best guessed by those who know history.

You did, in a brief span when you began, display remarkable resilience and refreshing freedom from inhibitions while handling difficult issues, national, and international, although I am afraid grave errors haunt your naive steps. Optimism is not opium, and so, I feel that if flaws in policy are brought home to you the vanity of consistency may not forbid your will to navigate the ship of state along a wiser course. In this hope, I pen these words of concern and correction before tragic sequelae complicate the situation. You may misunderstand my motive, may disrelish my diction and may even be dyspeptic about my irreverence. I assure you that my purpose is to place a point of view before you. Nor am I so opinionated as to delude myself that my opinion is impeccable. My object, in this long letter, is to persuade you that the Shah Bano nullification bill is born in communalism and will perish in communalism but the processes are often perilous. I pray that you pre-empt the evil by advance wisdom. "History is a cruel stepmother, and when it retaliates, it stops at nothing." When forces of destabilization and injustice seek to hold our nation as hostage to reaction and divisive politics is fuelled by fundamentalists and chauvinists we cannot afford the luxury of myopic mistakes. The best gift for national disintegration and incendiary communalism is the anti-secular, anti-Shah Bano amendment bill now under way. Please desist.

Let me explain a wee bit more the pathological potential of the nascent legislative exercise.

Section 125 Cr. P.C. is obviously a secular provision designed to salvage all divorced damsels in penurious distress, regardless of religion, from the throes of desperate destitution, which may drive them to prostitution and other survival alternatives. This provision is sustained by Article 15 of the Constitution and applies to all women equally. Any exclusion of one religious community is a plain violation of the fundamental right to equality. Illusory alternatives driving Muslim women to seek maintenance from their parents and from the wakf boards (most of which have little in the kitty) are clearly and substantially discriminatory. You could as well put Hindu and Parsi and Christian women under the same handicap and drive them to their religious trusts. Why pick on Muslim women? They are the major victims, as statistics show from a study of applications for maintenance under section 125 Cr. P.C.

You will easily appreciate that *this provision has no relation to liability to maintenance under the personal law.* The jurisdiction is different, the jurisprudence is different, the measure and procedure are different. One is rooted in family law, the other in public order and social justice. To confuse between the two is to be guilty of judicial cataract.

Section 125 Cr. P.C. is of British vintage broadened by the benign Parliament. The twenty-first century is a summons to move forward progressively, not to retreat regressively, frightened by sixth century primitivism. Section 125 rescues needy divorcees, rendered homeless, from moral danger and from resorting to a means of livelihood contrary to peace, tranquillity and social health. Such a provision is founded on the secular values of our republic and is expressly contemplated in Article 25, which empowers the state to make provision necessitated by public order, morality and health. To contend that section 125 is for or against any religion is a crass caricature of the scope and purpose of the law. To invoke 'religion in danger' to resist a provision based on the constitutional concern for public order, morality and health envisioned in Article 25 is to draw the red herring across the trail. Three decisions of the Supreme Court, which have consistently affirmed this approach, are enough authority to negative the fundamentalist distortion. Masculine obscurantism, Muslim or Hindu, should accept the law laid down by the highest Court explaining the *raison d'être* of the measure.

True, some ayatollahs of India and their political muktiars are making noises as is their wont, as if Islam would decline, if women in distress were kept contented! What a travesty of truth! Many hundreds of Muslims and many organizations of Muslim and other women have, to my personal knowledge, applauded the Shah Bano ruling and have been outraged by the reversal of the ruling through the legislative process. It is a grievous error to exalt the strident few reactionaries and pachydermic communalists as the sole representatives of the masses of women. Women's status is at stake; kindly discover the truth before it's too late. There is bitter disappointment among Muslims and total disenchantment among women consequent on the surrender of the prime minister to a handful of surrogates in Parliament whose 'sound and fury' scare him and make him deaf to the deeper feelings of the broader community.

What is more, there is a terrible danger of Hindu communalism being whipped up on this score. The temperature is hotting up. Bigots on both sides are busy. I implore you not to let down our secular stability, the political motive being transparent. Nehru said at Calicut, as prime minister, that the Muslim League is a dead horse. Should you, as prime minister, use it as your mentor? Cliques and claques may later betray.

I see ominous signs of passions rising and feel nervous about the backlash of communal conflicts and poll verdicts. After all, the Supreme Court has interpreted and there is no provocation for scuttling a salutory decision. Kindly note that in Kerala, as elsewhere, the Muslim intelligentsia and women have been awakened and large numbers of responsible people are denouncing the pseudo-Shariatariat. May I entreat you not to stand on prestige, which is a poor defence in crisis, but base yourself on human rights and social justice, so that principled politics may overpower communal politicking?

You rightly stress that communalism shall not be a political tool. But deeds and words must match. Whatever your assertions to the contrary, the present 'Muslim' bill is blatantly communal. *Et tu Brute!* may be history's comment. When the genetic code of this alleged 'Protection' bill and its communal DNA come to be decoded, I have little doubt about the analyst's report. Already communal passions, on this bill, are beginning to convulse. Why punish innocent Muslims and Hindus? You have shown dynamic departure from previous wrong policies and so may I humbly summon your statesmanship?

Let me tell you that the bill is a sin against the Quran and the constitution of wakf. Many Islamic scholars hold that the Quranic command to husbands to pay upkeep expenses to divorcees beyond the period of iddat is clear. Again, wakfs are religious and charitable trusts by pious Muslims to perform specified holy acts for their spiritual benefit. It will be a sacrilege to divert these funds for maintenance of other people's wives. Many wakf boards are themselves poor and it is an illusion to make them caretakers of jilted and jettisoned wives. The whole project is a legislative tamasha! Please don't stultify our great Parliament. Already the Supreme Court judges have been insulted by minister Ansari in Parliament.

May I conclude with a prayer to you on behalf of Indian women, human rights' defenders, secularist radicals and constitutional advocates?

The bill to kill the Shah Bano decision of the Supreme Court is the unfortunate political product of a creative·genius for multi-dimensional injustice. The bill is an injustice to our republic's secular principle; it is an injustice to women's basic rights and therefore, violative of human rights; it is an injustice to the egalitarian policy in our Constitution in Article 14, 21 and 25; it is a vindicative injustice to Muslim women selling the soul of the state's humanism to obscurantist fundamentalists; it is an injustice to the holy Quran which insists on payment of maintenance of divorced women in distress; it is an injustice to the twenty-first century because it throws us back to the sixth century to buy Islamic votes through the noisy illusion of electoral support of fundamentalists whose hold on the liberal Muslim intelligentsia and the suffering masses of women is marginal; it is an *ultra vires* injustice to the law of wakfs because wakfs are not trusts to look after privatized wrongs inflicted by irresponsible talaqs; it is an injustice to family integrity because it is fraught with potential for litigation between close relatives.

It is an injustice to a pragmatic working of the law because, functionally speaking, the provisions lead the destitute to several cases in search of a pittance; it is an injustice to national stability, because the secular credibility of the Government will be a casualty. The dictate of the social dialectics of India today leaves no choice. But as Karl Menninger put it:

> The voice of the intelligence is soft and weak, said Freud. It is drowned out by the roar of fear. It is ignored by the voice of desire. It is contradicted by the voice of shame. It is hissed away by hate, and extinguished by anger. Most of all it is silenced by ignorance.

With kindest regards,

Yours sincerely,
Sd/- V. R. Krishna Iyer

Excerpt from *The Telegraph*
4 March 1986

THE GOVERNMENT MUST NOT CAPITULATE
L. K. Advani, M.P.

In his Bombay speech at the Congress session, Mr Rajiv Gandhi admonished Congressmen for allowing basic issues of national unity and social change to recede into the background. "Instead," Mr Gandhi said, "phoney issues, shrouded in medieval obscurantism, occupy the centre of the stage. Our Congress workers, who faced the bullets of British imperialism, run for shelter at the slightest manifestation of caste and communal tension."

Very well said. But the country is entitled to ask: How is Mr Gandhi himself and his ministers responding to the tide of obscurantism sweeping the country in the wake of the Shah Bano judgement?

On December 20, 1985, the last day of Parliament's winter session, the Lok Sabha witnessed history of sorts being made on the floor. In the course of a single ministerial speech, the Chair had to interrupt on as many as four different occasions and order expunction of remarks which were regarded as unparliamentary or otherwise offensive! The minister was Mr Z. A. Ansari, and the occasion was a discussion on a private member's resolution seeking to undo the effect of the Supreme Court's judgement in the Shah Bano case.

What was struck off the proceedings was patently obnoxious, and cannot be quoted. But even what has been allowed to remain on the record adds up to a vicious diatribe against the Supreme Court, and more particularly, against the former Chief Justice, Mr Chandrachud.

Directing his barbs at Justice Chandrachud and his co-judges on the Bench, Minister Ansari observed: "If you have a tamboli doing the work of a teli, things are bound to go wrong. If you entrust a carpenter the job of an engineer and have him design a bridge what kind of a bridge will he design? They (these judges) know nothing about Islamic culture and its ethos, and they are quoting the Quran, the Haddis" (original speech in Urdu). Mr Ansari roundly denounced the Shah Bano judgement as "a prejudiced judgement", and "a discriminatory judgement."

The minister went on: "The real issue now is that if His Lordship (Chandrachud) begins interpreting the Quran, he will say tomorrow that the Quran does not require circumcision, and pronounce the day after that Quran does not require burial of dead bodies! So why not cremate them? Then, (he may say) why do you chant Allah-o-Akbar, Allah-o-Akbar again and again at the namaaz?"

The minister made this speech in Parliament, and so enjoyed immunity. If a speech of this kind had been made by an ordinary member it would have been bad enough. But for a minister to do so, and yet be none the worse for it, shifts the liability from the individual minister to the Government as a whole.

The Muslim orthodoxy is up in arms against the Shah Bano judgement. The Supreme Court is being accused of sacrilegious trespass into a field out of bounds for courts and for that matter for the legislature. Yet prior to the coming of the British, Muslim law covered every field. The British introduced uniformity in all spheres except personal law, and this was accepted without demur.

Even with respect to personal laws, *Constitutional Law of India*, vol. I, edited by the former chief justice, Mr M. Hidayatullah, records:

.... Till 1935, the Muslims of NWFP followed the Hindu law; the Shariat Act was applied to them only in 1939. Similarly, up to 1934 the Muslims in UP, CP and Bombay were governed by Hindu law in matters of succession; the Shariat Act was applied to them only in 1939. In North Malabar, the Marummakkathayam law applied both to Hindus and Muslims. The Khojas and Cutchi Memons followed the Hindu customs and were highly dissatisfied when the Shariat Act was applied to them.

The enactment of the Dissolution of Muslim Marriages Act, 1939, was an important legislative step towards Muslim law reform. The act conferred on Muslim women the right to divorce in certain circumstances. There was a great deal of opposition from Muslim orthodoxy to this law also, but it went through, and today no one questions it.

From time to time the courts also, by their constitutional right of judicial review, have been making their contribution, extremely constricted though it be, towards reforming Muslim law. One had hoped that leaders of Muslim public opinion would view the Shah Bano judgement in that light. Instead, they have unleashed a vitriolic anti-Supreme Court campaign.

The primary sources of Muslim law are the Quran and the Hadith (traditions of the Prophet). Ijma (consensus of jurists) is supposed to come next. Shortly after his retirement from the Supreme Court, the former chief justice Mr M. H. Beg kindly gifted me a learned treatise titled "Minorities and the Law" published by the Indian Law Institute, and edited by Mohammed Imam.

In this Mohammed Imam observes:

Muslim law was never intended to be static. It had its own rules of law development and if they have become obsolete or impracticable in the context of the present constitutional set-up and law enforcement machinery, they should be supplemented by other techniques that are used for developing any other branches of law. Muslim law should receive its evolutionary growth through the courts and the legislatures. The role of Mujtahid may have to be conceded to our legislatures and courts.

Those who are opposing the Shah Bano judgement are certainly annoyed with what the Supreme Court has said on the maintenance issue. But their anger is even greater over the Court's comment with regard to a uniform civil code. In a forthright statement, the Supreme Court regretted that Article 44 of the Constitution has "remained a dead letter", and observed:

> A belief seems to have gained ground that it is for the Muslim community to take a lead in the matter of reforms of their personal law.
>
> A common civil code will help the cause of national integration by removing disparate loyalties to laws which have conflicting ideologies. No community is likely to bell the cat by making gratuitous concessions on this issue. It is the state which is charged with the duty of securing a uniform civil code for the citizens of the country and, unquestionably, it has the legislative competence to do so.

A small section of Muslim intellectuals favours Muslim law reform, but is opposed to a uniform civil code. They strongly advocate reform in Muslim laws in India in the matter of polygamy, divorce, etc., to bring these in line with the laws in Turkey, Pakistan and other Muslim countries. But the anti-uniform civil code campaign that is being systematically built up draws its strength from leaders and sections who are opposed to reform as such, and who question the very competence of courts and legislatures to deal with the subject.

A prime task at the moment, therefore, is to mobilize powerful public opinion in favour of a uniform civil code. In building up this campaign, people will be fulfilling a duty to the Constitution which the rulers have failed to discharge.

Dr Ambedkar, the principal architect of the Indian Constitution, was of the view that the provision relating to a uniform civil code should be included in the Fundamental Rights chapter, and this should be made justiciable. In fact, in the sub-committee dealing with the framing of the Constitution, the desirability of a common civil code for all Indian citizens was unanimously accepted. The point at issue simply was whether this should be incorporated just as a long-term objective, or whether the nation should commit itself to its time-bound implementation.

The Fundamental Rights Sub-committee was so sharply divided on the question that the matter had to be decided finally by a vote. By a five to four majority, the sub-committee held that the provision was outside the scope of fundamental rights. The four distinguished members of this nine-person sub-committee who constituted the minority were Dr B. R. Ambedkar, Rajkumari Amrit Kaur, M. R. Masani and Hansa Mehta. The latter three, in a dissenting note, wrote:

We are not satisfied with the acceptance of a uniform civil code as an ultimate social objective set out in Clause 39 as determined by the majority of the Sub-committee. One of the factors that has kept Indians back from advancing to nationhood has been the existence of personal laws based on religion which keep the nation divided into watertight compartments in many aspects of life. We are of the view that a uniform civil code should be guaranteed to the Indian people within a period of five or ten years . . . .

The campaign against the Shah Bano judgement is clearly rooted in medieval obscurantism. Religious fanaticism provides it with dangerous teeth. Communal passions are being worked up. The Assam voting pattern has aggravated panic. Instead of acting up to the bold counsel he has given his partymen, the prime minister himself is considering amending section 125 of the Criminal Procedure Code.

It is this provision which enabled Shah Bano to knock at the doors of the court and get relief from her husband who had first thrown her out and later divorced her. After this Shah Bano verdict, a large number of Muslim divorcees have gone to court to claim relief under the same section. The proposal under active consideration with the Government of India is that section 125 Cr. P.C. be so amended as to bar its application to Muslim women.

If any such step is taken, it would be cowardly capitulation to the forces of obscurantism. Public opinion must assert itself to ensure that nothing of this kind happens.

Excerpt from the *Indian Express*
7 January 1986

WOMEN'S RIGHTS ARE FAR SUPERIOR UNDER SHARIAT TO THOSE PROVIDED BY SECTION 125 Cr. P. C.

Badar Durrez Ahmed (Advocate, Supreme Court)

The way has been marked out.
If you depart from it, you will perish.
If you try to interfere with the signs on the road,
You will be an evil-doer.

Jalaluddin Rumi

Mr X: Hello Mr Y. How are you?
Mr Y: Oh, hello!

Mr X: You don't look too well?

Mr Y: I'm all right; only a bit confused and perplexed.

Mr X: What about?

Mr Y: Oh, this issue of section 125, the shariat and the Muslim divorce bill that everyone seems to be discussing with inflamed emotions.

Mr X: But Mr Y, the whole affair is quite clear.

Mr Y: Not to me. Not to me! You see the politicians say one thing, self-styled jurists say another and journalists appear to have lost their bearings.

Mr X: Whatever the politicians, jurists or journalists may say there is no scope for confusion because section 125, the shariat and the Muslim divorce bill are all available in black and white for everyone to read.

Mr Y: You forget, Mr X, that unlike you, I am not a lawyer; nor do I find myself capable of sifting through these books and provisions and of culling out a logical and comprehensible meaning. Perhaps you could help?

Mr X: Most willingly.

Mr Y: Now, tell me, first of all, who maintains a divorced wife or woman under the shariat?

Mr X: Well, the husband does so during the period of iddat. Thereafter, he becomes a stranger and his liability to maintain ceases.

Mr Y: You mean to say that a Muslim woman who has been divorced will get maintenance, under Muslim law, only during the iddat period?

Mr X: No, no! What I said was that she would get maintenance from her "husband" only till iddat. Thereafter, she will be entitled to receive maintenance from her relatives within the prohibited degrees such as father, mother, brother, sister, son, daughter etc.

Mr Y: Now, let me be clear on this. You say that under the shariat or Muslim personal law, a divorced woman will get maintenance from her "husband" till iddat and thereafter, from her family.

Mr X: Yes.

Mr Y: What if she has enough resources of her own to maintain herself?

Mr X: In so far as the "husband's" liability to maintain her during iddat is concerned there is no change. Whether she can maintain herself or cannot does not affect his duty to maintain her. However, if she has enough resources of her own then her family and relatives are not bound to maintain her in the after-iddat period.

Mr Y: Suppose the husband does not have sufficient means then who maintains her during iddat?

Mr X: Whether the husband has or does not have sufficient means he has to maintain her during iddat.

Mr Y: But how?

Mr X: She can, for instance, even pledge his property or she can take loans on his name which he will have to repay.

Mr Y: Suppose the iddat period is over and the divorced woman has returned to her family and her father is very poor. Will the father have to maintain her?

Mr X: No. Except in the case of a husband and a father of a minor, maintenance is never due from those who are themselves very poor, and deserving of maintenance in their own right.

Mr Y: Then who is to maintain her?

Mr X: Her other relatives within the prohibited degrees and in accordance with the share of their inheritance from her.

Mr Y: What happens if she has no relatives within the prohibited degrees?

Mr X: Then she has a right against the Public Treasury of 'Bait ul Mal'.

Mr Y: Wait a minute. This right of hers against the Public Treasury can accrue to her only in an Islamic state.

Mr X: Yes, but in a secular democracy like ours her right of maintenance will be exercisable against the Muslim community.

Mr Y: From what you have told me it appears that under the shariat the maintenance of a divorced woman who is unable to maintain herself never fails. She is saved from destitution at all costs. Her right to receive maintenance never dies, only the source vis-a-vis which this right is exercisable is liable to change.

Mr X: Absolutely.

Mr Y: Before I ask you questions about section 125, Mr X, please tell me what is the maximum maintenance allowance that may be fixed under the shariat?

Mr X: There is no maximum. Whatever is fair and reasonable in keeping with her social status.

Mr Y: This maintenance allowance is quite apart from mehr, is it?

Mr X: Yes. Mehr has to be paid by the husband. You see, under Islam a woman's property is her personal property and her husband has no right over it. Whatever gifts etc., that are made over to her or are received by her are her personal and private property which she is entitled to take with her at the time of divorce.

Mr Y: So, would I be correct if I said that under Islam not only does the divorced woman have a right to maintenance from one source or the other, but she also gets her mehr, if not already paid, and she gets to keep all her property including cash, jewellery and other movable and immovable property?

Mr X: Yes. Moreover, if she has an infant at or after divorce, her ex-husband being the infant's father has to maintain her for two years as she would be feeding his child. The custody of infants is always with the mother.

Mr Y: Now tell me about section 125. What does it say about divorced women?

Mr X: Under section 125 a divorced woman is entitled to receive maintenance from her ex-husband if he has sufficient means and if she is unable to maintain herself.

Mr Y: If the husband does not have sufficient means — then what?

Mr X: It depends.

Mr Y: In what way?

Mr X: The divorced woman or girl may be a minor or she may be an adult and the consequences under each are different.

Mr Y: Let us consider these cases separately. What is the position where the divorced woman is a minor and her ex-husband does not possess sufficient means?

Mr X: In such a case, under section 125, the liability of maintenance shifts to her father provided the father has sufficient means.

Mr Y: Then, this is the same as under the shariat?

Mr X: No. Under the shariat, during the period of iddat, the husband is bound to maintain her whether he has sufficient means or not. Then under section 125 the liability of the father to maintain her would cease on her attaining majority. She would have no right of maintenance at all. Whereas under Muslim law her right to maintenance would continue even after she becomes an adult.

Mr Y: So, while under section 125 she becomes destitute upon attaining majority, under Muslim law she is saved from destitution as maintenance never fails.

Mr X: That is correct.

Mr Y: What happens in the case of an adult divorced woman when her ex-husband does not have sufficient means?

Mr X: Under section 125 there is no 'second line of defence'. This means that if the ex-husband does not have sufficient means then no order of maintenance can be passed against him. In fact, the woman's right to maintenance is extinguished.

Mr Y: What are you saying! You mean to say that in such a case the woman is not entitled to receive maintenance from anyone even though she may be starving?

Mr X: Yes. Unfortunately, that is the position under section 125.

Mr Y: Is it the same under the shariat?

Mr X: As I told you earlier, during iddat the husband is duty-bound to maintain her and after iddat the duty shifts onto her family and, as a last resort, onto the community. Her right to maintenance is fully secured.

Mr Y: Another thought just occured to me. Tell me, Mr X, what would happen if after divorce the ex-husband died or disappeared?

Mr X: Under section 125 the divorced adult woman would be without a right to maintenance.

Mr Y: And under the shariat?

Mr X: Her right would survive against her family members etc., as I explained earlier.

Mr Y: Hmm . . . . This is all very interesting. Under the shariat, women seem to have an unfailing right to maintenance and a guarantee against destitution. I'm afraid this is not so under section 125. This certainly does remove the halo that is being painted around section 125.

Mr X: That is the simple truth.

Mr Y: Since we are focussing on women tell me what are the rights of maintenance of a married woman, you know, a woman whose marriage is subsisting?

Mr X: Under section 125 or the shariat?

Mr Y: Both.

Mr X: Under section 125 as well as the shariat the liability to maintain her is on the husband. However, if the husband does not have sufficient means then under section 125 no order of maintenance can be passed against him. In the case of Muslim law the wife is entitled to maintenance from the husband in any event — she can pledge his property or take loans to be repaid by him.

Mr Y: What about unmarried women?

Mr X: Let us take the case of the minor unmarried girl. She is entitled to maintenance from her father both under the shariat and section 125. But her right is extinguished under section 125 if her father does not have sufficient means. This is not so under Muslim law. The minor girl's right to maintenance never fails.

Mr Y: Does her maintenance continue even after she becomes an adult?

Mr X: In so far as the shariat is concerned — Yes.

Mr Y: And under section 125?

Mr X: It depends upon the physical and mental condition of the adult unmarried woman. If she is unable to maintain herself due to some physical or mental abnormality or some injury then she is entitled to maintenance from the father. Not otherwise.

Mr Y: Are you saying that under section 125 an unmarried adult woman who is physically normal and mentally sane, but is unable to maintain herself, does not have any right of maintenance whatsoever?

Mr X: Yes.

Mr Y: You know something? Contrary to the mistaken belief that is being bandied about, women's rights under the shariat are not only inferior to those limited rights under section 125 but are, indeed, much superior. It is very clear to me now.

Mr X: I told you at the beginning.

Mr Y: But tell me just one more thing. What is this Muslim divorce bill all about?

Mr X: In a nutshell it basically seeks to enforce the rights that are available to divorced women under the shariat.

Mr Y: Which, to my mind, are more than what are available under section 125. One more thing. Would I be right if I said that while there is a time limit to the maximum monthly maintenance that may be ordered under section 125 no such ceiling exists under the shariat and the Bill?

Mr X: Yes.

Mr Y: Frankly speaking by implementing section 125 we are in fact depriving Muslim women of the better and wider rights that they have under their personal law. After this discussion with you I fail to see how anyone can oppose the bill on principle.

Mr X: Haven't you heard of Sufi Al-Ghazali's saying that "People oppose things because they are ignorant of them"?

Mr Y: Oh! Thank you for clearing my confusion.

Mr X: You are welcome.

Excerpt from *The Telegraph*
29 April 86

THE MUSLIM WOMEN BILL

Danial Latifi

The Muslim Women (Protection of Rights on Divorce) Bill is premised upon a supposed summary of the Supreme Court's judgement in the Shah Bano case. This summary is contained in the statement of objects and reasons of the bill. According to this summary in that case the Supreme Court "has held that although the Muslim law limits the husband's liability to provide for maintenance of the divorced wife to the period of iddat, it does not contemplate or countenance the situation where the divorced wife is unable to maintain herself after the period of iddat . . . therefore . . . she is entitled to have recourse to section 125 of the Code of Criminal Procedure . . . this decision has led to some controversy as to the obligation of the Muslim husband to pay maintenance to the divorced wife. Opportunity has therefore been taken to specify the rights which a Muslim divorced woman is entitled to, at the time of divorce and to protect her interests...."

But this is not a correct presentation of what the Supreme Court decided in the Shah Bano case. The former husband, Ahmed Khan's case was that he had already paid Shah Bano "the whole of the sum which, under the customary or personal law applicable to the parties, was payable on . . . divorce" as provided in section 127(3).

The only question before the Supreme Court was whether Ahmed Khan had paid this entire sum. The answer to this question is given by the court in paragraphs 15-23 of the judgement.

The historic contribution of the judgement in the Shah Bano case is its recognition of the right of a Muslim divorced woman to mataaun bil maaroof – a reasonable and fair provision to be made and/or paid to her, on divorce, as provided by the Quran II: 241.

The court held that the husband, Ahmed Khan, having failed to discharge his obligation aforesaid, "to make provision for or to provide maintenance to the divorced wife" had failed to fulfil the condition stipulated in section 127 Cr. P. C. namely, to discharge "the whole of the sum which under any customary or personal law applicable to the parties was payable on . . . divorce". In the circumstances the court held that the maintenance order, passed in favour of the divorced wife by the magistrate, must continue.

It thus appears that the statement of objects and reasons of the bill proceeds on an incorrect reading of the judgement of the Supreme Court, which seems to have held the exact opposite view.

If some doubts exist as to what the Supreme Court actually held, the matter could be clarified in another case. Actually one such case is now pending in the Supreme Court.

At this point, it may be useful to set down the gist of the argument at the bar, in the Shah Bano case, where I had appeared for Shah Bano Begum and certain interveners.

The main objections raised by Mr Yunus Saleem, counsel for the Muslim Personal Law Board, were two:

First, he said, that the amount of mataa referred to in the Quran II: 241 was a lump sum payment and not a recurring amount. This point was easily answered because it was not really in issue in this appeal. It was nobody's case that Ahmed Khan had paid any sum, whether lump sum or recurring by way of mataa to Shah Bano. A careful reading of the judgement of the court will show that this question has not been decided and it is still open.

Secondly, Mr Yunus Saleem, relying on the Privy Council judgement in *Agha Mohd* v *Kulsum B* (1827) IA 196 argued that, according to him, the payment of mataa under the injunction of the Quran II: 241 was optional, and not compulsory. To this my reply was, that the great Shia jurist, Imam Jafar as Sadiq had declared the mataa referred to in the Quranic verse II: 241, as fariza wajiba (obligatory duty). Mr Yunus Saleem conceded this, but said that this ruling applied only to Shias. I then said that I also had the ruling of Imam Shafei, acceptable to all Sunnis, to the same effect. Upon this the chief justice, Mr Y. V. Chandrachud, interjected that since the Quranic verse itself was so crystal clear, it seemed unnecessary to go to other sources.

I acquiesced in this view, and did not insist upon citing the authority of Imam Shafei which I had ready in my mind. I may say that both the citations and full references to Imam Jafar as Sadiq and Imam Shafei were contained in my written arguments which I had filed in court and supplied to all parties.

This is a sound and ancient rule of Muslim jurisprudence, evolved in the period of the Umayyad and Abbadid monarchies, to limit judicial discretion within ·the parameters of the rulings of the great jurists of Islam. This was to prevent extravagant constructions being put on Quranic verses by judges' pressurized by corrupt rulers.

Here I may mention that Article 18 of Egyptian law No. 100 of 1985, passed only last year by the Egyptian parliament, after full discussion with the scholars of the renowned Al Azhar University of Cairo, entitles a divorcee, over and above her mehr and maintenance, to a compensation from her former husband amounting to minimum two years' maintenance (with no maximum). The husband may be permitted to pay this amount in instalments.

Let us now see what the present bill actually seeks to provide: section 2(a) of the bill defines a "(A) 'divorced woman' to mean a Muslim woman who was married according to Muslim law and has been divorced by or has obtained divorce from her husband in accordance with Muslim law". Section 2(b) says that "iddat period" means, in the. case of a divorced woman, "(*i*) three menstrual courses after the date of divorce, if she is subject to menstruation; (*ii*) three lunar months after her divorce, if she is not subject to menstruation (*iii*) if she is enceinte, at the time of her divorce, the period between the divorce and the delivery of her child or the termination of her pregnancy, whichever is earlier".

These provisions appear to be patent violations of Muslim law, for the following reasons.

The Muslim law provides a number of procedures for divorce. Among these the most important are: mubarraat (divorce by mutual consent), khula (divorce at the wife's instance), faskh. (divorce by court, now regulated by the Dissolution of Muslim Marriages Act, 1939) and talaq (unilateral divorce by the husband). Of talaq there are three kinds, talaq ahsan (least disapproved by the Prophet); talaq hasan (less disapproved by the Prophet) and talaq-ul-bidaat (forbidden by the Prophet, but allowed by the present interpretation of the Hanafi school of law). (See *Mulla's Mohammedan Law*, 18th ed. by Hidayatullah pp. 329-331.)

The last of these, the talaq-ul-bidaat is the dire "triple talaq", pronounced in one breath, that is a nightmare for every Muslim wife subject to it. It was illegally smuggled into the law by fatwas issued at the behest of the Umayyad monarchs and is today, alas, continued as the favourite practice of the elements sponsoring the present bill. Talaq bidai is regarded as sinful by all schools of Muslim law and is held illegal by all Shia schools.

In the talaq ahsan, (least disapproved by the Prophet) the three month iddat (probation) period, which is provided for enabling reconciliation of the spouses, precedes and does not follow the divorce. During the iddat period the woman is not known as a muttalaqata (divorcee) but as a muattuda (woman in probation).

Thus reading together sections 2(a) and 2(b) of the bill, the result would be that at least the talaq ahsan would cease to be a recognized mode of divorce and, possibly, so also the talaq hasan. Hereafter only the universally execrated talaq bidai would hold the field. No doubt this is the form that some of our maulanas seem to favour. But the law ministry should know better. These kinds of technical flaws abound in almost every section of the bill. This makes it eminently desirable that it should be subjected to detailed scrutiny by experts in Muslim law, among others, before it is further considered by Parliament.

The most serious objection to the bill is its purported "definition", actually mutilation of the Muslim women's right on divorce against her husband, as secured to her under her personal law, and as declared by our highest court.

This is done by sub-sections (a) and (b) of section 3 of the Act. The former, in a seemingly deliberately garbled sentence, offers the woman: "a reasonable and fair provision and maintenance to be made and paid to her within the iddat period by her former husband." It is difficult to understand the purpose of inserting the words "within the iddat period" in this sub-section.

Alternatively one may say, it is difficult to understand the purpose of jumbling together two distinct ideas and concepts in a single sentence. These two distinct ideas and concepts are: (1) a reasonable and fair provision (which could be a capital sum, property or usufruct) and (2) maintenance for iddat period.

The latter is not applicable in the case of talaq ahsan where the wife is kept and maintained in the divorcing husband's house in the same status as before in the terms spelt out in Quran LXV: 1-7.

The two distinct rights enumerated in two distinct provisions in the

Quran, namely II: 241 and LXV: 1-7 are sought to be jumbled and telescoped into one sentence in the Muslim Women (Protection of Rights on Divorce) Bill with a sacrifice of clarity and introduction of possibilities of error and adverse judicial determination.

It is difficult to see why the legal draftsman has tried to compress so much into a single sentence in this clause which is perhaps the most important in the whole bill.

As the law now stands, a Muslim divorcee is entitled to reasonable maintenance during the iddat period and also, as held by the Supreme Court in Shah Bano's case, to mataaun bil maaroof, which may be translated correctly as "a reasonable and fair provision". However, by the strange juxtaposition of words it has been made possible for a husband to argue that section 3(1)(a) of the bill restricts this amount to a provision only for the iddat period of three months.

Now, is the "reasonable and fair provision" and maintenance one provision or two distinct provisions? If the latter, why not deal with them separately in two sub-sections? If the sub-section deals with only one indivisible right then why so much verbiage? Is it that the wife is entitled to a reasonable and fair provision in addition to maintenance for the iddat period? If so, why does it not say so in plain language?

I have already pointed out the anomaly of referring to the iddat period as being subsequent to the divorce. The talaq ahsan is done by the husband pronouncing a single talaq while the wife is in a free state, and thereafter living with her under the same roof for three menstrual courses without resuming cohabitation. Upon the expiry of the iddat period in this case the talaq becomes final and irrevocable. But the parties are free to remarry. Such remarriage cannot be repeated more than twice. This was the form of talaq recommended by the Prophet, as already stated.

The other provisions of the bill may be dealt with briefly. They read like pages from *Alice In Wonderland*. Section 3 (I) (B) says that a divorced woman shall be entitled — "where she herself maintains the children born to her before or after her divorce, a reasonable and fair provision and maintenance to be made and paid by her former husband for a period of two years from the dates of birth of such minor children."

It is not clear whether this refers to the children of the divorcing husband or to the children of some other man.

If this refers to the children of the divorcing husband then the Muslim law has always insisted upon the liability of the father to maintain them during minority no matter in whose custody they are. So this bill is also an attack on the rights of children.

Section 4 of the Act makes a provision for relatives, including collaterals, maintaining a divorced Muslim woman.

So far only the Hanafi law has had such a provision (see Fatwa Alamgiri) but such obligation is limited to relatives within the prohibited degrees. The draftsmen of the bill have overlooked this limitation. The Shia and Shafei law further limit such obligation to ascendants and descendants. (See *Imameeah Minhaj at Talibin* vol. 3, pp. 93-7). This provision would be most cumbersome and in practice difficult to enforce particularly for a magistrate's court, on account of difficult and complex questions of law and fact.

It would appear that any relative charged with an obligation under this section who wished to escape from it, could easily do so by registering his marriage (if married) under the special marriage act! So in any event the woman would get nothing from an unwilling relative. The willing ones would support her anyway. The provision invades the rights of Shias and Shafeite Sunnis. It is an exercise in futility and should be scrapped.

Lastly, there is the provision also in section 4, making a divorced woman's maintenance a charge on Muslim waqfs. The law of Islam is very strict on the point that a benefaction must be applied to the purpose specified by the wakif — the founder of the trust. It cannot be changed by anybody. Legislative interference in the objects of trusts is an outrage against constitutional principles. It would, *inter alia*, violate Article 30 of the Constitution, which Muslims have, in the past, fought to uphold.

All in all, the bill as it stands is obnoxious to Islamic principles, derogatory to human rights, violative of the rights of the minority community to establish and administer charitable and educational institutions of their choice. It may, if persisted in, involve the political leadership and the country as a whole in increasing difficulties and may founder on the bedrock of our Constitution. The earlier it is withdrawn the better for all concerned. The bill as drafted is an insult to the traditions of Islamic civilization.

Excerpts from *The Times of India*
12 – 13 March 1986

MUSLIM WOMEN BILL EVADES ISSUES

Zarina Bhatty

March 8 is observed all over the world as International Women's Day. Schemes are initiated to improve women's lives, seminars are organized to discuss women's problems, and processions are taken out to highlight women's plight.

March 8 means different things to different women. What does it mean to Salma, a 55-year-old housewife from Aligarh? Salma was married in her teens and produced four children. She came from a middle class family and was not provided much education beyond elementary skills in Urdu. Her husband, an intelligent boy, was sent for higher education. He did well in life and secured a job with an international agency. He had money and status, and had postings mostly abroad.

Salma stayed behind in India, reared their four children including a spastic one. She looked forward to settling down with her husband at least when he retired. But her husband being a Muslim exercised his own options. Why live with an old spent woman after retirement? So when he came back, he married a younger woman, bought a house in Delhi and decided to enjoy his second youth.

What does March 8 means to Fatima, another Muslim woman married for nearly 30 years, who was sent home only because her husband found her to be unattractive and unsuitable for his growing economic status?

What about poor Shakila, who was one of too many children in her family? She was married off as soon as she turned sixteen — at least one mouth less to feed. After all poor Hamid was getting old and earning less. His sons were good-for-nothing. He had even managed to give her a bed and two chairs, besides a few sets of clothes (a gift from a relative in the Gulf) in dowry. Six years passed, Shakila produced two daughters and a son in quick succession. Wasn't it an expression of her husband's affection for her?

On fine morning, she returned to her father's house with the two girls, half of her body bearing scars from burns. Her husband had been torturing her in order to get a scooter from her parents. She had refused, knowing they could not afford it. Ultimately the husband threw her out.

How many Shakilas, Salmas, Fatimas and Shah Banos can be lined up in India? A Muslim can keep up to four wives, and divorce one without giving reason or maintenance. The religion allows it, the law of the land allows it. But do they act as Muslims? Do they fast for a month every year? Do they pay zakat (Islamic obligation to give away two and a half per cent of their capital to charity?) These are irrelevant questions. What is relevant is that they have kept their identity by practising the Muslim personal law. The Muslim community should maintain its distinctiveness in continuing to be male chauvinist and unkind to women!

What is the relevance to Indian Muslims of the fact that Islamic countries like Pakistan, Turkey and Indonesia are examining the outmoded and discriminatory social and legal practices like polygamy and unilateral divorce, and modifying their personal law? After all India is not an Islamic state. Therefore Indian Muslims must retain their right to remain backward, clinging to outmoded and unjust practices.

There is a vigorous feminist movement in this country. Indian feminists adorn chairs at international conferences. Can they do anything about Salma, about Fatima, about Shakila? What can an Indian Hindu woman do about her Muslim counterpart?

There are innumerable schemes sponsored by the Government for women's development. There is a separate ministry of women's welfare headed by a woman minister and run by a woman secretary and a woman joint secretary. What can it do for Indian Muslim women?

There is the Constitution, the most enlightened constitution in the world, which guarantees "equality irrespective of caste, colour, creed, or sex" for all Indians, but what can it do for Indian Muslim women? Are they only Muslim, not Indian?

There is a young, truly enlightened, utterly sincere prime minister dedicated to the development of women. He has women in his cabinet, he has women in his secretariat, but what can he do for Indian Muslim women? Is there anyone who can do a thing about this deplorable situation in which Muslim women live in this country? Must it be a lonely fight by the Muslim women alone? Should it not be the concern of all enlightened secular-minded Indians, men and women? These are some of the relevant questions that need answers.

The fundamentalists have given an assurance to the prime minister that a divorced woman's maintenance is well organized in the shariat. The husband is required to maintain her for the period of "iddat" (three months and a few days); then the father; and failing him the brothers; failing them, the nephews, and if all these relatives fail her, then waqf property can be used to provide maintenance. Many educated men and women, Muslims and non-Muslims, are unable to see that this pretty assurance is most undesirable both from a practical and ideological point of view.

From the practical point of view, Shakila's case mentioned above is self-explanatory. Even in middle and upper-middle classes, how many brothers, leave alone nephews, would support a relative for life? Is it not known what happens to waqf property, and how it is misappropriated? On what basis can one believe that in the case of divorced women the waqf authorities will become competent, honest and selfless? Many of us may not know that nearly 90 per cent of the prostitutes in this country are Muslims. What a way to maintain an identity!

On the ideological level — and this is the real issue — accepting the fundamentalist view amounts to encouraging Muslim women to go round with a begging bowl. Is the principle of equality and dignity of a person not involved? We totally exonerate the man of any responsibility in marriage towards his wife. Muslim fundamentalists take pride in the fact that the Muslim marriage is a contract. But it is an unequal contract which places no obligations on the part of the male.

The issue is not that of providing two meals a day to a helpless divorced woman but of equality between men and women in marriage and in society. Is marriage not a two-way relationship which establishes a family and brings new life into this world? A breakdown of this relationship only at the will of one person hurts not only the wife but also the children. Should any religion or society or legal system allow the unilateral decision of only one member of the family to destroy the whole unit?

Even if maintenance after divorce was made obligatory on the man, it may not serve the purpose. As long as the man is allowed polygamy he need not divorce a woman; he may just abandon her or let her hang around and take another wife. The termination of marriage by talaq and khula has another discriminatory element. If the termination of marriage is initiated by the husband, the payment of mehr (dower) becomes obligatory. But if it is by khula, that is, at the initiative of the wife, then mehr is not obligatory.

Therefore, as long as bigamy and polygamy are allowed, a man need never utter talaq. He can conveniently marry again and let the first wife rot until she herself asks for khula. Besides, even if a man does initiate divorce and pay the mehr it amounts to a pittance. In the first instance, many fix the mehr according to the Sunnah, the amount which was fixed for the Prophet's wives, which has been calculated at a few rupees. Mehr has acquired a status connotation also: in many families mehr is fixed in lakhs, which has nothing to do with the ability to pay. In such cases, even if a woman goes to court and demands mehr, she will not receive lakhs from her husband who probably does not even have Rs 10,000.

Islam makes it incumbent on the man to pay at least part of the mehr before consummating the marriage. Some clever but pretentious men blackmail their wives, by refusing to consummate the marriage, unless they "forgive" the mehr. Therefore, the provision of mehr as part of a marriage contract cannot provide financial security to a woman.

There can be no two opinions that the interpretation of the Quran in the form of the shariat is extremely male-centred and negates the principle of equality between the sexes. It is, therefore, the duty of all enlightened Indians to examine Muslim personal law in the light of equality and social justice enshrined in the Constitution and not to leave it to the uneducated, ill-informed Muslim mullahs.

Excerpt from *The Times of India*
8 March 1986

BEHIND THE VEIL

Seema Mustafa

On Tuesday at 5.30 p.m, just after the Government introduced the
Muslim Women (Protection of Rights on Divorce) Bill in the Lok Sabha,
the minister of state for energy, Mr Arif Mohammad Khan, walked out
of the House and resigned from the council of ministers. He sent a long
explanatory note to the prime minister, Mr Rajiv Gandhi, regretting
that, while the Government claimed to have consulted "leaders of the
Muslim community", it had given credence to the views of only the
conservatives and ignored the progressive and secular opinion within
the community. He also challenged the Government's definition of
Muslim "leaders" maintaining that no effort had been taken to obtain
a cross-section of views on this very important matter.

The next morning, Mr Khan, driving his own car, and followed by
the official car, went to his office. He deposited the keys and left. The
energy minister, Mr Vasant Sathe, was immediately informed by puzzled
bureaucrats and he rushed to the prime minister to urge him not accept
the resignation. It was Mr Sathe who broke the news to the Congress
(I) members in Parliament even as efforts were on to persuade Mr Khan
to withdraw his resignation. Mr M. L. Fotedar, Mr Arun Singh, Mr
Arun Nehru and others were sent by the prime minister to the 35-year-old
MP from Uttar Pradesh, to impress upon him the disastrous results his
resignation would have for the party, particularly at this time. Mr Khan
refused to surrender his principles and when it became clear to all that
he was adamant, the prime minister advised the president to accept his
resignation.

The news sent shock waves through the party even as the Government
not only introduced the bill but hotly defended it. The resignation put
life into paralysed limbs and the Congress (I) MPs, most of whom are
totally opposed to the bill were suddenly activated into calling a general
body meeting without consulting the party president. He was informed
of the decision, through a letter, by the Congress (I) Parliamentary
Party (CPP-I) secretary, Mr Harikishen Shastri, who sought to convey
the "strong resentment" of the members to the prime minister. If held
as scheduled, this would have perhaps been a historic meeting, but
adroit party 'managers' were successful in whittling the dissent down to
a mere whimper, at least for the record.

The sequence of events leading to the union minister's resignation
can be traced back to last year's Supreme Court judgement which granted
Shah Bano, an old destitute from Indore, maintenance from her husband

who haa aivorced her after more than four decades of marriage. The court on the basis of a progressive interpretation of the shariat, decreed that destitute Muslim divorcees were entitled to maintenance from their husbands, that the husband's responsibility was not limited to the iddat period, that mehr (dower fixed at the time of marriage) could not be taken as compensation for divorce and above all, that if there was any conflict between sections 125 and 127 of the Criminal Procedure Code (Cr. P. C.) and the Muslim personal law (MPL) the former would prevail.

This was widely hailed as a progressive judgement. It had its echoes in the Lok Sabha which was at the time discussing a private member's bill, introduced by Mr G. M. Banatwala (Muslim League) and directed against a uniform civil code and section 125 of the Criminal Procedure Code (Cr. P.C.). After the judgement, the discussion on the bill focussed on it. Impassioned arguments both for and against, were heard in the House, but the first authoritative answer to the conservative stand came from Mr Khan who was then the minister of state for home affairs.

In an excellent speech, Mr Khan challenged the mullahs on their own ground by quoting solely from the Quran and the Haddis, seeking to prove that maintenance rights were available to the Muslim divorcee under her own religion as well. He said that it was absolutely wrong to hold that the husband's responsibility concluded with the iddat period of three menstrual cycles, maintaining that this argument went totally against the concept of Islam. He regretted that the 'thekedars' (self-appointed guardians) of the religion were very upset when reminded of their responsibilities under the religion, but did not raise their voice when the shariat provisions were wrongly interpreted to enslave women and deny them their rights. He regretted that the "experts" on shariat never raised a voice when women were divorced and thrown out into the streets in complete violation of the MPL, but got very agitated when some maintenance was awarded to them under the same law.

The speech was hailed by all progressive members of the community. It reaffirmed their faith in the Union Government's commitment to secularism. It was clear at the time that Mr Khan had spoken at the direct behest of the prime minister who even sent him a letter congratulating him on his "excellent" speech.

The speech, however, fuelled the protest movement against the judgement organized by conservatives belonging to the Muslim Personal Law Board, Muslim League, Jamaat-e-Islami and other similar organizations all over the country. Black band demonstrations were held and fiery speeches castigating the Supreme Court and the Union Government were delivered. Mr Khan was singled out for personal attack by a section of the Urdu press. He was gheraoed and stoned at Hyderabad airport. The conservatives, who have consistently opposed progressive change throughout the history of this country (a parallel can be drawn with the opposition to the reforms brought about by the Hindu Code Bill), came together to attack secular institutions and individuals.

It is from here on that a change was noticeable in the Government's thinking on the subject. Shortly after Mr Khan made his speech, two men close to the prime minister — Mr Shiv Shankar and Mr M. L. Fotedar — began organizing the Muslim Congress (I) MPs to persuade Mr Rajiv Gandhi that in supporting the Supreme Court judgement he was acting contrary to the interests of the Muslim community. This, it was argued, would lead to a total alienation of the Muslims from the ruling party. Such a development was bound to adversely affect its electoral performance. The prime minister bought the argument and agreed that it was time for another Muslim minister to contradict Mr Khan's secular assertions in the Lok Sabha. The choice fell on Mr Z. R. Ansari.

The Government changed its mind in the period between the monsoon and winter sessions of Parliament. It decided to support the conservatives and Mr Ansari was allowed over three hours to argue that the Supreme Court judgement was against Islam. He asserted that the divorced Muslim woman, under Islam, had to be maintained by her father, brother, or whoever, but definitely not by her husband whose responsibility ended with the iddat period. He not only reiterated the conservative opinion but also criticized the former Supreme Court chief justice, Mr Y. V. Chandrachud, in insulting language.

Mr Ansari's speech was applauded by orthodox elements in the Muslim community. He was at one with Mr Banatwala and Mr Sulaiman Sait. The gap had been bridged and Mr Shiv Shankar, Mr M. L. Fotedar, and others took great consolation in the fact that their palliative for reducing the aggressiveness of the Muslim communal attack had been accepted. The Congress (I) defeat in the Kishanganj parliamentary by-election in December, where a known proponent of Muslim conservatism Syed Shahabuddin (Janata) was elected, merely strengthened this lobby's argument that Mr Khan and others like him within the party and outside were completely out of tune with the times. Moreover, the secularists being politically passive could easily be ignored, as their dissent, it was argued, cannot influence the votes.

And once Mr Rajiv Gandhi accepted this line, he did not look back. Mr Khan and those who shared his progressive views were unceremoniously 'dropped'. The prime minister made no pretence of defending his minister against attacks from the conservatives and instead with Mr Shiv

Shankar and Mr Fotedar close at his side, began the process of "consultation". In meetings with the Opposition leaders, he agreed to prepare a background paper on the entire debate on such issues in the past, on the views of all sections, the legal opinion and the Shah Bano judgement. He assured the Opposition as well as a women's delegation that no decision would be taken without a "nationwide" debate.

But the process of consultation was cut short. In actual fact the prime minister reportedly consulted not more than six persons, all known conservatives who have always resisted any attempts by the community to progress. In fact, those seeking a progressive interpretation on the shariat are, according to these leaders, "non-Muslims". They were Maulana Ali Mian, chairman of the Muslim Personal Law Board, Mr Minnatwala Rehmani, secretary of the board, Mr G. M. Banatwala and Mr Sulaiman Sait of the Muslim League, and, on occasions, Syed Shahabuddin. Not a single Congress (I) Muslim leader was consulted. Certainly not Mr Khan, but not even Mr Ansari, Mr Abdul Gafoor, Mrs Abida Ahmed, or Mrs Najma Heptullah. Nor was any other Muslim leader in the Opposition consulted. Muslim academicians, scientists and leaders in other fields were not contacted for their opinion. The promised background paper was forgotten.

Mr Khan was called over three weeks ago by the prime minister's office and informed that an 'agreement' had been reached with the Muslim Personal Law Board. He was not asked for his views; he was not even given a copy of the agreement; he was merely told that, as a disciplined member of the party, he was expected to cooperate when the bill was introduced in Parliament. This courtesy was not extended to Mr Ansari, but then the prime minister's office probably realized that it was not necessary as he would conform. The fact that Mr Khan had been first asked to take a stand, that he had done it on the floor of the House and could not very well withdraw without jeopardizing his principles and his reputation as a politician, was not taken into consideration. Incensed at this attitude, it is believed that the young minister had decided at the time that he would resign when the bill was introduced in Parliament.

On Tuesday, most of the Opposition members resisted the introduction of the bill but their views were ignored. Mr Indrajit Gupta (CPI) summed up the secular sentiment by wondering how the Parliament of India committed to a secular Constitution could even think of introducing a legislation whereby rights were denied·to a section of the women and fundamentalist arguments endorsed. The union law minister, Mr Asoke Sen, defended the bill as being in response to the demand of the majority of Muslims, maintaining that the Government had reached a decision only after consulting all Muslim leaders.

Mr Khan, who had not even been approached for his views, left the House to submit his resignation letter. His action helped bring to the surface the dissent within the party on the bill and, for the first time, MPs were emboldened to speak out openly against the draft legislation. A general body meeting was called threatening a crisis in the party.

Mr Rajiv Gandhi's aides swung into action. The first step was to postpone the meeting by a day with the argument that the prime minister wished to consult the different sections of opinion first. He called a meeting of women MPs only to inform them that he could see no point in withdrawing the bill. As one young MP said after the meeting, "You see, most of us had not really read the bill and we do not understand the Muslim law so we could not counter his arguments." She also said that the support extended to the bill by a few Muslim women members made "it difficult for us to oppose it". Mrs Margaret Alva is amongst those to have voiced her strong objections to the bill. Mrs Rajendra Kumari Bajpai is another minister who is extremely unhappy with the bill. Mrs Mohsina Kidwai is playing it safe by adopting a totally ambivalent stand.

This was followed by group meetings of Congress(I) MPs with the home minister and law minister throughout the day. That this exercise was meaningless became clear the same evening when Mr Rajiv Gandhi, completely ignoring the views of the members, stood up in the Lok Sabha to defend the bill on the grounds that it was secular, that it did not deprive Muslim women of their rights but was superior to even section 125, Cr. P.C. and that, as Hindus, Parsis and Christians had modified bills why should this be denied to the Muslim women.

Those who oppose the bill argue that it is not secular. It is retrogressive as it seeks to take away the minimal rights given to the Muslim divorcee by the Supreme Court. It is anti-women as it seeks to make Muslim women second-class citizens by taking away their option to appeal under secular laws. As Mr Indrajit Gupta had pointed out, section 125 does not compel a woman to seek justice from the court. She is still free to go the qazi if she so wishes. So what is the point of bringing in a legislation to deny her this option? Moreover, the Hindu Code Bill is progressive legislation which gives rights to women and does not take away certain rights as this bill seeks to do.

As for the argument that the majority opinion in the community favours the bill, the answer was best given by a Congress (I) MP from Uttar Pradesh who said, "Well, if the majority view amongst the Hindus favours sati will they legislate to allow it once again?"

The Congress(I) Parliamentary party met on Friday to hear the prime minister reiterate his commitment to secularism and to the bill. No one who could cause any embarrassment to the prime minister was allowed to speak. In fact, after the 12 hand-picked members, had concluded their speeches, former Uttar Pradesh chief minister Sripat Mishra, who has been opposing the bill, stood up to have his say. The prime minister cut him short by pointing out that no time was left to continue the discussion. And so Mr K. K. Tewari, while briefing reporters later, could safely state that the meeting had "unanimously" left the decision about the bill to the prime minister.

Mr Khan did not attend the meeting. His supporters, or at least those who are at one with his views were not allowed to speak. Mr Rajiv Gandhi will push the bill through by issuing a party whip which no Congress(I) man today has the stature to disregard and the draft legislation will soon become law.

Excerpt from *The Telegraph*
2 March 1986

SEPARATE PERSONAL LAWS DO NOT DILUTE SECULARISM

Kuldip Nayar

That Arif Mohammad Khan has done tremendous service to the cause of secularism by resigning from the ministership is not disputable. For a Muslim to stand up against his community's overwhelming demand for a law to bypass the Supreme Court's judgement on maintenance in the case of Shah Bano is both courageous and commendable. But the issue that has come to rouse the nation is not a mere personal law; it is not even communalism versus secularism as it is sought to be made out; it is communalism versus communalism, Hindu fundamentalism versus Muslim fundamentalism.

A uniform civil code is an ideal which the Constitution framers included in the Directive Principles of state policy. But just as many other directive principles, including the right to work, have remained on paper, the one dealing with a uniform civil code also has. Arguing that since most Muslims are not in favour of it, they are fundamentalists, is like arguing that those who do not participate in the efforts to secure a social order for the people's welfare, another directive principle, are opposed to the Constitution.

Certain things are not clear cut, neither black nor white. The opposition to the Muslim personal law, which is being spelled out to ensure that section 125 of the Criminal Procedure Code regarding maintenance of a divorcee or widow, is not because the Muslims are not open to progress, but because in their mind it is an onslaught by the majority community on them, a minority. Sometimes it is Aligarh, sometimes Urdu and now the Shah Bano case; they are symptoms of the disease, which is the feeling of insecurity.

The point to look into is why, even after 37 years of independence, the Muslims feel insecure and how to get them out of their ghetto attitude. It is the responsibility of the majority to give a minority a sense of confidence; it is not that the minority must avow loyalty all the time to make the majority feel secure. The hub of the problem is that the Hindus have not forgiven the Muslims for having supported the demand for Pakistan and the general feeling is that the Muslims in their heart of hearts owe loyalty to Pakistan; also since the Muslims have "got" Pakistan, they have no claim to anything else in India.

Many mullahs in mosques and leaders among the Muslims only strengthen the impression of being disloyal by preaching separatism or by picking up a minor irritation to poison the community's mind. The unlocking of the Ram Janam Bhoomi at Babari mosque in Ayodhya was bad enough, but the way some of the Muslim leaders threw down the gauntlet was worse and what happened in Jammu and Kashmir is unforgivable. Surprising, that no Muslim leader has condemned the happenings in Kashmir and the UP government has not gone in appeal against the district judge's verdict on the unlocking of Babari mosque.

Coming back to the controversy over the Muslim personal law, I am at a loss to understand how secularism is in danger if the Muslims have their personal law, which they otherwise follow except for the aberration in the case of maintenance for a divorcee. For that matter, I do not think that the heavens will fall if the Sikhs also have a separate personal law, though I am opposed to it. A common civil code is desirable but if the two communities want to have their own personal law, it is not a point on which the country should go into a frenzy. Separate personal laws do not dilute secularism; the bigotism noticed among all communities, including the Hindus, does.

I do not like it, but the fact is that today more than 95 per cent of Muslims support the new bill on maintenance, etc.

Should the country join issue with the community on a point which is a non-issue? Some argue that one thing will lead to another; probably it will if we continue to concentrate our attention and energy on non-issues like maintenance of a divorced woman in Muslim society.

Passions may not have risen so high if Prime Minister Rajiv Gandhi had not rushed to introduce the bill; he should have allowed a countrywide discussion, as Jawaharlal Nehru did on the Hindu Code Bill. He could have referred the matter to a larger bench of the Supreme Court. But so irked was he by the general remark that he is indecisive, that he wanted to show he is not.

The introduction of the bill should, however, make us ponder over why communalism is raising its head once again. True, secularism, like liberalism, requires time to take root. But we must find out where we have gone wrong and what steps need to be taken to set things right. It is no use bringing in the example of Pakistan all the time because that country is a theocratic state; we have opted for secularism which gives equal rights to followers of all religions. Why our forefathers chose to be secular was because in a nation of many climes, colours and religions as we are, only secularism can ensure a democratic set-up. Secularism cannot be a cover for Hindu raj, which ultimately will be the rule of the upper caste.

No doubt, most Muslims have not risen above the tug of communalism and even the most liberal among them are afraid to speak out. But as the example of Arif Mohammad Khan has proved, some of them are asserting themselves and breaking the shackles of separatism to join the mainstream.

The Hindus have to give them time and also see how the Muslims come up economically and socially because the conditions which they face in business or profession and in which they live give birth to a feeling of persecution. The way out is not to deny them a personal law but to create a condition in which they themselves reform their own religion and where they awaken to the call of a liberal society.

For the Muslims in India, there is no going away from secularism and, even if the Hindus become communal, the Muslims have to be secular because in the clash of bigotism, it is number which wins.

Excerpt from *The Telegraph*
15 March 1986

SECULARISM SEGREGATED IN RAJIV'S INDIA

Nikhil Chakravartty

Communalist forces have occasionally raised their heads in different parts of the country, seeking to undermine the fabric of national integrity, but never before has their revival been the direct outcome of the Government's action as it has been in the last few months. The national scenario as it unfolds itself today shows that secularism is being forced into segregation in Rajiv's India.

The storm that has broken out over the so-called Muslim Women (Protection of Rights on Divorce) Bill sponsored by the Government in Parliament is ominously significant. For, it brings out that not only is the Rajiv Government bereft of any firm stand on the need to combat communalism, but it can be moved not by forward looking forces but by the obscurantist lobby.

Details of this sordid story are known and only the landmarks need to be mentioned: one year ago, on March 15, 1985, the Indian Union Muslim League secretary Banatwala brought forward a bill in Parliament to nullify the positive provisions of the Supreme Court judgement on the Shah Bano case which had granted certain relief, however small, to the hapless divorced Muslim women. This was definitely a retrograde move on the part of the Muslim League leadership whose commitment to communalism has throughout been unwavering.

Against the Banatwala bill, a groundswell of Muslim opinion could be visible and in this background Arif Mohammed Khan, the young minister of state, very convincingly opposed the proposed Muslim League bill and courageously debunked both in Parliament and in public the obscurantist standpoint which made a target of him. Although Arif had started his campaign in defence of the Supreme Court verdict with the knowledge and consent of the prime minister, it was soon clear that the Rajiv establishment got cold feet at the onslaught of the communalists. It was amazing to find that with the prime minister's clearance, one of his ministers, Ansari, not only attacked the Supreme Court judgement but the Supreme Court itself.

After this, the rake's progress continued culminating in the Government's introduction last month in the Lok Sabha of the Muslim Women (Protection of Rights on Divorce) Bill. The title of the bill itself is patently dishonest, because if anything it puts the divorced Muslim woman in the category of a second-class citizen. The law minister introducing the bill on February 25 had no qualms in saying that the Government had given priority to the views of the "leaders" of the Muslim community — thereby dismissing the very large section of Muslim opinion in the country. In other words, the Rajiv Government has thought it fit to accept the communal, obscurantist elements of the Muslim community as its leaders, thereby repudiating the clear stand taken by the Congress 40 years ago, in rejecting the Muslim League's two-nation theory. This has been a case of blatant betrayal of the principle of democracy — not to speak of secularism — which had throughout led the Congress leadership not to accept the Muslim League as the voice of the Muslim community.

Dissimulation has been carried further when Rajiv Gandhi made the preposterous claim in Parliament that the bill under attack is secular in character, making a total mockery of the concept of secularism. The prime minister obviously could make no sense to his own flock as could be seen by the principled resignation from the council of ministers by Arif Mohammad Khan, whose stature as a crusader against communalism has undoubtedly gone up today in the same measure as the prime minister's has gone down.

And it is not only Muslim communalism that is getting a fresh fillip under the present dispensation. The manner in which the so-called Ram Janam Bhoomi campaign has been allowed to spread its unalloyed communal virus throughout the Hindi belt brings out the Government's incapacity if not unwillingness to curb communalism. The UP government which is presided over by one of Delhi's yes-men did not bother to even seek an immediate high court injunction against the unwise verdict of a lower court in a portracted legal battle over a small patch of ground claimed by the rival communities as their respective place of worship.

The Hindu communalist claim that the spot was the exact birthplace of Rama is unsubstantiated by historical research; even if legend is to be conceded as history, there was no reason at all for the Government to sit idle when the entire campaign took a dangerously communal overtone. Similarly, the Muslim claim that this was the site of a mosque built by Emperor Babar, could have been handled with care and not ignored at all. Any responsible and competent authority could have brought about a reconciliation satisfying the rival contentions with persuasion and firmness, qualities which the present chief minister of Uttar Pradesh singularly lacks. What is extraordinary is that Rajiv Gandhi's Government has permitted the intensification of communal tension over this issue which need not have brought about a critical situation.

In snow-bound Kashmir, a crisis-point has been reached with the rampaging fundamentalists trying their best to stir up communal tension. For the first time in its chequered history, communal poison has entered the countryside in the Kashmir valley. The provocative action of the fundamentalists in attacking the minority Hindu homes and property could hardly be combated by the Ghulam Shah ministry propped up by Rajiv Gandhi's mandate to the Pradesh Congress(I). From the beginning it was known to every careful observer of the Kashmir scene, that Ghulam Shah with his known links and proclivities would lend a protective shield to the fundamentalists as a counterweight to the lack of solid support that he could not muster in the National Conference itself. But the continuation of this ministry with its dubious record until Friday was entirely due to the helping hand that the Centre had throughout extended to Ghulam Shah even in the teeth of objection from the Pradesh Congress(I) party.

The emergence of fundamentalists in the Kashmir valley adds a new dimension to the country's security problems. It is no secret that the fundamentalists in the valley derive their sustenance from across the frontier from the Pakistani authorities. If these fundamentalists can consolidate their base in the Kashmir valley — a target which they could never reach before — that will virtually amount to an invitation to massive Pak infiltration into the valley, which in turn would strengthen the secessionist forces in the area.

No doubt, the prime minister is now worried about the future of the Kashmir valley, but one can legitimately ask why this was not seriously looked into in the last one year when the fundamentalists were, step by step, building up their political stockade in the valley. The measures that have now been taken by the Centre — including the removal of the Shah ministry — could have been far more effective in dealing with the fundamentalist challenge, had they been taken even six months ago. The over-all picture is serious, very serious. But one does not get the feel in the capital that the Rajiv establishment is aware of the magnitude of the communal menace it is facing, and that it realizes its own substantial contribution towards promoting this menace.

In the struggle against communalism, the time-tested strategy of encouraging and supporting the enlightened, non-communal and anti-communal sections within a community seems to be now being given the go-by in favour of some sort of understanding with the rabid obscurantist elements or their allies. This could be seen as the current Congress tactic in Kerala where the rickety Karunakaran ministry has been desperately trying to buy peace from the communalist groupings masquerading as political parties.

In Punjab, Rajiv Gandhi has let his accord with Sant Longowal be capitalized by the extremist Akali fanatics whose armed gangs are campaigning for Khalistan, with the Barnala ministry acquiescing in all that and the Centre presenting the picture of a helpless bystander. There is no advance planning, no careful assessment of a mounting crisis: and when the moment would come for intervention, there is the danger of some hare-brained adventurism which might prove disastrous not only to the Government but to the nation as well.

This is indeed a sad state of affairs, rather dangerous not only for the morale but for the integrity of this great nation. What is emerging in the consciousness of a growing section of the public is that the Rajiv Government does not seem to have a command over the happenings in the country and, confronted with difficulties, is desperately trying to come to terms with forces which are themselves its potential adversaries. The portrait of a highly mismanaged establishment which began its career one year ago with a lot of fanfare about its being studded with super-management wizards.

Excerpt from *The Telegraph*
14 March 1986

INTERVIEWS

PRIME MINISTER RAJIV GANDHI
SPEAKS TO M. J. AKBAR

Three months ago everything seemed to be going right for you. After that, suddenly everything seems to be going wrong. Why?

I don't think everything is going wrong, though there's such a perception in certain groups. The fact is, certain hard decisions have to be taken. Perhaps these have upset some people.

Hard decisions of what kind?

Like, for example, Vishwanathji's action against certain business groups. That seemed to be the turning point in the attitude of the press.

No, there is also the Muslim personal law. We'll come to that. But it has been alleged that part of the reason remains your ignorance of what is called 'real' India.

I don't think so. The point is that we have to break through what has become a vested interest in almost every set-up — whether it is Government, whether it is private industry, whether it is public sector, farmers, wherever, the whole lot. The system is being brought to a grinding halt by vested interests. We've got to break it.

But are you going to give in to pressure?

No.

That again has been alleged, as for instance on the Muslim personal law you succumbed to pressure and . . . .

Oh, I don't agree at all.

What was the rationale in that case?

I feel that the law that we've brought in fact gives women much more rights. But the bill is in Parliament and I do not think an interview is the right place to get into the details of this.

One of the reasons why people are getting worked up is because of the support you seem to be getting from people like Banatwala on this subject.

Well, it's not only Banatwala. The majority of Indian Muslims, the average Muslim, is very worked up about it. The Muslims had felt at the time of independence and soon after, that India will protect their system ——

Or their identity——

Their identity, their culture in a way. And if this (controversy) has made them feel threatened in India, that this is the first step towards really finishing Islam in India, I think it's a very dangerous thing. Because our intention is not to encroach on that.

So you see this then as a part of a larger reassurance rather than a specific question of the rights of women in Islam?

Very much so.

What is Arif Mohammad Khan's future going to be?

He is a member of our party. There is no problem on that.

How did you take his resignation?

It was up to him to decide. I thought that he over-reacted a bit, because I had talked with him earlier and after the introduction of the bill and we discussed the bill; and I thought that he felt, after having gone through it, that the bill was not as fundamentalist as he had originally thought. So, I was a little surprised. But apparently he felt very emotionally . . . . He is an emotional person.

But also quite honest.

He is honest, yes.

One belief that has created problems is the feeling that Banatwala helped to draft the bill.

No. Not at all. The bill was drafted by the law minister, Asoke Sen, and Banatwala was not really involved in it at all.

What has been the Opposition's role in this whole controversy?

Well, unfortunately, and this was one of the things I did say in Parliament while answering the President's address, they have not played a positive role. The issue was women's rights and the rights of indigent women and unfortunately it has been projected in a totally different colour. They converted it into a religious issue almost and it has made the Muslims in India·— I don't say all the Muslims but a very large majority of Muslims — feel that their system may be threatened within the Indian framework. This cannot be allowed to happen.

Which becomes another issue altogether.

Which becomes a totally different issue.

You didn't consult your own MPs apparently on this issue.

We did. We consulted a number of MPs. Those MPs whose views we knew very clearly we didn't talk with them too much about this. But with the others, we did. Muslim MPs plus other MPs. There is a reaction among certain group of MPs. But I think that reaction in fact represents what we are trying to fight.

This actually follows from the larger allegation that you don't meet your MPs often enough, and that you don't consult them often enough.

Well that's not true. I have been meeting them daily now. I think I must have met at least half the number since Parliament started . . . . It must be close to 200 odd MPs — individually, and not as groups; apart from meeting them in groups.

How do you see the problem of dissidents which seems to be rising in the party?

I don't think it is dissidence. You see, what we are trying to do — the party has traditionally not been an outspoken party, and this is true not only of the Congress, but is so of all other parties also. When we won the election last year we got a huge majority, and the result was that there was no Opposition in the Lok Sabha. I thought it was necessary that we allow something to come up, otherwise we would drift off on a tangent and not know that we were going on a tangent. So we have deliberately asked our MPs to be outspoken and to say something when they feel that it is important . . . .

Excerpt from *The Telegraph*
12 March 1986

Arif Mohammad Khan
Speaks to Seema Mustafa

What do you think the Government has achieved by passing the Muslim Women (Protection of Rights on Divorce) Bill?

This only the Government can tell you. How can I say what it has achieved? The ministers while making their speeches during the course of the discussion said — I don't know if they were making any accusations — that an atmosphere of tension and communalism was being created and in order to ease that tension the bill was brought in. This is the Government's aim, this is what the ministers are saying, and I hope that this tension is diffused.

So in a sense by giving this argument the ministers were saying that in their estimation the majority of Muslims were creating this tension and posing a threat to the unity and integrity of the country?

I do not know what they had in their minds.

But it sounded like that?

No, I don't think it sounded like that, but it definitely gives a hint about the activities of the persons who were organizing this agitation (against the Supreme Court judgement). The leaders of this agitation were not using the normal channels available in a democratic society but, according to the Government spokesmen, they were creating communalism and tension in society, which compelled the Government to bring in a measure which could diffuse that tension. I won't say that the charge was being levelled against the community as a whole, but the responsibility of the leaders cannot definitely be minimized. And I think they were being held responsible (by the Government).

But the one point made by all the ministers during the debate was that the majority of Muslims were for the bill. Nowhere in the debate did they differentiate between the leadership and the masses; their whole argument was that the masses were for the bill and because of the resulting tension the Government had no choice but to pass the bill.

They did say that. You are not asking me whether I agree with that viewpoint, are you?

Yes, I am asking you precisely that.

I definitely do not believe that the majority of the Muslims are posing a threat. I don't agree with that viewpoint. There might be some leaders, there might be some individuals masquerading as leaders of the community who may be speaking the language of communalism, but definitely the ordinary Muslim is not. He or she has many other problems. I think so far as the self-appointed champions of the Muslim interests are concerned this was a wily device to relegate to the background their security, honour, property. This leadership used the bill to divert the attention of the Muslims from the real issues which it has failed to solve, which it has never tried to solve. In fact, it has not been able to help the community in any manner to overcome those problems which the community is facing.

How do you think a similar situation would have been handled by Jawaharlal Nehru or Mrs Indira Gandhi?

This is very difficult to say, because I have experience only of the present situation.... I do have experience of being in the Government of Indira Gandhi, but in her time I do not think communal pressures on any issue were as strong as they have been on the issue of the

Shah Bano case. And you know comparisons are always odious. In a given situation you cannot depend on old solutions.

As you are speaking against the bill it is obvious that you don't agree with this measure. Do you also agree that the Government is appeasing the fundamentalists in the community?

No. I believe what the Government is saying. So far as the provisions of the bill are concerned, even the Government is not defending them. And my objection is to the provisions of the bill. As for the political reasons which have been given in defence of the bill — well, I may agree with some. In fact, I have myself said that the blame lies with people like me who after having spoken in Parliament did not go out to mobilize public support against the activities of the communalists and fundamentalists. Whereas all this time these people kept themselves busy whipping up communal feelings and tension and they finally succeeded in bringing undue and undesirable pressure on the Government, and they succeeded in creating this impression that if their demand is not accepted they will become a threat to public order. This is what the Government has said in defence of the bill.

In fact, one of the ministers linked it with the question of internal security. That in itself is an admission that the agitation built against the Shah Bano case judgement and in support of the bill was posing a threat to internal security. And in order to deal with that threat . . . .

You agree to their demands?

This (bill) amounts to that.

Exactly. But if . . . .

Not that you agree to their demands, but this (the bill) is a measure to diffuse the tension and to stop these forces from possibly translating their verbal threats into action.

But is it not a fact of history that the more you appease communal forces the more you strengthen them?

No, the Government is not saying that they have been appeased.

But the bill is an appeasement measure?

Well it is open to all kinds of interpretations.

What is your interpretation?

My interpretation is the stand that a colleague of mine had taken in Parliament. Ziaur Rehman Ansari who is a minister, had taken this line. He had demanded not only the exclusion of Muslims from section 125, but he had also questioned the authority of the Supreme Court in interpreting religious law. My question is that since the Government has agreed to codify the religious law, who is going to interpret it? And if interpretation by the Supreme Court in the Shah

Bano case was not acceptable to these people because it amounted to interpretation of religious law, will the interpretation by the courts of this law not amount to the interpretation of Islamic law? Will this be acceptable to them now?

Section 125 is a law which is rooted in social justice. The purpose is to prevent destitution and while interpreting a provision which is rooted in social justice, the Supreme Court also had a look at the teachings of the religion to see if it was not prohibited. The court's interpretation was of a law not rooted in religion but in social justice but then they (the fundamentalists) said that it amounted to the interpretation of Islamic law.

Mr Ziaur Rehman Ansari called me names, and now that the Islamic law has properly been codified who will interpret this? If the Supreme Court gives its intepretation, this will be open to attack again. Now if someone raised the demand for the setting up of religious courts to interpret this law that will be in keeping with the statements of Mr Ansari.

And the fundamentalists have already started saying this?

Not just them but a minister of the Government has said this. By implication he means the same thing.

You agree that the majority of Muslims in this country are neither progressives nor fundamentalists, but fence sitters who have to be educated about their rights and interests?

Even a fence sitter knows about the other two positions . . . .

I meant ignorant.

There I agree with you. He does not know about reform or even the traditional law. If you conducted a survey in any Muslim town, before this controversy started, 99 per cent of Muslims, even among the educated, you would have found, did not even know about the procedure of divorce as laid down in the Quran. They knew only about the irrevocable divorce which becomes effective instantly.

The question of payment of mehr: These leaders have taken the stand that mehr becomes payable after divorce whereas the requirement of the teachings of the religion is that mehr should be paid before the consummation of marriage.

The question is if a small decision in the Shah Bano case can infuriate them so much that they can raise the slogan of religion in danger, why does this non-payment of mehr according to the teachings of Islam not stir their conscience? And this irrevocable divorce which does not find sanction in the Quran and is a punishable offence under the shariat, why does this not upset them? And has the Muslim Personal Law Board which was set up 13 years ago been able to educate the Muslims about their law? Not a single pamphlet has been issued by them, in fact people came to know of the board only after the Shah Bano judgement. Who are they to legislate on our behalf? What is their legal acumen and legal knowledge? Only because they are teaching in some madrasah should we hand over our destiny to them?

So you agree that the majority of Muslims do not have any concrete opinion about the bill?

Why only the majority? Even those (MPs) who have taken part in the voting and were supporting the bill, the majority of them also do not have any idea about the provisions of the bill.

There is a progressive movement against the bill amongst the Muslims. Why is it that the Congress(I) decided to support the fundamentalists instead of strengthening the hands of progressives?

Well, there I might differ with the approach of the Government. But I can give you the reason. The reason is that the progressive section which you are talking about, does not have the capacity to create tension in society. It can't incite people to indulge in violence and become a threat to the internal security of the country.

This can become very dangerous if it is taken to its logical conclusion. Any section which has the capacity of creating trouble can then automatically get its regressive views accepted.

There I may not agree with you. (*laughs.*)

There has been a certain amount of dissidence in the party leading to the expulsion and suspension of some members. Are you at all associated with it?

I think all this dissidence is only about two weeks old, whereas the stand I had taken on this issue is very old . . . . I had spoken in Parliament on August 23 last year and since then I have been very consistent about my stand. I resigned on the day the bill was introduced. Even when the bill was being passed and I had decided to follow the whip of the party, I made my position clear and gave expression to my views. So I don't think that this issue should be linked with the question of dissidence.

Because of your view on this bill have you been subjected to any kind of pressures or checks? It is believed, you were going to Kerala, but had to cancel the trip because of some instructions?

No, no one gave me any instructions to cancel my visit but I came to have this impression that I was not opposed to the passing of any bill which aims at codifying the law, I was opposed to the denial of this right available under section 125 to a woman who is unable to maintain herself. I had come to have this impression that possibly this right will not be taken away. I thought if this was so then on principle I will have no objection to the passing of the bill.

But this right has been taken away?

Now, I agree it has been taken away, but at that time when I cancelled my Kerala visit I felt that this right may not be taken away. In fact in the original bill, section 125 was not mentioned, but now in the Government's amendment . . . .

Which is quite ridiculous.

It has added a novel concept to our system of jurisprudence where the consent of the accused has to be obtained now before launching prosecution against him. It is like saying that if someone picks your pocket then you obtain the consent of the pickpocket to prosecute him.

Why didn't you speak in the Lok Sabha at length? You only made some clarifications in which you attacked the bill.

I think that after making an hour long speech I would have brought them to the conclusion that the bill is anti-Islam, it denies the rights of women which Islam has been given them and that is why I said this pushes them back to the pre-Islamic era when they were treated like animals. Section 125 is for the destitute. You are claiming that your scheme is sufficient to meet the requirements of all women and that no woman can remain destitute. My point is, then why are you putting a blanket ban on (access to) section 125? You say that the community will look after the divorcees, the only proof that the community is fulfilling its role would be if no woman appealed for maintenance under section 125. Presently hundreds are seeking justice in the courts (under this section).

Secondly, the Constitution guarantees freedom of religion but this cannot be converted into imposition by the state. Now they are imposing a form of religion as interpreted by a particular group of people and they are asking every Muslim that, if you are Muslim, you will have to accept this form.

How is this going to affect you politically? There are reports that you received a very poor reception in your constituency Bahraich. Is this true?

I don't think I am going to lose any Muslim vote because I am absolutely clear in my mind that the provisions of this bill are in total contravention of the provisions and teachings and spirit of Islam. And when this atmosphere of tension and communalism which has been built by them goes and normalcy is restored, then Muslims will realize what this bill actually is. So in the long run I am hopeful that I am not going to lose Muslim support, I am going to gain Muslim support. But even they are not saying I have lost general support.

130 The Shah Bano Controversy

They are only claiming support of a certain section and even in that section it is the male support they are talking about. The community does not consist of men alone.

For instance, the other day I addressed a meeting in Kalighat (UP) which was, according to the people, a historic meeting. But one MP from that area was telling some other people that there were barely 60 persons. About Bahraich, I think the people have been very nice to me but at no other time was the response so tremendous and overwhelming as this time when I went after my resignation from the Government. In fact the video cassette is with me, anyone can see it.

Is the bill a greater issue amongst the Muslims of Uttar Pradesh, where you come from, or is the opening of the Ram Janam Bhoomi temple agitating them more?

It is the Janam Bhoomi issue which is engaging everyone's attention at the moment. The bill became an issue only after it was introduced in Parliament.

And all the communal riots are taking place because of the Ayodhya issue?

Definitely.

So that will have a bigger influence on the votes than the bill in the final analysis?

I think you are right.

Excerpt from *The Telegraph*
13 May 1986

Baharul Islam

Interviewed

What exactly is your stand on the Shah Bano judgement?

In my view, the interpretation of the Supreme Court on section 125 Cr. P. C. was absolutely correct. However, it unnecessarily made two other observations. It said that a Muslim man could divorce his wife at any time without rhyme or reason and also that he can marry four wives. Both observations were wrong and contrary to Quranic law.

On marriage, the Quran says, "Wed thee from among the women ye would, by two's, three's and four's, but if you fear, that you cannot be fair to all of them, then only one" (*Sura Al Nisa* 4 : 3). Now, with our modern knowledge of psychology, science, physiology, particularly female psychology, and sexology, I have grave doubts whether any man can claim that he can treat four women, or even two, equally.

Equal treatment does not depend on the honesty, sincerity and so-called capability of the man himself. It also depends on the receivers, the four women. The immediate test would be that if you are a married man, ask your wife if she doesn't mind you marrying a second wife. What would be her reaction? I am sure she would say no.

Now, with regard to the court's observation on talaq, it is absolutely wrong. I was possibly the first judge of the Gauhati High Court to write a judgement on talaq. The old law laid down by the British was that a Muslim man could divorce his wife at any time without rhyme or reason. It was accepted as current law. I was shocked.

I thought Islam was the youngest religion. It appeared to be very up-to-date and practical. Could it be so harsh towards women? I therefore thoroughly researched this aspect in the Quran. To my great relief, I found Quranic law to be very modern. It says that if a quarrel arises between husband and wife and the question of a dissolution of the marriage comes up, the husband shall select an arbitrator from his side and the wife would pick one from her side. They would strive for a reconciliation. If this is not possible, talaq is permissible. That is the law. That is why the court observation was wrong.

In this context, what do you think about the bill?

When I addressed the women before Parliament on February 25, I said nothing about the bill. I told them, I congratulate you, welcome you, because you have come out to emancipate the wretched Muslim women who are being exploited. I told them may God bless you and help you in this.

So far as the bill is concerned, I feel it should be more modern and must not give way to obscurantist ideas. Women must be given real justice. Section 125 Cr. P.C. says that if a husband is capable of giving maintenance and if the wife cannot maintain herself, then and only then will the court give orders directing the husband to give a reasonable maintenance.

At present, the bill says the woman's relatives will be directed to give maintenance. The very idea behind this is that the woman will be treated as a chattel, being driven from pillar to post. And the second clause is that if the relatives are not capable of giving maintenance, then the waqf boards must.

But I personally know the condition of one waqf board — that of Assam. It has no finances. So the woman will just run from pillar to post, even if she gets a court order. There will be no justice for her at all. Therefore, the bill is not correct. It is possible that our party may be in difficulty, being a democratic party and being influenced by the majority opinion.

Don't you think a principled stand is called for, instead of giving way to what you call the tyranny of the majority?

In a democracy this is always so, unless the minority, or a single person, is of exceptional calibre of power, like Gandhi or Nehru. For other people, it is very difficult to withstand the pressure of the majority.

As a Muslim leader, do you really feel that a majority of your community is against the provision of maintenance to divorcees?

Most Muslims are influenced by maulvis and Ulamas. So if their opinion is taken today, most would favour the bill. But an enlightened section will be against it.

What about the Muslim women though, who constitute half the Muslim population?

I can tell you that if they were allowed to express their opinion secretly, 100 per cent would oppose this bill. They are forced to say yes out of social compulsion. You saw in the papers that one day Shah Bano said she favoured the Supreme Court judgement, and the next day she said she opposed it. I believe that all Muslim women would like to be liberated from this exploitation.

Is there any conflict between the shariat and the provision of maintenance as laid down in the Shah Bano judgement?

The Quranic verse says that the husband will pay reasonable maintenance for his wife. The expression 'during the period of iddat' is not there. It was interpolated in later commentaries and is not a part of the Quran.

What is your comment on the status of women in Islam now and as was provided for?

The present practice is that they do not have equal rights. My view of the Quran is that it gives equality to them. There are five fundamental principles of Islam, five pillars: kalma (article of faith), namaz (prayer), roza (fasting), Haj (pilgrimage) and zakat (charity).

The provisions of each are identical for men and women. It does not say a woman should believe half the kalma or say their namaz two-and-a-half-times. The Muslim is to observe a month of fasting, both man and woman. The same law applies for Haj and zakat. But so far as inheritance is concerned, the Quran says especially that a mother of a deceased will get half of what the husband does and a son will inherit twice as much as a daughter. Therefore it appears that a woman is half as important as a man.

But this is not the case. The laws have to be interpreted in the context of the situation prevailing in Arabia before the advent of Islam, when the status of women was very low. They were treated as chattels. A man could have any number of wives and keep any number of concubines and could divorce or discard at will; Islam raised women out of this plight.

Further, the Quran does not enjoin that only half of what a man gets should go to a woman. What it says is that not less than half, at least, should be given.

For example, the Quran says you must say your prayers five times a day. This does not mean it would be a sin if you said them seven times. It would be a virtue still. If you gave equal proportion of property to women, it would be in consonance with the Quran and also the Constitution.

The general impression is that the Congress and the Centre are following a policy of compromise with the fundamentalists.

As a disciplined party man I had better not comment on this.

Excerpt from *Current*
8 March 1986

Dr Tahir Mahmood
Interviewed by Kuldeep Kumar

What is your opinion on the Muslim Women Bill? Some people say that it will not stand the test of the Constitution and is bound to be nullified if challenged in the Supreme Court.

I don't know why some people are saying that but . . .   so far as challenging (the bill) is concerned, you can challenge anything in the Supreme Court. However the question is: what will be the response of the court? Suppose, Parliament passes it again after the Supreme Court strikes it down. Then, what would happen?

There is a view that the bill is violative of the Articles 14 and 15 of the Constitution.

On this, one can have one's own personal opinion. I do not find the bill contravening the provisions of Articles 14 and 15 for the simple reason that the bill relates to personal law and these two articles do not apply to personal law.

The bill does not give any new right to the Muslims. It partly codifies the existing Muslim law, the traditional and conventional

Muslim law on the rights of a divorced woman. To that extent, the interpretation would be that now onwards, if a divorced Muslim woman comes before a court, her rights will be determined by the provisions of this act if it is passed. And to the extent the provisions of this act are contravened by sections 125 and 127 of the Cr. P.C., this act will have supremacy, but only in the limited sphere of a divorced Muslim woman's rights.

Which means that you subscribe to the view that sections 125 and 127 do come into conflict with Muslim personal law.

Yes, of course. You see, the state and society have two options, either you scrap the personal laws and move to an absolutely uniform civil code which has nothing to do with either Hindu law or Muslim law or any other personal law, or every community may have its own personal law. You call it Hindu law whether it has been imported from Scandinavia or the Soviet Union or whatever. And not only do you call it a Hindu law, but under that law you treat conversion by a man or a woman into a non-Hindu religion as a ground for divorce. Under that law you say that a Hindu cannot inherit from a non-Hindu, that a Hindu mother on becoming a Muslim does not remain a guardian of her children. So what is it? Is that a personal law or not? Therefore, so long as the Hindu personal law is there, the Christian personal law is there, the Muslim personal law is bound to claim application and protection.

But there are different interpretations of Muslim personal law.

All that is bunkum.

But people like Mr Arif Mohammad Khan and Mr Danial Latifi quote extensively from the Quran to prove that it is obligatory upon the former husband to pay maintenance to his divorced wife?

So far as the second name is concerned, Mr Danial Latifi is a well-read person and a very senior man, but this is his personal opinion. But so far as Arif Mohammad Khan is concerned, my very clear-cut reply is: this whole controversy envelopes two things — law and religion. Now, Arif Mohammad Khan may be knowing anything else but he does not know law or religion.

There is no quarrel that the Supreme Court's decision may be in accordance with the provisions of the Criminal Procedure Code or to the judges' conception of equality and justice but it is not in conformity with traditional Muslim law.

It is said that a number of Islamic countries too have laws which make it obligatory upon the husband to pay maintenance to his divorced wife.

This is absolutely nonsense. If anybody has said that a Muslim woman in any of the Islamic countries can seek maintenance from her former husband after the expiry of the period of iddat with or without the help of the court, it is absolutely baseless. The only country that introduced some reform in this respect was Egypt. A law was enacted in 1979 which said that if a husband has divorced his wife, on proof that the husband had arbitrarily acted against a very good wife, on proof that the wife is not at all responsible for the divorce, on proof that the wife has nobody in the family of her birth who can provide her maintenance, the former husband may be required to pay her a lump sum amount which would be enough to maintain her for a period of two years from the date of divorce. The law was made by the Egyptian parliament in 1979 but was struck down by the Egyptian Supreme Court as an unconstitutional provision and there is no second country where there has been any rethinking on Muslim law.

There is a conceptual difference between the legal culture of Islam and the legal cultures of other communities living in India. The traditional Hindu law, and I am not criticizing it, has its own ethos, its own social culture which Islam does not share. According to Hindu law, a girl is transplanted into the husband's family after marriage. She becomes a part and parcel of her husband's family, so much so that when the husband dies, the responsibility to maintain her is of that relative of the husband who would have been responsible to maintain the husband had he been a minor. So, the girl has no tie with the family of her birth. Marriage effects a perpetual transplantation of the girl into her husband's family. This legal system, incidentally, had no concept of divorce. Marriage was not known to be a dissoluble union. But modern Hindu law, on legalizing divorce in the 1950s, thought of this question of a Hindu woman's post-divorce rights. This was guided, and should have been guided, by the Hindu concept of a family. And in the fitness of things, it was decided that the husband would provide maintenance to the divorced wife.

But Islamic law had a very different concept of marriage, a very different concept of divorce and a very different concept of family. Here there is absolutely no question of transplanting the girl from one family to another family. Even after marriage, the girl belongs to her father's family. She does not become a part of her husband's family. Legally, she is related only to her husband.

The in-law relationship is not known to Islam. So much so that there are no words in the Arabic or the Persian language for mother-in-law or father-in-law, for these relationships do not exist in Islam. The girl marries an individual, not a family. And her marriage with this individual is not a perpetual union. Islamic law, without any hesitation or vengeance, allows dissolution of marriage at the instance of both husband or wife.

In consonance with this view, Islamic law provides that all the rights and privileges of a girl in the family of her birth remain intact even after her marriage except the right of being maintained by her father. The right of day-to-day maintenance is transferred from the father or the guardian to the husband. Unlike her Hindu sister, she retains her inheritance rights in her father's family. The only thing that is suspended, not abolished or transferred, is the right to get day-to-day maintenance from her father.

These are the two socio-legal systems. The question is: why should one of these be regarded as the only ideal system, as the only secular system, as the only national system, as the only Indian system fit enough to be imposed on every other Indian who does not belong to this culture?

This is the legal position. But do you disagree that most Muslim women face tremendous hardships after divorce?

There cannot be two opinions about the fact that the problem does exist, as much as among the Hindus, as much as among any other community. There is a very serious problem, and that is why, when a remedy was provided in 1973 under the Criminal Procedure Code, then, not realizing that it was in conflict with Islamic law, Muslim women started taking benefit of this provision.

Don't you think that in a lot of cases, the woman is wronged and the husband abuses the right to divorce?

That is the crux of the matter. Everybody seems to be interested in the post-divorce rights while they should be interested in the law of divorce itself. In 99 per cent cases of divorce by Muslim husbands in our country, the husbands flout the Islamic law itself. They exercise their right to divorce in violation of open provisions of Islamic law of divorce. If you can check that, there is no need to regulate the post-divorce rights of Muslim women. Actually, the area which needs control, and reform, is the husband's powers to divorce.

Do you think Muslim leaders should do something in this regard?

They must. If they don't, they will have to face situations like this. If they don't put their own house in order, they will have to agree to it being demolished.

Can the law do something to ensure that the Muslim husband does not misuse his right to divorce?

Yes, and this is what has been done in some Muslim countries which is being talked about these days. This bill partly codifies a very limited aspect of Islamic law — the post-divorce rights of a Muslim woman. But what about divorce? The first thing which should have been codified is the divorce law because that is being misused. If you codify them and strictly enforce them, the problem of divorces will be automatically solved.

What about the statement issued by 125 eminent Muslims against the introduction of this bill?

Are they really eminent? Anyway, they are entitled to their opinion. But they should not project it as the religious or the Muslim viewpoint.

But a number of Muslim women are also campaigning against the bill.

(*Raises his voice*) What about those Muslim women who had been asking for this bill? You do not know about them because what they say does not appear in the national press. I would recommend to the Government to put this bill to a referendum among the Muslims. I tell you that it will be approved by not less than 95 per cent majority.

What about a uniform civil code? The directive principles of our Constitution say that the state should strive towards a uniform civil code. What would you ideally like to have — different personal laws or a uniform code? It is also said that you dropped a chapter on the uniform civil code from your book.

Yes, it is correct, my answer is that if the majority community in this country starts projecting its mythology as the national history, minorities are bound to dissent from it. Just look at it. Who is demanding a uniform civil code? The Rashtriya Swayamsevak Sangh, the Hindu Mahasabha. Doesn't it speak for itself? Are they asking for a secular law? They know they have their own concept of history.

But there are a lot of other progressive sections among Muslims who are demanding it.

There are two kinds of people who demand a uniform civil code. The Hindu fundamentalists or those who have no idea about it but who think they are advocating something very progressive. They want to project their image as progressive and support the demand without knowing what they are talking about.

But people like G M Banatwala and others who support this bill are also called Muslim fundamentalists. Do you agree with this description?

Well, that way I may also be called a fundamentalist. My answer is that, yes, I am a fundamentalist because I have got some fundamental rights under the Constitution.

Excerpt from *The Sunday Observer*
9 March 1986

Hemwati Nandan Bahuguna
Interviewed by Siraj Mirza

As there is great deal of talk about Muslim personal law these days what is your opinion about it?

It is a religious problem and in India a religious problem is extremely sensitive. We have no right to express our opinion on this. I know this much that the English rulers had made the Mohammadan law and also in their own way they wrote commentaries on Islamic law but our Government should refrain from doing this. Not only Muslims but also Hindus and tribals have their personal law and they want to lead their social life according to it. And so they should be left to do that. Only those who have expert knowledge of the religion of Islam, its law and fiqh can speak.

There are many things to do for the Government. It should strive to improve the material conditions of common people rather than attending to personal law. Let alone material prosperity, let it work for fulfilling the basic necessities of life. But our Government, instead of doing this, raises religious problems. It is not without reason. The Government wants the people to be busy in such things. Muslim leaders also knowingly or unknowingly walk into this trap. This way all Muslims will be angry and excited. Then the Hindu communalists will incite the Hindus taking advantage of such a state of affairs and the peaceful atmosphere in the country would be disturbed and for few days they will forget how to make a living. The Government also wants this. For such things every government has its own strategy. It is called dirty trick division . . . .

Arif Mohammad Khan is a promising young person. In his 90 or 100 minute speech he referred to the Quran and the hadith. It was a pleasure to know that such conditions arose that he had to study holy books of his religion. But it was not correct use. He tried to silence Muslim Leaguers or those who are raising their voice in favour of the personal law. In my opinion he wants his party to do this job by vanquishing the Muslim League. Even if this happens, let alone other Indian people, how would even Muslims benefit? Of course, the Government would benefit. If he were a wellwisher of the people, and not of the Government, he would have certainly said one or two things in his long speech which would have exposed the weakness of the Government. No, he wouldn't do that. That way he would lose his power.

Excerpt from *The Urdu Blitz*
29 September 1985

Mohammad Yunus Salim

Interviewed by Anis Ahmed Safdar

What is your opinion about the bill which has been introduced due to persistent efforts made by the MPB and united but peaceful agitation launched by Indian Muslims.

This bill fulfills all the requirements of the shariat. There is no question of opposing this bill. Only those will oppose it who do not consider it necessary for Muslims to follow the shariat.

What is your opinion about the criticism in the English press on the question of provision for the divorcees from the wakf.

In fact in fiqh (Islamic jurisprudence) provision is to be made from *bait al-mal* (state treasury). In some countries the social security department arranges for it as it is in Libya etc. Here as there is no such department which can look after the needy, the alternative of wakf was resorted to. The wakf board charges 6 per cent from the mutawallis, for administrative purposes; the provision for the divorcees can be made from it. This will happen only when there is no relative at all. There may be one or two cases in lakhs. Awkaf will be rarely responsible for it.

There aren't wakf boards everywhere.

Such things are being raised from those areas where Awkaf are quite rich. I know in Maharashtra one mosque has income in lakhs. This is being said only to spread wrong understanding.

What if the relatives washed their hands off from the responsibility of payment?

If the woman is rich the relatives readily share in her wealth so why should they not share (her misery) when she is needy?

You had appeared in the Shah Bano case in the Supreme Court on behalf of the MPB.

Before this, in the Tahirabi and Fazlunbi cases we lost and nobody paid attention. When it had become a trend in the Supreme Court it was necessary to prepare well for the case though I got the files very late in this case. Nevertheless I tried my level best . . .

In this country, the life and property of Muslims, their honour and the economic condition are some of the basic questions. It appears as if deliberately their attention is kept on issues like the Aligarh Muslim University or the Babri mosque.

If the Government wanted, the Shah Bano case controversy would not have been prolonged so long. Section 125 of Cr. P.C. and its wrong interpretation could have been corrected. In my opinion, Rajiv Gandhi should have been given enough time to fulfil his promise.

This is my reading.

Was it not better that this happened as a result of united efforts on the part of Muslims?

Undoubtedly the Government realized the significance of public opinion and the ruling party felt that if the feelings of Muslims were not respected it would not be possible to get Muslim votes. They had to surrender before the Muslim demand. . . .

In The Times of India *a highly debatable statement by your old colleague Mr Latifi has appeared. What is your opinion about it?*

Alas! my old colleague Danial Latifi has, in his *Times of India* statement, said many misleading things. In my opinion, any person who does not have command over fiqh, hadith and tafsir (exegesis), should not give an authoritative opinion by simply reading (all this) in translations. Latifi saheb is not right in his discussion of intricacies of fiqh. I ' will insha Allah soon throw light on this in my article. Mr. Latifi was not honest in presenting the parts of my presentation. . . . He should have put forward the whole thing. . . . I had said before the Supreme Court that even if we accept Abdullah Yusuf Ali's rendering of mataa as maintenance, no time period has been mentioned. For this we will have to refer to the hadith of the Prophet and sayings of the Imams. . . . So referring to Hedayah (a standard book of Islamic law of the Hanafities), I referred to the saying of Fatima bint-e-Qais and, based on the sayings of Hazrat Umar and Hanafi jurists and Imam Shafei argued that the difference between the Shafi and Hanafi jurists is this much that whether maintenance should be paid to the divorcee during the period of iddat in case of a revocable divorce and irrevocable divorce also and that Imam Shafei is not in favour of giving maintenance even during the period of iddat in case of irrevocable divorcee . . . . If he (Latifi) thought of referring to my discussion of mataa he should have referred to the whole discussion. . . .

Excerpt from *Inquilab*
23 March 1986

SURVEYS

MOST MUSLIMS IN U.P. OPPOSED TO BILL

Hasan Suroor

Only the Government and that particular section of Muslims on whose advice it has formulated the controversial bill on divorced Muslim women's rights can pretend that it reflects the majority opinion in the Muslim community. For even many of those who had opposed the Supreme Court judgement in the Shah Bano case find the bill obnoxious, and there is a widespread feeling in U.P. that it is an attempt to appease · the conservative Muslims, after their hysterical reaction to the reopening of the disputed shrine at Ayodhya to Hindu devotees.

However, there is a tendency not to take a public stand for fear of the "mullahs". Even a section of Muslims within the ruling party is unhappy over the manner in which the two issues have been handled by the Government. Some go to the extent of hinting that this is part of a "conspiracy" by disgruntled Congressmen to "destabilize" Mr Rajiv Gandhi.

"I am not pretending that the bill on women's rights was not Mr Gandhi's own idea but the manner in which it has been projected and the drama enacted by Mr Arif Mohammad Khan certainly suggests that some ambitious partymen are trying to make political capital out of it at the expense of the prime minister. For example, it is interesting to note that the Vishwa Hindu Parishad, which by no stretch of imagination can be called a progressive organization or a friend of Muslims — either men or women — has come out in support of Mr Khan. Similarly, in the case of the Ayodhya shrine, some influential local Congressmen played a decisive role when they could have easily averted the situation," says an articulate Muslim Congress MLA who does not want to be identified.

How well-founded the "conspiracy" theory is, is debatable, but there is no doubt that Mr Rajiv Gandhi's popularity among Muslims here has suffered some erosion. While the conservative Muslims are still agitated over the Ayodhya issue — obviously the Government's somersault over the Shah Bano case has not helped assuage their sentiment — the liberals find it odd that an avowedly secular prime minister who is so passionately hooked on the 21st century is allowing himself to be manipulated by the communalists in both communities by pandering to Hindu reaction in Ayodhya and to Muslim fundamentalism in Shah Bano's case. "If elections were to be held right now, I doubt if the Congress would get very many votes," says a retired Muslim army officer.

A visit to some of the towns and villages in U.P. shows how tenuous is the claim that the bill enjoys the majority support in the Muslim community. The fact is that a substantial majority of the common Muslims is not even aware of the provisions of the bill, and even in Bahraich which Mr Arif Mohammad Khan represents in Parliament, not many seem to have a clue to the issues which led to his resignation from the union ministry. A waiter in Bahraich was all praise for Mr Khan's "bold" stand for he mistakenly thought that he had resigned over the "Ayodhya issue." But when told about the real reason, he said: "Sahib hamen isse kya lena dena, ham to garib log hain" (what do we have to do with such things; we are poor people).

And yet the "mullahs" claim not only to know the mind of the Muslim masses but also the right to speak on their behalf. They argue that the "true" believers of Islam would never tolerate any interereference in their personal law, and it is therefore safe to assume that they favour the bill as it attempts to nullify the Supreme Court judgement which interfered in the Muslim personal law.

"If you are a Muslim you believe fully in the Islamic code — lock, stock and barrel. You cannot say that you are a Muslim but do not believe in the Prophet or the shariat or any other aspect of Islam," says Mr Mohammad Amir Mohammad Khan, Raja of Mahmoodabad, and one of the more emancipated Congress MLAs, having studied in the West and taught at Cambridge University until his recent entry into politics.

Thus the ostensible support for the bill is based on a series of arbitrary assumptions: (*a*) that providing maintenance to a divorced Muslim woman is a religious issue and a secular approach amounts to interference in the Muslim personal law; (*b*) that the Muslim masses however ignorant are "true" believers (whatever that might mean) and since they are not in a position to understand the divine right, to make up their mind for them instead of making any attempt to help them understand the problem in its proper perspective; and (c) that the liberal Muslims fall outside the pale of the "millat" and they are either Communists or in league with the communal Hindu elements who want to impose a uniform civil code on the Muslims.

Far more insidious is the attempt to suppress the views of Muslim women who are directly affected by the bill. A senior lawyer admits that his daughters are bitterly opposed to the bill but they cannot express their views because they are married to conservative men. "If they take a public stand or talk openly about it they might end up getting a divorce themselves," he says.

Miss H. Zamin, a senior bank executive, says that the bogey of shariat and "Islam in danger", has been raised only to mislead the illiterate Muslim masses: "If are they so much committed to the Islamic laws then why don't'they also insist that all Muslims who are caught stealing will have their hands chopped off? But if the law is applied to Muslims, the same mullahs will call it discrimination."

An elderly school teacher, Mrs Sahiba Rahman, contests the claim that the bill enjoys majority support and says: "When they say this, they simply ignore the views of countless Muslim women whose voice is muffled by their fathers, husbands, and the mullahs."

Many women don't buy the argument that since the husband becomes a total stranger to a woman after divorce it is beneath her dignity to accept money from him. "Whose dignity are we talking about? The dignity of a destitute divorcee who is either forced into vagrancy or or prostitution to keep her body and soul together," asks a very angry Miss Rana Parwez, a student of Lucknow University.

It is pointed out that there have been cases where a man has tried to force a relationship even after he has divorced his wife. "Only last night, a woman killed her former husband because he tried to rape her," says Dr Abdul Rahman Khan, a young doctor in Bahraich.

In fact, there are a large number of Muslim men in Bahraich who are opposed to the bill. Mr Ejaz Ali Khan, president of the U.P. Non-Gazetted Employees' Association and brother of a Congress MLA, says that there is widespread support for the "bold" stand taken by Mr Arif Mohammad Khan. "The opinion among the young educated Muslims is that a man has a social responsibility to maintain his former wife." "The problem is that the mullahs are out to destroy the community. There was a time when the same mullahs opposed family planning on the ground that it was against Islam but when the Government managed to persuade them they took the opposite stand. How can you believe such people?"

Of course, there are people who have been carried away by the cry of "Islam in danger" and even those who do not know anything about the shariat say: "We believe in Hadith and we will not tolerate any interference."

Hakim Mohammad Siddiqui, who has a small clinic in Barabanki, admits that he does not understand the issues and would abide by what his mentor, Maulana Kaleem Ullah says. "Agar woh din ko raat bata den to main woh bhi maan loonga" (if he says that instead of day it is night, I will accept that also).

This is the target group of the mullahs and they are exploiting it to the hilt in the name of religion.

Excerpt from *The Statesman,*
7 March 1986

WAITING FOR CRUMBS OF RELIEF (TALAQ BILL-II)

Pramod Pagedar, Anand Agashe and Rupa Chinai

In Bombay and Pune, the number of maintenance cases filed remains constant, without showing any sudden spurt. In Nagpur, the pace has somewhat quickened.

The judicial magistrate's court in Nagpur has jurisdiction over Nagpur's Central Avenue, Mominpura, Panchpavli and areas in the neighbourhood, where a bulk of the city's estimated one-and-a-half lakh Muslim population lives.

In 1984, Court No. 4 had registered 86 cases. The following year it rose to 93 cases. In the first quarter of the current year, 18 cases have been registered. Court No. 5 admitted 17 cases last year and three during the current year.

Majhar Khan, a middle-aged clerk at Court No. 4 and the court employees' union leader, makes no bones about his being a 'kattar (fundamentalist) Mussalman'. Yet, when he deftly thumbs through the register of maintenance cases meticulously kept by him, he does not hesitate to admit that the Shah Bano verdict and the furore over the new bill have had no discouraging effect on the Muslim divorcees knocking at the court's doors. The cases are coming here all right. "They (divorcees) know very well where to go for help when they are driven out by their husbands," he asserts.

Normally it takes one year for a maintenance case to be resolved in a lower court at Nagpur, despite a Bombay High Court directive stipulating a time limit of six months. Going beyond the lower court can be time and money consuming. But this does not appear to deter the Muslim women from continuing their legal battle at the appellate court level.

As many as 131 revision cases were filed under section 125 of the Cr. P.C. with the Nagpur Sessions Court as on September 1, 1985. Interestingly, out of these only three were filed by Muslims divorcees. The rest were by married Muslim women either deserted by or separated from their husbands.

The number of maintenance cases with the Nagpur bench is much lower, but impressive, considering the interminable procrastinations involved. Out of a total of ten maintenance cases (revision) admitted by it since 1983, only two have been disposed of so far. Of the total seven application cases admitted last year, three are still awaiting decision.

In Pune, the rise in maintenance cases is negligible. For instance, the number of such cases filed in the Pune court during 1985 is 557, out of which only 78 are from the Muslim community. Similarly, among the 170 cases filed in the Khadki court last year, the number of Muslim divorcees seeking maintenance is only 24. The comparative figures of earlier years also indicate the same proportion.

Advocate Madhumita Chowdhary, who has been fighting maintenance cases for Muslim divorcees over the years, explains this intriguing phenomenon. "Thanks to the rampant illiteracy, it took quite some time for the news of the Supreme Court judgement to percolate to the Muslim women. Whatever news reached them was distorted. On the other hand, Shah Bano's somersault, which was widely publicized by the mullahs, came as a great shock and paralysed them totally."

That Muslim women are well aware of their right to approach courts for maintenance, to seek custody of children or to demand divorce was evident during the survey conducted in Bombay and Bhiwandi. In many cases, this was despite the pressure of the jamaat which tried to ensure that the cases were settled through them and not through courts.

"The jamaat stopped me from going to court. They said they would throw me out of the samaaj," complains Nafeesa Adam Athania, who defied their verdict. Her husband had told her, "Take a lump sum and keep quiet." Her maintenance case has been pending for the past three and a half years.

The widespread pressure of the jamaats against approaching the courts was confirmed by the Bhiwandi judicial magistrate Mr N. G. Pawar. In the wake of the Shah Bano judgement, the jamaat had listed the cases registered under section 125 and engineered withdrawal of many of them with the promise of an out-of-court settlement.

Both the Bhiwandi court and the Mazagaon court of Bombay, which are situated in areas where Muslims predominate, further confirmed that the majority of women filing cases under section 125 were deserted rather than divorced.

In the two courts of Bhiwandi a total of 124 maintenance cases are pending. On an average, of the 50 cases filed per year, 60 per cent are Muslim and 40 per cent Hindu. The cases stem mainly from Malegaon and Bhiwandi towns. "This does not reveal the true number of divorce or desertion cases in the area, since most families do not come to court except as a last resort," Mr Pawar points out.

The three courts at Mazagaon revealed that within the last three months of 1985, 14 Hindus and 17 Muslims have filed cases under section 125. The court records further revealed that during 1985, 91 Muslims,

56 Hindus and two Christians filed maintenance cases. While the number of Muslims both in Bhiwandi and Mazagaon courts is obviously higher, these figures, when compared with court records, are indicative of the steady stream of cases coming there for the past three years.

The basic awareness of a divorced or deserted woman's right to appeal to court for maintenance was apparent amongst those interviewed in Bombay and Bhiwandi, but not in Nagpur. Although the latter too preferred to go to court, it was the fathers who decided on the course of remedial action.

When 22-year-old Shahnazbano, hailing from Nagpur, was thrown out by her well-educated husband Babbukhan from their Kalmeshwar town residence, just three months after their marriage in June 1981, she returned broken-hearted to her parents' home.

Her father, Aslam Khan, a senior technician with the city division of the State Road Transport Corporation and head of a large joint family, first tried to reason with his son-in-law. When that failed, he filed a court appeal.

Soon a local mullah called on Aslam Khan and tried to talk him out of the idea of waging a court battle. The mullah's argument was that approaching a court of law on the matter was a direct violation of the shariat, and it would further weaken the Muslim community "already under attack from the courts and the nose-poking Government".

When this logic did not work, the mullah dropped subtle hints for Aslam Khan's benefit, threatening that the latter was "buying trouble". But Aslam Khan stuck to his guns, went through a four-year-long court ordeal, and successfully obtained a court decree granting Shahnazbano a monthly maintenance of Rs 200.

Dismissing the mullah's arguments regarding "honour of the community being at stake", Aslam Khan indignantly says, "Neither he, nor the community would help me look after my divorced daughter for the rest of her wretched life. If I had accepted his admonitions and avoided going to court, I would have been worrying about my daughter's fate until I died."

Aslam Khan's mood is not, however, shared by Sheikh Fateh Ahmed, a 52-year-old worker in a workshop in Pune. Both his daughters were married in the same family in Junnar town of Pune district and were abandoned within months, one after the other. Though he admits that he cannot maintain them as he had four sons and one daughter to look after, Fateh Ahmed is not prepared to move a court to seek maintenance from his sons-in-law because "I am sure I won't get anything from the boys as neither of them earns much." He feels remarriage of the girls is the only way out, but wonders how this can be honourably achieved.

All prospective sons-in-law are multiple divorcees in their 40s or 50s, he points out.

Perhaps one of the reasons why Muslim parents of Nagpur are more adamant about approaching the court to secure maintenance for their daughters, is because the court there has been increasingly adopting a sympathetic posture on such cases. They have awarded maintenance even in cases where the woman is alleged to have taken the initiative for a divorce and consented to it after giving up her right to claim mehr, as was the case made out by Shahnazbano's huband. The Nagpur bench ruled that Shahnaz qualified for maintenance even if her signed statement (she was duped into signing a blank paper by her husband before being chucked out of the house) was legally deemed as her consent to divorce.

During the course of the survey in Nagpur, it was found that many women preferred to settle for a lump sum payment to end the harrassment from their husbands. Taking advantage of the loopholes in the system, the husbands resorted to umpteen ways to delay the proceedings and the payment, thus forcing the harassed ex-wife to settle for a compromise to end the ordeal once and for all.

A lone voluntary organization Stree Atyachar Virodhi Parishad, operating in Nagpur, has so far handled 26 cases of Muslim divorcees, a majority of them belonging to poor families from around Vidarbha. While seven women, through the assistance of the Parishad's free legal aid cell, have obtained maintenance decrees from courts, the rest are awaiting the verdicts. While maintenance in the seven cases has ranged from an incredibly low Rs 35 to 190 per month, Mrs Seema Sakhare, a member of the Parishad, states that even this pittance is important for a dejected divorcee, providing her with some consolation.

Mrs Sakhare was critical of Congress (I) leader Najma Heptullah's insinuation that Muslim husbands, like their Hindu counterparts, would start burning their wives to death if they were compelled to pay maintenance against the tenets of the shariat. Muslim husbands are already proficient in the art of bride burning, she comments wryly. The parishad had detailed records of 25 Muslim housewives who were brutally burnt to death by their husbands.

Excerpt from *The Indian Express*
24 April 1986

TORN BETWEEN RELIGION & REALITY (TALAQ BILL-III)
Rupa Chinai

Be it in the fundamentalist-controlled mohallas of Bhiwandi, the cloistered gulleys of Bhendi Bazar and Madanpura, or the Tulsiwadi slums of Bombay, the ordinary, illiterate Muslim women were united in their verdict that deserted Muslim women must retain the right to approach courts. This was because only courts could decide who was right or wrong, and grant justice. The consensus was that even if women are denied maintenance, the man has to financially support his children until they become independent. The new bill which was neither according to the law nor according to Islam, would give greater freedom to men and cause greater 'zulum' (injustice) to women, they feared.

During the course of our detailed interviews and discussions, one thing became quite obvious: Muslim women were wholly ignorant of the provisions of the proposed bill. However, when enlightened on the implications of the bill, their response was intelligent and well measured.

"This is 'ulta kanoon' (justice in reverse)," said Bilkiz Bano, a housewife of Madanpura. "Why should one lie? In which book is it written that only the parents are responsible for the girl and her children?" In a situation where neither the jamaat nor the panch has any control over men and discard wives like old clothes, were else could women go except to the court? Unlike in the past, today's Muslims live in singular units. No one is concerned about the welfare of others, she asserts.

Introducing her neighbour, Mariam Bee, who claims to be at least a hundred years old, Bilkiz Bano points to her plight. Although her husband was a rich weaver, his wealth was divided amongst his brothers and nephews after his death, leaving the childless Mariam Bee penniless. Today it is only because of her kind neighbours that she can eat two meals a day. Endorsing Bilkiz Bano's view that the burden of maintenance cannot be put on the parents, Mariam Bee irreverently states, "Such a law may be right for the panch, but it is not right for us."

Attacking the fundamentalists for formulating such a law, Mariam Bee said, "What the mullahs say is not all right. Today there is no honesty left among them. Only two or four out of a hundred are honest. Now in the masjid we have to pay Rs 6 instead of Rs 2. It is Allah's house. Why have the prices been raised?"

Representative of the radical younger generation of unmarried Muslim women, Munna Inamdar, a final year law student in Pune, asserts that the new bill is "truly draconian for the would-be brides". "I have found that several male chauvinist husbands have already started using the impending bill as a bogey to force their wives into submission."

As the new bill absolves husbands of any responsibility of supporting their divorced wives, once it is passed, there would be no stopping the males, who even now enjoy an indiscriminately superior status in Muslim society, Munna observes. "As an overwhelming section of our community is poor, illiterate and generally backward, the new bill will undoubtedly abet crime, particularly prostitution," she feared.

According to a group of young mothers living in Byculla — none of them has studied beyond the SSC level — Islam has given a high place to women in society. Hence their present bondage and low status did not stand to reason. Accepting the view held by certain Muslims that the shariat, written several hundred years after the death of the Prophet, was an interpretation of the Quran by ordinary mortals, they felt a change in the shariat was necessary. If maintenance for women is included in the shariat, it is a good thing. But maintenance and inheritance rights of the children should definitely be there," asserted one of the group.

But would such changes in the shariat not put Islam in 'khatra'? To this commonly-heard refrain, one of the mothers replied, "How is this issue putting Islam in danger? It is men who will be endangered!"

This flexibility of approach toward Islamic laws in today's context was, however, not visible in the group of nine women met during a three-hour discussion at a home in Bhendi Bazar in Bombay. Although they understood the plight of deserted or divorced women, they were firm in their belief that to accept maintenance from a man who had discarded them was 'haraam' (shameless), because the Quran said so.

Their refusal to accept any other interpretation of the Quran, than the one they had been taught to believe, brought the discussion to naught. Asked what they would do if tomorrow they or their daughters were divorced or deserted, they had no answer.

"No woman wants to go against Islam. In fact, women enjoy a high place in Islam. They are very free. Everyone knows there is misuse (referring to oral talaq and polygamy). It is true that women are not always to blame. But if it comes to changing Islamic law, were are helpless. The shariat was written at the same time as the Quran. It should remain as it is. For women the only solution is to educate our daughters so that they can stand on their own feet," said the wife of a qazi, who summed up the views of other women.

Were the middle-class Muslims, such as members of this group coming from a more stable background, unable to understand the suffering of the really poor amongst whom greater divorce rates prevailed? Refuting this impression one of the young mothers in the group hit back: "I am living with my parents, who are supporting me and my children. When one of my children died, I could not even afford a 'kafan' (shroud), I too know what suffering is."

The Muslim women of Tulsiwadi slum did not fight shy of declaring their views. "Men must give maintenance to women and to children, for it is men who create the 'lafda' (trouble). Without support women can be left with no alternative but to go astray," warned a middle-aged woman.

She pointed to the prevailing practice where men, on the first night of the marriage, coerce women into giving up their claim to mehr by getting her to say, "I forgive you, and my God forgives you". "We were stupid enough to agree to saying this," she regretted.

Upholding the right to approach the court as at present, and the right to get maintenance for children until they become independent, a middle-aged housewife living in one of the maze-like mohallas of Bhiwandi asserted, "The new law is wrong. We do not want it. Tell the Government not to bring such a law. Men will become more free. They will not care for their children. What the court has been doing so far is according to Islam. Divorced girls cannot accept to live dependent on their parents or brothers. Oral talaq should be banned. This law will create greater 'zulum' on women. Give me the names and addresses of those who have written such a law. I will write and tell them that the new bill is neither according to law, nor according to Islam."

Excerpt from the *Indian Express*
22 April 1986

GOOD IN PARTS, BAD IN MOTIVE (TALAQ BILL-IV)

*Anand Agashe, Sarita Rai, Radha Srivastava,
Arif Shaikh and Charudatta Deshpande*

Opinions of the intellectuals and activists among the Muslim community are, perhaps, summed up best by Bohra reformist Asghar Ali Engineer: "The current controversy is political and not religious. There is nothing in the religion that prevents people from paying maintenance beyond three months. That amounts to 'ahsan', which is good according to the Quran," he says.

Ms Nasreen Fazalbhoy, doing research at the Women's Study Unit of the Tata Institute of Social Sciences (TISS), feels that the way different groups of people have reacted to the issue raises doubts about their ultimate objectives.

"I wouldn't call it only politicization. Various other issues are coming to the fore — such as a common civil code, rights of minorities, the real intention of the Government. The question of maintenance and divorce goes down in terms of priority. Each group seems to be using the issue to satisfy some underlying intention of its own," she says.

"It is not that Muslims are not pained by any unfair measures, or that they don't want to oppose the bill. They are reacting not just to the issue, but to the various related issues which seem to threaten their identity," she adds.

Most of them, barring the activists of the Muslim Satyashodhak Mandal, were opposed to the introduction of a common civil code. "Why shouldn't such a vast population have its own law," asks Ms Kamila Tayabji, citing the example of the USA, where there are different laws in different states. Admitting that certain provisions of the Muslim personal law needed reform, she says it was none of the Supreme Court's business to cast aspersions on it.

"India is a bouquet," says Mr Ahmed Zakaria, chairman of the Islamic Cultural Centre, Bombay Unit. "Let all the flowers bloom and give their fragrance. In what way does it affect others, when only 0.1 per cent of Muslim women are involved and are affected by the bill?"

However, members of the Muslim Satyashodhak Mandal do not agree with him. Such a code should 'evolve' in the long run, they maintain. "We have been demanding a common civil code since 1966 and we had also taken a morcha to the Vidhan Sabha in this connection," Ms Mehrunnissa Dalwai, wife of the mandal's founder, the late Mr Hamid Dalwai, says.

A common civil code should be based on humanitarian principles, insists Razia Patel, a progressive Muslim social worker of Chatra Yuva Sangharsh Vahini in Aurangabad, who has spearheaded many agitations for equal rights of Muslim women in Maharashtra. She, however, expressed concern over the involvement of communal Hindu organizations in this issue and asked how come they had become overnight-sympathizers of Muslim women, when in the past they had done nothing to alleviate their plight. Their intention is rather different, she alleged.

Mr Anwar Rajan and Mr Sayed Bhai, Muslim reformists from Pune, feel that a common civil code is imperative to extricate Muslim women from the dungeon they are languishing in. "Reforms always have to be enforced at first," they point out. Mr Taher Poonawala, another reformist leader, however, feels that such a code must evolve from within the community, instead of being imposed on it.

Mr Asghar Ali Engineer argues that the general feeling among Muslims is that a common civil code would mean imposition of the Hindu code. "There is no need for a common civil code," he says. "What is important is justice to women. As long as it can be done within the framework of the Muslim personal law, why abolish it?"

Ms Fazalbhoy feels a common code would not solve any problem, but only complicate and confuse matters further. "It will be an imposition upon Muslims and will be viewed as violative of the rights of the minorities," she says. Ms Tayabji suggests setting up of a committee to study the problem of the Muslim community, adding that retired Muslim judges of the Supreme Court or High Court should be appointed on the committee.

Are they opposed to the new bill? Most of them have their reservations on the issue. "The new bill has its plus and minus points," says Ms Fazalbhoy. "The general trend these days is to discredit the bill completely and uphold section 125 of the Cr. P.C. as the solution. But this is a very simplistic attitude. Section 125 helps only certain women up to a point. In practice, very few women are able to get alimony through this avenue."

"I am opposed not so much to the content of the new bill as to the high-handed manner in which it is being pushed through in Parliament. The prime minister had promised that there would be a committee to go into the Muslim personal law and view it from every possible angle. However, the bill has been formulated without this, and hence it is bound to be inadequate in certain respects," she says.

"One good feature is that it does not limit a woman in getting support. She has a lot more sources open to her; but this also leads to a practical problem. By this new bill, a divorced woman can take her parents of court if they do not provide for her; but it is impossible that any woman will actually do this," Ms Fazalbhoy asserts.

"Clause 3(b) of the proposed bill talks of giving maintenance to women for two years, if she is looking after the children. I would like to know from where they have taken this provision and why the time lag should be limited to two years? Moreover, if the mother looks after the children, it seems logical that, apart from providing for children, the man also has to make some provision for the mother, who has to be fit enough to look after the children," she argues.

Ms Shama Zaidi points out that every Muslim country has its own different laws. "However, most countries do have maintenance in their laws. They have interpreted it that way. But our prime minister unfortunately has got a set of followers who are very backward and literally interpret the Quran. There are many schools of thought. The so-called fundamentalists — it is a misnomer — are actually Habis. Habis are a most puritanical sect. They get money from Saudi Arabia and many other sources. They have got clout."

Opposing the bill, Mr Engineer says pronouncing divorce in one sitting itself is unjust. "Why should the parents and relatives of the women be punished? Why should the parents and relatives of the women be punished? Why should the husband's arbitrariness be excused? A referendum on the subject is possible only after a continuous educational campaign. The Arab custom of woman returning to her parents after divorce is a weak argument. Any knowledge will not ascribe it to Allah. The bill should not be passed. Provisions of section 125 should continue to apply to Muslim women," he says.

Ms Tayabji feels that the bill would be struck down by the Supreme Court. "I am amazed how the prime minister has supported the bill," she says. Voicing the same reservations as those raised by Mr Engineer, she says the bill was full of fallacies and would not benefit anybody. "It is ridiculous to say that the waqf funds should be utilized to pay the maintenance of the woman, if her husband, parents and other relatives fail to pay. The waqf funds are not sufficient to meet the expenses."

On the other hand, the amount of mehr should be fixed at the time of marriage, apart from granting the right of divorce to both the parties, Ms Tayabji suggests. Ms Dalwai feels that the bill would put Muslim women under the dictatorship of their husbands and the mullahs, and would curtail their freedom. "It will widen the gulf between Hindus and Muslims and give Muslims a different identity," she opines.

In the name of religion the bill gives men licence for exploitation of women, says Razia Patel. "If the prime minister proceeds with this bill, it will certainly be a death knell for the rights of Muslim women in democratic India," she opined. The bill will give unlimited powers to men and complete insecurity to women. "The Government should not sacrifice the rights of women for the vote bank of fundamentalists," she adds.

Mr Anwar Rajan, a Khoja reformist from Pune, is of the view that though the bill would affect the entire community, its impact would be felt less by the Khojas. "Being, by and large, a wealthy and educated community, the incidence of oral talaq among the Khojas has always been on the lower side."

A tightly-knit hierarchial controlling structure of local councils, regional councils and a federal council appointed by the community head, Prince Aga Khan, also helps in checking the divorce rate, Mr Rajan points out. According to the custom prevalent among the Khojas, he explains, the husband has to seek permission from the council for a marriage which does not come easily.

Mr Taher Poonawala, the Bohra reformist, had a similar tale to narrate about his community. "Ours is a microscopic community," he explains. "There are only 10 lakh Bohras all over the world, about seven lakh of whom stay in India. The head priest, the Syedna, therefore, finds it easy to control all the activities within the community. Since every act has to get the prior approval of the Syedna, those seeking divorce are discouraged because of the long time taken by the approval process."

"The prime reason why the new bill is not dreaded by the Bohras is that there is no stigma attached to remarriage among them unlike in other communities. This makes the new bill of little consequence to us," Mr Poonawala points out.

And yet the Syedna has welcomed the bill? "That is only a gimmick to express solidarity with the other sections of Muslims," Mr Poonawala asserts. "Secondly, the Syedna stands to gain out of it because the bill would further strengthen his stranglehold on the Satyashodhak Bohra community."

Both Mr Rajan and Mr Sayed Bhai of the Muslim Satyashodhak Mandal view the new bill as a "definite retrograde step that is bound to destroy the integrity of the country". "Omission of Muslims from the purview of section 125 would amount to an abject surrender to the Muslim fundamentalists, who seem bent upon creating a pre-partition situaition," they feel.

Mr Zakaria, however, is all for the bill. "It is mainly the so-called intellectuals among Muslims who use the shariat to their own convenience. The new bill, in fact, favours the individual rights of Muslim women," he said. However, he did not elaborate in which way the bill enhanced the individual rights of Muslim women.

"Personally speaking" — Ms Fazalbhoy had her own argument — "in spite of being a divorcee myself, I would never think of asking for maintenance from my husband. Not because it contravenes the Islamic law, but because I would hate to be dependent on my husband in any way, when I am able to look after myself. My conscience would not allow me to seek maintenance," she asserted.

Excerpt from the *Indian Express*
23 April 1986

OPINIONS

HOW DO MUSLIMS VIEW THE DIVORCE BILL?

*Interviews by Paromita Ukil, Yubaraj Ghimire,
Lekha Dhar and Prashun Bhaumik*

Syed Shahabuddin *(MP, General Secretary, Janata Party)*

What is your opinion on the Muslim Divorce Bill?

It's a welcome step of the prime minister and I am in favour of the bill. The bill intends to safeguard the majority voice of the minority community as the prime minister has heard the Muslim leaders who, obviously, should have a decisive voice on the bill that relates to their personal law.

Are you fully satisfied with the bill?

There are still some "ambiguities" in the bill and there is scope for their rectification. It, at least, intends to nullify the Supreme Court verdict in the Shah Bano case that showed utter disregard for Muslim personal law.

But the minority within the Muslim minority feel let down.

In fact, there is a very feeble voice that sometimes finds an echo among some Muslim elitists who have lost all contact with the masses.

What about Mr Arif Mohammad Khan?

His is a thoroughly opportunistic move. If he is sincere, he must resign his Lok Sabha seat as well. Others who recently submitted a memorandum to the prime minister protesting against the bill are just fellow-travellers and do not represent the Muslim community.

What will be your individual stand if the Janata party issues a whip to vote against the bill?

It's true that there are very strong feelings about the bill in the party. But I do not think that the party would compel any of its members to overrule their conscience.

Since you admit there are some ambiguities in the bill, are you in favour of the bill being referred to the joint select committee of Parliament?

I am totally against that. It's a very sensitive issue touching the entire community's sentiment. Time-taking procedures should be avoided and Parliament should take a quick and convincing stand. It's a belated move to the Government to rectify the Supreme Court judgement. In fact, while the Government does not have the right to change or interfere in the personal law of a community, it should nullify any such moves either from the court or from any other quarter.

Dr Anwara Khatun *(eminent gynaecologist)*

Do you think the bill is against women?

The bill certainly discriminates against Muslim women. If other women in India can enjoy the privileges of sections 125 and 127 of the Cr. P.C. then why can't I? I am an Indian first, an Indian second and an Indian last. But the Government does not want to regard me in that light. How can you call it secular then?

Should the Government initiate progress or should it come from the community?

The Government should at least support the progressive section of a community. Agreed that the progressive section is always in a minority, but didn't Toynbee say that it is the dominant minority? What one historian of Irfan Habib's stature says is certainly more important than the opinion of one lakh conservative Muslims. But will Mr Asoke Sen care to listen to the progressive viewpoint? After the Supreme Court verdict in the Shah Bano case many Hindus also came out to support it. Isn't that also a significant step towards national integration? But our respected prime minister chose to ignore it despite all his pledges.

Are you in favour of a uniform civil code?

It has been 38 years since Independence. I think it is high time that we had a uniform civil code. I am a humanist and not a theologian. All I am concerned about is that the bill proposes to throw 40 million women into the hands of fundamentalist wolves.

Syed Mustafa Siraj *(eminent Bengali novelist)*

Is the bill against women?

It is definitely against women; it will drive the helpless Muslim women to the streets. The wakf board will certainly not take care of the poor women. Moreover, the board offices are all in the big towns. From where do you think a penniless woman of Murshidabad will get the money to come to Calcutta?

Is the bill secular?

How can the bill be called secular when it makes two classes of Indian citizens? In every other country there is only one law of the land which holds good for every community. Muslims are a minority even in the U.S., Britain, Canada, China, the Soviet Union, Yugoslavia and Albania. Do fundamentalists dare to seek separate laws there?

History has already proved that Jinnah's two-nation theory was all wrong, but Rajiv Gandhi seems to be following in his footsteps and repeating the same mistake. And what is most unfortunate is that a section of the Muslims is helping him to establish a Hindu state.

Should the Government wait for the community to itself evolve reforms?

Laws are never framed on the basis of the opinion of the people. They are based on the opinion of the progressive and educated (in the real sense of the term) sections of the administration. When the people oppose progress and their opinion is not in keeping with the moral values of the age then it is the Government's task to intervene. Will the Government ever sanctify human sacrifice the name of tribal rights?

Remember when sati was abolished in the nineteenth century, only a handful of liberals were in favour of the move. The majority of the Hindus had opposed Raja Rammohan Roy. The British government did not pay any heed to the conservative view then, but Rajiv Gandhi now is giving much more importance to orthodox opinion.

Are you in favour of a uniform civil code?

Certainly. I think that India must have strong civil and criminal codes. The nation today is headed for another partition.

Hashim Abdul Halim *(Speaker, West Bengal Assembly)*

Is the bill against women?

The bill is not only against women but also against the basic principles of the shariat. Nowhere in the shariat is it written that the father, brother or wakf board should provide maintenance to a divorced woman. The bill denigrates the position of the woman by reducing her to a beggar in the house. It is the most retrograde bill since partition and will free the man of all liability. He will marry today, divorce tomorrow. Instead of heading towards the twenty-first century, the Government is passing a bill which will take us back to the era before Christ.

Does the bill go against secularism?

The bill will divide the country along communal lines and hence should be opposed by all democratic and secular minded people and even devout Muslims. A group of fundamentalists are practising a fraud on the community and the prime minister is surrendering to these forces. These fundamentalists who are not the real representatives of the people are misdirecting and misguiding the people. They have no authority to take away basic rights. Today it is the Muslims, tomorrow the Hindus will make similar demands. Why should not the Hindu Endowment Board then be asked to support the Hindu divorced woman? You cannot have separate codes and the Government should be more pragmatic and firm in its commitment to the people.

Should the Government take the lead in evolving reform?

Communities should evolve their own reforms through the real representatives and not by an isolated section of people. The Government under no circumstance should take the lead in this direction. The demand for a common code, too, must come from the people.

Zoya Hasan *(convener, Committee for Protection of Rights of Muslim Women)*

What is your opinion on the introduction of the bill?

It was not at all necessary at the moment. It is against women. It undermines the rights of Muslim women. It exonerates the main culprits — the husbands who divorce their wives. It seeks to pass on the responsibility to maintain the divorced Muslim woman to her natural family.

What's wrong with that?

It will encourage conflict within a family. Suppose the family fails to maintain the divorcee, she will have to go to the courts against her own family. That is time consuming; moreover, once she is abandoned, it is unlikely that she will get the required treatment and care from her natural family.

What if the bill ensures all protection to divorcees?

The very fact that it has been brought indicates that it cannot ensure protection. Section 125 Cr.P.C. is much stronger and provides requisite protection. But the bill protects the husbands who would divorce their wives without recognizing the contribution they made all their lives in the process of family building. The constitutional provision ensures maintenance beyond the period of iddat while the bill takes that away. It is very unfair, unjust and discriminatory and violative of Article 14 of the Constitution which stands for "equality before law". Now Muslim women would be unequal before the law.

But some Muslim leaders have welcomed the bill on the ground that it ensures the "freedom of religion"?

In the guise of freedom of religion, Muslim women are being denied constitutional and human rights.

Does the bill go against secularism?

I would say that it is based on a dubious definition of secularism.

Do you think that the Government should wait for communities to themselves evolve reforms or should it take the lead in this matter?

The question is irrelevant. It is not the question of the personal law of a community, but that of the abandoned getting social justice. As interpreted by the Supreme Court, it should strictly come within the purview of the criminal law.

What do you expect of the majority of the Muslims?

They would be against the bill. We have already submitted a memorandum to the prime minister with the views of prominent Muslims from all quarters.

But the Congress Parliamentary Party meeting unanimously supported the prime minister's stand . . . .

It was a rigged meeting and I think no one was allowed to express his free opinion.

Abdur Rauf Ansari *(West Bengal Congress (I) MLA)*

Is the bill against women?

No. It gives adequate protection to the rights of divorced Muslim women and provides more relief than ever before. I fully support the prime minister on the bill.

Is the bill opposed to secularism?

The bill is fully in keeping with the secular policy of the Indian National Congress.

Are you in favour of a uniform civil code?

Within the existing laws and the secular nature of our country, every individual has a right to practise his own faith. The question does not arise in this context.

Ismat Chugtai *(eminent Urdu writer)*

Why are you opposed to the bill?

If there is to be a bill, the period of maintenance should be extended to a lifetime or till the women marries again. And I want it to be equal: equal amenities for all. There should be no difference between Hindu women and Muslim women. If there is a separate bill for Muslim husbands, Hindu and Christian husbands can object. Why should there be such a difference? And such a bill? The fight should be for a uniform civil code.

What is secularism? It means that there should be no difference between Muslims and Hindus; there should be no mention of religion. We are all Indians. We should all have the same rights. The bill is against this principle.

It is argued that the bill is pro-Islam.

It is an insult to Islam. Yes, the Quran says that the women is to be paid maintenance till she marries again. But who will marry a 75-year-old woman? Why should she be thrown to the dogs?

In Pakistan if a man divorces his wife, he has to pay her maintenance till she marries again. So why not here? Why are we being so narrow-minded? If they want to retain a separate personal law, then what about the rest of the shariat? You cannot choose the good and leave out the bad to suit yourself.

Ali Sardar Jafri *(well-known Urdu writer)*

Does the bill really protect the rights of Muslim women?

I would not categorically state that the bill is against women. I have a feeling that Muslim women will be deprived of some of their rights by the application of this bill. Every talaq (divorce) has to be legally scrutinized, if the bill is to be passed. The harmful effects of the bill will be minimized if each talaq is scrutinized in court.

Does the bill strengthen secularism?

I think it is against the declared aims of secularism. According to our Constitution, we have socialism, secularism and democracy. If we practised all three, there would be no need for these laws.

But section 125 of the Cr.P.C. does not violate the fundamentals of Islam, according to which every needy person should be provided for by anyone who can afford it.

In principle, there should be a uniform civil code. But we live in an uneven society, where three fundamental changes—economic, social and political—have to take place. Only then can there be a uniform civil code. Otherwise no.

Excerpt from *The Telegraph*
3 March 1986

SURRENDER TO FUNDAMENTALISTS

Interviews by Madhusri Das and Ajai Sahni

Prof. Agwani

It is believed that the interpretation of the shariat in most Muslim countries is more progressive than in India. Is this true?

The basic difference in the status of Muslim women in India and in the Muslim countries is due to the fact that in all the latter, evidently, the Muslims are in the majority. As a result, they don't have a minority complex. In India, however, such a complex exists. And therefore the community is constantly on the defensive.

Some Muslims express the fear that the uniform civil code might, in fact, be the Hindu civil code and that, perhaps, there is a conspiracy to impose it on Muslims. Thus, there is an automatic resistance to any changes in the laws, especially (to) those relating to marriage and divorce.

I believe that the time has come for a draft to be prepared for a uniform civil code. This must not be the same as the Civil Marriage Act. It must incorporate healthy elements from Muslim traditions, Hindu traditions, Christian traditions and others.

And it has to have an Indian flavour; it must reflect Indian customs. Unless this is done, people will talk only in the light of their fears and apprehensions. But once we have a draft civil code for public debate, I think discussions will be more concrete.

As for Muslim countries, till the nineteenth century many were part of the Ottaman Empire. This had started reform of personal law in the latter part of the century. They started bringing religious laws under the application of unifying codes.

Later, when the Arab world became independent, in countries like Egypt, Lebanon, Syria and Iraq, the trend was that instead of having a shariat code and Christian code and other codes, they evolved one unified code to adjudicate all personal laws.

The approach has been not to touch personal law itself but to build administrative regulations around it so that it would not be misused.

The Quran says you can have more than one wife provided you can do justice to all of them, but, if you cannot, then only one wife. Well, Syria, Egypt and Tunisia made an administrative regulation that, since history, experience, and even the Quranic text suggest that a man cannot do justice to more than one wife, it will not be permitted.

Another thing they have done in Egypt is to discontinue the practice of divorce by the formula of repeating talaq thrice. The courts there do not take note of such divorces. Until a man satisfies them on the reasons for the divorce, they will not register a second marriage unless he tells them why he is taking a second wife. So, without touching the shariat, they have made these rules.

In India such changes have not been introduced. They are possible in Muslim countries as there is no question of the minority being deprived of its identity, culture or religion. But in India, the fear that Muslim identity may be wiped out has stalled such reforms. In this sense, there is a vast difference between India and the Muslim nations.

What do you think of the Shah Bano judgement in this context?

I don't think anyone would have objected to the provisions of section 125 Cr.P.C. if the honourable court had not gone into other issues. That was both uncalled for and very tactless. Many judgements had not made news because they were not seen as questioning the shariat. The Supreme Court unnecessarily invited trouble. That is why section 125 has now become a bone of contention.

What changes do you envisage in the Indian context?

Well, India being an open society, the change must be initiated by the women themselves. I have been studying changes among the Dawoodi Bohra community in Udaipur. They have progressively cast off the control of the Syedna by themselves. About 60 per cent of the community there insisted that the Syedna should give an account of all the money they had donated. The Bohra youth movement has an active women's component.

Saifuddin Choudhary

You had spoken vociferously against the proposed bill in the last session of Parliament. Now that it has been introduced, in the budget session, what have you to say?

It is nothing but communalism being practised by the Congress for political interests. Rajiv Gandhi has been completely exposed. There can be a strong backlash against this bill. Sikhs can also demand a separate personal law, as can the Hindus. The young MPs of the Congress should take a brave stand on this issue.

Why do you think the opposition parties have come together on this issue?

Because everybody is concerned about the human aspect of the issue. It is not a question of religion at all. It's question of women, humanity and secularism. All parties are combined on this. And Muslim intellectuals should come forward so that women can be saved. If things are not set right, the country will disintegrate. The CPM took a strong stand against this matter earlier. Why should fanaticism be allowed to flourish? It should be left strictly to religious institutions.

What will be the repercussions of this bill on Muslim women?

Well, they are being repressed. Now, a husband can pay a woman even Re 1 as alimony and get away with it. Where does that leave the wife? If a deserted or divorced woman becomes a prostitute, which religion will come forward to save her?

When divorce is granted in a Muslim country, there is a public notary to record the statements—the whole process is legal. There is no such provision in this country. Section 125 of the Cr.P.C. should be applicable to all Indian women. Can Hindus go back to the laws of Manu?

The Muslim leaders of this country should realize the grave damage they are doing. They have not thought of the matter in the long-term perspective at all—to parties like the Muslim League, the issue of maintenance to Muslim women has become a basis for political survival, a means of keeping themselves in the public eye.

Prof. Rais Ahmed

What did you think of the Shah Bano judgement, which led to the introduction of the Muslim Women (Protection of Rights on Divorce) Bill in this session of Parliament?

At first, I thought that it is an ordinary judgement and the Supreme Court had passed a justifiable order. Later on, it was clearly evident that political parties were exploiting the judgement.

They have to periodically assert their importance. In this issue, no long-term interests of the community are at stake. What is being talked about is only the shariat law, which is a tradition and not really a law. It was formulated centuries ago but it has no place in the modern industrial society of today. In my view, the fundamentalists of Islam are not being challenged. It is the outdated traditions that are being challenged. This regression will surely make the Muslims in India march backwards.

Do you agree with the widely-held view that Rajiv Gandhi has succumbed to the lure of Muslim voters?

If he has, it's a misconcieved factor. This bill cannot under any circumstances be regarded as long-term bait to trap Muslim voters. Voters would be forthcoming anyway, if voting is based on rationality.

Do you think that the status of Muslim women in India will be greatly changed by the new bill?

No, I do not think so, if there is a strong fight against such unjust measures. There is no difference between the average Hindu woman or the Muslim in this country. Both are poverty-stricken and illiterate.

Excerpt from *The Current*
8 March 1986

CONTROVERSY OVER THE UNIFORM CIVIL CODE

ISLAM IN INDIA TODAY

GROWING INSULARITY AND INCONSIDERATION

Badr-ud-din Tyabji

To one who has lived through three critical periods of our country's history — the decade preceding Independence; then the one following during which its form and substance were shaped; and finally the subsequent decades — functioning in various capacities, if not as a major participant, at least as a ringside observer, the painfully slow development of social consciousness retain among our people has been a source of constant distress and alarm.

The progressive development and refinement of such consciousness for the effective and harmonious working of this kind of policy that we have wisely chosen for ourselves is an obvious *sine qua non*. The tripod of "democracy, secularism, and socialism" on which it is precariously poised in this vast country, with such a diversity of cultures, religions, ethnic groups and, not least, historical memories, cannot possibly remain steady, let alone consolidate itself, without a much more sustained growth of civil social consciousness of each other in our diverse population than is now in evidence.

We have not even reached a stage when it is possible for anyone belonging to a particular religion or ethnic group to dissect or analyse the beliefs, customs and way of living of another group, sect or religion, however sincere and well-equipped intellectually or morally he may be to do it. His objective may be wholly laudable; to bring a particular ethnic or religious group or sect up to the level of what he considers the necessary social norms to enable it to form a homogenous and cooperative element in the polity of India governed by its three basic principles. But more likely than not, he will immediately be attacked for presumptuous interference in matters that do not concern him, or worse, of blatantly attempting to do down another community; in brief, of being a rank communalist — a term with many meanings in India, none unfortunately other than pejorative.

It was, therefore, a pleasant surprise to attend a seminar on "Islam in India since Independence" organized last month by Kashmir University's Iqbal Institute under the able stewardship of Professor Ale-Ahmed Suroor. In a way it was a sequel to the Institute's 1981 seminar on "Islam in the Modern World — Problems and Prospects". Though the participants were predominantly Muslim academicians and scholars, a few distinguished non-Muslims also participated. What its organizers called the keynote address was delivered by me and I reproduce something of the substance.

Speaking in Srinagar, where Islam is the predominant religion, and in a gathering where the majority of those present were Muslims, it was important to bear in mind that the real value of Islam as a moral and regenerative force as enunciated in the Quran can only be judged fairly and justly, in the context of its impact on all the people living in the area dealt with. That meant India and encompassed all Indians.

It is often conveniently forgotten by many zealots that Islam is not meant to be a blessing only for Muslims but for all mankind. Therefore, unless Muslims by their conduct in community with the tenets and spirit of Islam palpably demonstrate that the religion they profess is also a benefit to, and a blessing for, both Muslims and those who profess other religions, Islam is not fulfilling the role ordained for it in the Quran, and propagated by the Prophet.

Muslims are not alone in not being able to see themselves as others see them. This inability is very human and almost universal. After being in a number of countries and seeing a great number of people, Muslim and non-Muslim, I have to conclude that nowhere is its lack more widespread or more endemic than in India. Our inability or disinclination to subject ourselves to any degree of self-introspection before judging the conduct of others on similar issues has almost become a national characteristic; a seemingly self-protective carapace of the Indian psyche. It inhibits us not only from establishing mutually agreeable and beneficial working and living relations with foreigners, but even amongst ourselves.

It is easy, and perhaps even to some extent justifiable, to attribute this largely to the effect on the Indian psyche of the continuous and large-scale waves of foreign incursions into the subcontinent, and of the subsequent colonial regime whose survival depended so much on the success with which it could divide and rule us. But this is only as Ghalib says: "Dil behlaney ke-liye yeh khial achha hai!" (To cajole oneself, this is a pleasing thought.)

The main thrust of Islam, as enunciated in the Quran and propagated and practised by the Prophet, is its claim to being a soul satisfying and yet practical doctrine that will cater to the needs of, and benefit, all mankind, whether they are in formal terms Muslims or non-Muslim. Islam is not meant to be practised only for the benefit of "believers" but also of those who believe as sincerely in their own faiths and ideologies. Therefore, care has to be taken, and attention paid, to the point of view, as well as the convenience and the susceptibilities, of the non-Muslim communities with whom Indian Muslims co-exist.

Every latitude for the manifestation of their religious practices, customs and habits that Muslims claim, or allow themselves on the plea that these are integral elements of their religion, will have to be matched by conceding an equal latitude to the followers of all other faiths, or be adjusted with them for the mutual convenience and benefit of all citizens of India.

Ostentatious, arrogant and self-advertising displays of one's piety are always irritating to others. They do not win friends or influence people. Rather, they create antagonism and active dislike. When such a display is made in the name of religion, it unfortunately not only harms the person who indulges in it, but damages the religion under whose cover it is indulged. It also casts a slur on the reputation of others professing the same faith, who do not take any step to show their disapproval of such conduct on the part of some of their co-religionists.

Take, for example, the noise and din that some Muslims, even when living in the heart of a locality in which the majority is non-Muslim, make in the early hours of the morning when they are preparing themselves for the month-long Ramzan fasts. Instead of going about their business quietly, in a reverent spirit, they shout, beat drums, utter cries and in every possible way try to let the whole neighbourhood know what they have got up for. Their whole object seems to be to proclaim their own virtue, and also inflict as much discomfort on others as they themselves feel at having had to get up at that early hour.

Again, one sees in some of the busiest throughfares on a Friday or some auspicious day, Muslims insisting on saying their prayers on the road itself, blocking traffic and causing inconvenience to passers-by. The ostensible reason given for this is that they cannot all be accommodated in some small mosque on that particular road. There is, however, no special reason why they should pray only at that particular mosque and, when that is full, do so in the public ground adjoining it. But they will do it. Are they really more concerned about the sanctity of their prayers, or their success in disrupting traffic, and hope that by their antics they will attract public attention?

When Muslims insist on indulging in such or similar anti-social acts on the ground that the free practice of their religion is guaranteed under the Constitution and the secular banner that floats over it, can they really be surprised when other communities and religions also insist on exercising their religious freedom rights in the same inconsiderate ways? And as non-Muslims are overwhelmingly superior in numbers and positions of authority in India, by doing so they tend to deafen and exasperate non-participants with public manifestations of their personal religious zeal. Incidentally, they encourage Muslims to forget the similar social transgressions committed by their own co-religionists.

Surely secularism does not mean unfettered liberty under the garb of religion for indulging in practices that cause inconvenience or discomfort to those who do not attach an equal importance to the performance of such rites? It would be worthwhile to draw up a balance sheet between the public demonstrative peace-disturbing manifestations of various religions to see how they compare, and then attempt to work out how they could be reconciled to each other for the mutual benefit of all.

As Muslims yearn, as they patently do, that their religion and culture should be understood and appreciated, they must on their part make a sincere attempt to understand those of the others among whom they live. No one really likes anyone unless there is some reciprocity of feeling between them in their understanding of common problems, and they make joint efforts for solving them. Iqbal in one of his flashes of brilliant insight exclaimed: "A Kafir before his idol with wakeful heart/Is better than the religious man asleep in his Haram."

Therefore, it is an essential duty and responsibility for religious-minded Muslims in secular India to become aware of the authentic teachings — not the street or bazaar manifestations — of the great seers, gurus, and saints of India. They should approach them in the true spirit of the Prophet's injunctions prescribing the reverence and the authenticity be accorded to the teachings of past prophets and teachers; and in a humble way, try to understand what their original message actually was, and how far it coincides with what Islam teaches them. This will promote a feeling of oneness between them and other fellow citizens.

A curious ambivalence seems to have developed in the attitude of Indian intellectuals towards the concept of nationalism and inter-nationalism in recent years. In the immediate postwar period, intoxicated by the heady rhetoric of the victors of what was then genuinely regarded as a victory of democracy over fascism, and the creation of the United Nations, "One World" became the slogan of the hour.

In this upsurge in favour of internationalism, Muslims did not lag behind, either in India or in the world. Gradually, however, the national mood all over the world changed. Nationalism began to displace it both outwardly and inwardly. In fact, inwardly, nationalism had never been supplanted by internationalism. Nationalism has always been and remains the main cohesive force that has both created modern states and kept them together.

In India, the political rivalry between Hindus and Muslims for overlordship of the subcontinent was only partially resolved by the partition of India in 1947. Not only have the wounds of that surgical operation not yet healed, but the new democratic form of government that was initially adopted in both countries soon began to take on an altogether different shape and character.

What needs stressing is that internationalism in the true sense is quite different from pan-Islamism; as well as from the intense, inevitable, but sometimes politically inadvisable interest of Hindus and co-religionists, whether in Pakistan, Bangladesh, Nepal, Sri Lanka or elsewhere. It is, however, impossible, human nature being what it is, for anyone not to be more concerned about those who are related to one by blood, religion and/or history, or past history, than with people with whom one has no such bonds.

Both Hindus and Muslims seem to have failed lamentably in understanding and making allowances for the feelings of each other. With more self-examination and introspection, many of the political crises that arose as an outcrop of this shortcoming should have helped to buttress our common nationalism, instead of creating suspicions about it on either side.

. Finally, to come to the question of Islam and democracy. An obvious point that needs to be emphasized is that in a democracy, ultimately, the will of the majority must prevail. Unless the minority is willing to abide with that condition, democracy cannot function; it will inevitably be supplanted by another form of government that will be infinitely worse for the minority than the previous one with all its failings.

On the other hand, all history teaches us that the majority, in any democracy worth the name, cannot and should not ride roughshod over the views of the minority, on issues fundamental to its survival as an ethnic, social, cultural, and, of course, religious entity.

Similarly, the minority cannot and should not hold itself aloof or be indifferent to issues that relate to the basic structure of the society, of which it is an indissoluble organic constituent, or those affecting that society's future evolution or character. It must wholeheartedly participate in debates on such issues, put forward positive proposals, and if it is a truly Islamic minority, strive to ensure that the fundamental axiom of the Quran that the teachings of Islam and its benefits are meant for all mankind, and not only for professed Muslims is achieved.

A striking, and to me painful, example of the failure to do this is the Muslim personal law issue. In season and out of season, this subject has been brandished before Muslims as a red rag to a bull. Unfortunately this is done principally by those Hindus who are less mindful of the warts and pimples by which time, history, and human frailty have succeeded in distorting and blemishing the pristine purity of their own great original conception of society, humanity, and tolerance, than of the shortcomings of others.

The Muslim reaction to such incitement has been almost equally deplorable. Instead of attempting to separate the wheat from the chaff in the criticism levelled against Muslim society, and to remedy what has palpably gone wrong with the personal practices that a few of them choose to follow, contrary to Quranic injunctions, and the whole spirit of Islam, most of them have fallen an easy prey to agents provocateurs. They have reacted blindly against all criticism, even when made by those whose advice they should have heeded and benefited from; if only for the sake of putting Islam back into its rightful position as a regenerative and creative force in the subcontinent.

In the directive principles of our Constitution, stress has rightly been laid on the desirability of framing a common civil code. Even tentative attempts to begin drafting such a code have, however, been thwarted by Muslim opposition to the very idea of such an attempt, on the ground that they have their own personal laws, that cannot be even explicated, let alone complemented by civil laws. Indian Muslims have become so different from the Muslims of old who were the torch-bearers of jurisprudence and law reforms that they have not even tried to work out any proposals by which a future common civil code of India might incorporate the features of Muslim personal law that are fundamental to Islam, and thus contribute to the wider dissemination of the benefits of those principles. Instead of that, the two sides — those who stand for the present form of Muslim personal law (corrupted though it may be by the accretions of custom, compromises and malpractices), and those who advocate a common civil code formed after all points of view and beliefs have been taken into account — continue their verbal and occasional physical assaults on each other.

I confess my inability to understand why Muslims should not participate uninhibitedly in a national debate for the framing of a common civil code, while insisting that such a code should conform to the basic principles of Islamic laws. Then, if they find that any part of it is unacceptable to them, because it transgresses against specific Quranic injunctions, they can be given the option to exempt themselves from the application of those provisions. All Muslims should have the right to opt for the application of the code in toto or to abide by their personal law in regard to the provisions of specific items in the code, by making a formal declaration to that effect, in a competent court, on reaching adulthood. That provision should remain in force for the next 20 years, after which the question should be reconsidered in the light of experience and the circumstances of the time.

Excerpts from *The Statesman*
10 & 11 November 1985

WHY MUSLIMS RESIST A COMMON CIVIL CODE

Som Anand

Now that the agitation against the Supreme Court judgement in the Shah Bano case has again been revived, it is time to reassess our attitudes and see why a simple issue of providing alimony to a divorced woman created such a row all over the country. There is now no doubt as to what Muslim public opinion in the matter is. No other issue has agitated the Muslim mind so much in post-independence India.

Muslim newspapers and journals are unanimous that by accepting Shah Bano's claim, the Supreme Court violated the laws of the shariat. More than the operative part of the judgement, Muslims resented the references in it to the need for a common civil code. This judgement, it was said, was an attempt to introduce such a code through the back door.

Another fallout of the Shah Bano controversy has been that many Muslims became conscious of the fact that non-Muslims in this country have a poor opinion of their community's personal law. Many Muslim papers have admitted in the last two months that customary practices of the community have contributed much to giving a wrong impression to other communities about the shariat. One conservative Urdu daily from Bombay said recently — almost as a confession — that some Muslims do treat their women as chattel and there is an urgent need to reform this attitude. There have also been appeals to the Ulama to help draft a code of conduct for the community.

Notwithstanding all this, an overwhelming majority of Muslims resist with great determination the idea of a common civil code. Any member of the community who pleads for such a code, or even for some reform in Muslim personal law, is considered an apostate and not given a proper hearing. This may explain why many Muslim radicals who had been so outspoken in favour of reform when the Shah Bano case began, now prefer to lie low.

It is important to remember that social reform cannot be brought about merely by legislation. Those who wax eloquent on the need to help poor Muslim women by reforming Muslim personal law should see how little the anti-dowry laws have helped to eradicate that evil from Hindu society. Social reform is assisted more by education and economic factors than by laws passed by legislatures.

We have to look at the backwardness of Muslims in education, and their poverty, to understand why several archaic customs survive. In

1983; the secretary of the Minorities Commission said that Muslims were ten times more backward in education than other communities. Our primary task, therefore, must be to remove this backwardness rather than to lament the excesses being committed on Muslim women by their husbands.

To know how deeply the Muslim masses are opposed to any change in their personal law it would be enough to see how the late Hamid Dalwai's efforts at reform failed to make an impact on the community. The people remain unconvinced by the moderates who plead that there is enough scope within the framework of the Quran for necessary reforms. As a matter of fact, all modernists, whether radicals or moderates, are regarded as renegades.

This conflict between the modernists and traditionalists is nothing new. A storm was raised in the nineteenth century when Sir Syed Ahmed Khan, founder of the Aligarh Muslim University, asked Muslims to learn English and reform their social customs. The Ulama were furious and Syed Ahmed Khan was virtually declared an apostate. In the end, though he succeeded to some extent in persuading the Muslim elite to receive modern education through English, his ideas on the religious thought and social customs of the Muslims had no impact on his community as a whole.

Much has changed since the days of Syed Ahmed Khan, and the Muslims of the subcontinent have accepted many practices which they loathed in those times. One of the greatest changes has been that the people of Pakistan have accepted considerable reform in Muslim personal law. Polygamy has been practically banned there and the traditional Muslim divorce, making it easy for a man to get rid of an unwanted wife, has been replaced by new laws. There are some other Muslim countries too where traditional laws have been similarly amended.

But these arguments cut no ice with Muslims in India. This is because Muslims live here amid a non-Muslim majority, and the Government, though elected by all communities, is largely non-Muslim in character. Therefore, although the civil laws in India may not have anything to do with religion, to the average Muslim they are all Hindu laws.

Not surprisingly, therefore, whenever there is any talk of reforming Muslim personal law or introducing a common civil code, Muslims fear that Hindu laws are going to be imposed on them. This fear, it must be said, is reinforced by the discrimination a Muslim has to face while dealing with individuals and institutions. This is a fact of life in present-day India; a Muslim cannot escape from it whether he is seeking a job or trying to do business with any organization. Widespread prejudice prevails against the community and, whatever the reason for this may be, it makes a Muslim feel like an alien in his own land.

This discrimination affects adversely not only the Muslims' economic welfare; the cultural heritage with which they have enriched life in India is also being eroded. The most glaring example of this is·the treatment being meted out to Urdu. Though the language has many non-Muslim protagonists, it is the Muslim community which has contributed to most of its growth and is consequently identified with it. A Muslim's love for Urdu is only second to the regard he has for his religion. But what we have done to the language claimed to be its own by the country's largest minority? In its home state (Uttar Pradesh) one cannot even make a representation in Urdu to any Government department.

A Muslim has also to live with the fear of communal riots whose rising graph tells us that even those areas which were earlier considered immune from the virus of communal hatred are no longer safe. Bitterness grows because a Muslim no longer expects the police force, with a negligible number of his co-religionists in it, to save him from marauding mobs. One has only to read the accounts (in Urdu papers) of communal killings in Meerut, Aligarh, Bhiwandi and other places to know what Muslims feel about the role of our police force. Moreover, state governments lack the political will to punish those who are guilty of instigating riots or participating in such killings.

All this makes a Muslim feel that the State in India, which is largely administered by the Hindus, is working to ruin and destroy him and erase his religious identity. We must remember this whenever we cite examples of those Muslim countries which have reformed their civil code. Whatever other difficulties those countries may have faced while introducing changes, governments there did not suffer from the handicap of being regarded as unauthorized to do so.

It will do us no good to relate the question of a common civil code to national integration or unity. We should have seen by this time that any effort to force such a law on the minorities will achieve the opposite. The Shah Bano controversy has already given a handle to obscurantist elements to inflame feelings.

Excerpt from *The Statesman*
25 February 1986

DON'T WE HAVE IT ALREADY?

Vasudha Dhagamvar

A uniform civil code is a Directive Principle of State Policy (Article 44). In our political and constitutional history is also a promise given by an earlier government to agitated Muslim leaders that Muslim personal law will not be touched without a demand from them. Ever since the UCC (uniform civil code) has become identified with the Muslims, it has indeed become a veritable battleground.

On the one side are ranged orthodox Muslim leaders and the Muslim masses, including women, whom they lead. On the other side are reformist Muslims who claim that the reforms they seek are well within the teachings of the Quran; orthodox Hindus; women's groups who are concerned for the helpless women with whom they work; and stray individuals who support the principle of UCC without reference to any holy book.

Then there are the fence sitters. In this category, liberal Hindus of the Government vie for first place. The liberal Hindus are a schizophrenic lot. They would like to be thought tolerant and broadminded towards other religions and other ways of life. At the same time they would like to be on the side of the underdog (namely, the women) and on the side of secularism in public life. The Indian Government stands on two stools and shift its weight from foot to foot. It is committed to a UCC (mercifully there is no deadline for it). But it is also committed to its promise to leave Muslim personal law alone.

Forgotten meanwhile, are the silent spectators who also have an interest in the subject: Christians, Parsis and Jews.

The UCC is a serious and complex subject. It is high time we had a serious nationwide debate over it. One can start by asking several questions.

About the laws: What is going to be in the UCC? Is there a draft of it? Is it true that we have no uniform civil laws at all? Is it true we have no uniform personal laws?

About the constituency: Who will be affected by the UCC?

The first three questions are relatively easy to answer: There is no draft on the UCC nor has there ever been one. But a concrete draft of the UCC may make both its defenders and denigrators change sides on specific provisions. As things stand we may all be tilting at windmills.

We do have a large number of civil laws that apply to all Indians. Among them are procedural laws like the Civil Procedure Code,

Evidence Act, Registration Act, etc; commercial laws like the Transfer of Property Act, Contract Act, Company Act, banking laws, tax laws, relating to income, sales, customs, excise, etc, miscellaneous enactments such as land revenue codes, and tenancy acts, and socially significant legislation like the Dowry Prohibition Act and the Bonded Labour System (Abolition) Act.

The expression UCC is perhaps a misnomer. It should have been called a Uniform Code of Family Laws. But even here we find that we have several uniform laws: the Special Marriage Act 1872 replaced by the Special Marriage Act 1955; the Indian Succession Act 1875; the Guardians and Wards Act 1890; the Indian Succession Act 1925; the Child Marriage Restraint Act 1929; and the Medical Termination of Pregnancy Act 1971.

Then there are service rules covering government employees and public sector companies which forbid polygamy; provident fund rules treat the wife as the sole successor, as does life insurance.

The Special Marriage Act of 1955 like its predecessor, applies to all Indians irrespective of religion. It enables persons of different religions to marry without either having to convert. It makes the Indian Succession Act applicable to those who marry under it. It also makes the Succession Act applicable to all those who have married under their personal laws and then at any later state have got their marriages registered under the Special Marriage Act. The effect of the registration is retrospective from the date of the religious ceremony. A Hindu man marrying under the Special Marriage Act ceases to be a member of his joint family for purposes of succession to his property.

The Guardians and Wards Act 1890 allows the civil court to appoint a guardian for a minor. While the court is required to have regard for the religion of the minor and the minor's personal laws, the welfare of the minor is paramount. Under the Indian Majority Act every minor is deemed to attain majority on completing 18 years of age. Every minor for whom a guardian has been appointed attains majority on completing 21 years of age, whatever his/her religion.

The Indian Succession Act applies in full to European and Anglo-Indians and Indian Christians. It applies with different exemptions to Parsis, Hindus, Muslims and Jews. Obviously it is not even possible to say that matters relating to family relationships and family property have never been brought under a common law.

I have deliberately included the Medical Termination of Pregnancy Act in this list. No personal laws permit abortion. The MTP Act not only allows it, but is so drafted that even an unmarried mother can avail of it. Nor does a married woman need her husband's consent – altogether as "immoral" an act as one can care to imagine.

Long though the list may be, the fact remains that Muslims who did not object to uniform personal laws enacted up to 1955 are doing so now. Debates erupt over Supreme Court judgements awarding maintenance to divorced women who happen to be Muslims. In both the cases of Bai Tahira and, recently, Shah Bano, the court had awarded maintenance under section 125 of the Criminal Procedure Code, a code whose universal applicability has never been challenged. While some Muslim leaders object to these judgements, others support them.

Meanwhile the idea gains ground that the UCC is all about protecting Muslim women from unilateral talaq, polygamy and denial of maintenance. Is that the truth? What about other minorities? What about children? Even the profile of the helpless, hapless woman beneficiary which is projected is faulty. She is obviously a middle-class or upper-class housewife. She is also childless. She must be because no one seems to press for a mother's right to custody of her children, leave alone the superior right of guardianship.

The only time that the child as an individual with its own rights and needs seems to have concerned the law makers was during the 1970s. From 1972 to 1980 the Adoption Bill was on the cards. It saw passionate debate, joint select committee deliberations, public hearings and two amended versions. Finally it fizzled out. The bill was first introduced in the Rajya Sabha in 1972. It was meant to apply to all Indians, and it was to permit inter-religious adoptions, the child taking on the religion of the adoptive parents.

Muslims and scheduled tribes objected to the bill. The tribal witnesses said that they did not want to adopt from outside their clan or killi, nor did they want to have to register the adoption in court. As things stand, scheduled tribes are not covered by the Hindu Adoption and Maintenance Act. Yet fake adoption of non-tribal boys by tribals is one way by which tribal lands pass on to non-tribals. As no one challenges the adoption, the non-tribal 'son' gets a share which in effect is controlled by his real family. Needless to say he marries in his own caste. So one can see the logic behind their demand. When it was pointed out that India had a large number of cultures, even tribal cultures, one of the witnesses remarked, "In that case let that which is best for the country, be done." Incidentally, some of them wanted their women to have the new, non-traditional right to adopt. A witness from Ranchi said that this might save childless widows from being murdered by rapacious relatives.

Muslims objected to the bill on the sole basis that their personal law did not sanction adoption. It was pointed out that the law, if passed, would not compel them to adopt and that they were being misled on this score. One witness said they did not want a civil law that would allow a Muslim to adopt in defiance of the shariat.

Witnesses were asked by joint select committee members how they or their community had not objected to the Special Marriage Act in 1955. The answer was that no one had asked them, otherwise they would have objected. When their attention was drawn to changes in personal law made in Pakistan, Iran and Turkey, the witnesses replied that those were dictatorships. India was a secular democracy and therefore should not interfere in the personal laws of the minorities — rather a strange interpretation of secularism.

In 1976, the joint select committee presented its report to Parliament, with certain amendments to the original bill. They exempted scheduled tribes from its application, but not Muslims. There was a furore, especially by Muslim intellectuals, at this unwarranted interference in their personal law.

In December 1980, a fresh Adoption Bill, which exempted the Muslims (but not the scheduled tribes) was introduced in the Lok Sabha. Even that did not go through. A debate which had raged for nearly a decade finally came to nought.

As the law stands today a non-Hindu child has no hope of finding a home. Since no one knows the religion of an abandoned infant, unless it goes to a Hindu orphanage — and thereby becomes a Hindu! It cannot be adopted. Even Christians in India cannot adopt.

The real casualty of the aborted Adoption Bill is the child. The Indian Penal Code too boldly lays down that kidnapping is an offence against guardianship — and not against the child. Something is very wrong with our perception of the UCC if we can leave out the child, whether as an individual or in relation to the mother.

At a recent seminar in Delhi, Subramanian Poti, retired chief justice of Gujarat, had suggested that a concrete draft of the UCC may allay the fears of the minorities — the nameless devil always being worse than the named one. In view of what happened to the Adoption Bill this seems unlikely, but we will at least realize how much wider is the scope of the UCC than we think now.

There are any number of civil and family laws which are applicable without regard to the religion of the parties. Further a lot goes on in rural India with which national leaders are not acquainted although they claim to speak on behalf of the nation or a nationwide community.

This is just as true of Muslim leaders. They belong to the "great" tradition, and do not always seem to be aware of what is happening in the "little" tradition. To put it simply the great tradition of a culture (which includes its customary law) is the one which follows from written sources — ancient texts and learned commentaries by scholars secular and divine, down the ages. It embodies the culture of the upper strata of society. It also spans a wide frame of time and space. The little tradition is an oral tradition. There would be reference to the biradari panchas or elders, who in turn would search their memories. Someone may cite a text, but it would not be accompanied by the kind of sophisticated discussion in which urban scholars would engage themselves. Thus the little tradition remains far more localized both in time and space. It is generally blithely unaware of the great tradition, which returns the compliment with compound interest, and less justification.

Thus it was that in the summer of 1980 I came across the practice of adoption amongst Muslims in the Santhal Parganas. I had not been looking for it. I was studying land settlement and overheard my hosts for the day, who were Muslims, talk about it. I asked for details. Some Santhal men present also participated in the discussion. It transpired that Muslims adopted, "just like Hindus".

What did that mean, I asked?

"The Hindus recite the Katha of Satyanarayana; we recite Milad — the story of the birth of the Prophet. Hindus distribute prasad. We distribute shirini. The grown-ups come for the religious function, the children for sweets, and everyone gets to know of the adoption."

Who was given in adoption? The answer was even more curious. I learnt that adoptions were intra-community as well as inter-community. If the boy was of a different community than the adopted father, the latter would ask the child's community elders if they had any objection to the adoption. If they said that they had none, then the adoption took place. Hindus, Muslims and Christians, all adopted and gave in adoption. I was given two instances of adoption of tribal children by Muslims and two of the adoption of orphan Muslim boys by Christians. In every such case the child was given the religion of his adoptive father.

I was still not convinced. Hesitantly I asked why, if this was the practice, their maulvis and leaders were objecting to the Adoption Bill. Silence fell upon my hosts. They were embarrassed, not for their leaders, but for me and my ignorance. But I was a guest so this had to be handled carefully. Came the reply: "Surely you are mistaken. If a poor boy goes to a good home who can mind it? His life is made. It is a good deed. No one can object to it."

After this there was no more to say. I did wonder then, as I do now, at our supreme confidence. Sitting in Delhi or Bombay the "national" leaders are absolutely positive that adoption is against their religious law and yet in the far-away Santhal Parganas, Muslims serenely adopt and give in adoption, even across religions. Their practice was in many ways uncannily identical with the provisions of the Adoption Bill.

National leaders are not even aware of the uses of courts and statutory laws in rural areas. When I was working on land laws in the Maharashtra villages, I found Hindu and Muslim peasants alike deposing before the Agricultural Land Tribunal that they were the karta of their joint family. As everyone knows, karta is purely a concept of the Hindu joint family.

I would like to give another example, this time from West Bengal. Reporting from a mofussil town the correspondent of an English daily from Calcutta told the story of a woman whose husband had gambled her away — a situation not uncommon in our country. What was strange, however, was the news that the wife had gone to the winner, "in order to honour her husband's promise". These words having aroused our curiosity, two of us set out in search of the young woman. We found that she had in fact refused to oblige. The husband had starved her. On the third day of her starvation she had escaped with her baby and run away to her father's village, some ten miles away. A few days later, after consulting the elders, her father took her to the court and she registered a document made on a stamp paper, divorcing her husband. When we visited her the husband had remarried and the community had accepted the divorce. It so happened that these people were Muslims. But that was hardly relevant, for no personal law recognizes this mode of divorce. Even so this divorce was accepted by everyone, including the religious leaders.

A registered document has enormous authority in village India, regardless of what its legal validity might be. That is why the sale of women by their menfolk including their husbands is registered in Gwalior, thinly disguised as agreements of domestic service against "advance" payment of "salary". Ninety-nine per cent of such sales are of Hindu women. These documents, legal pundits never tire of telling us, have no value at all. And yet they are honoured by all parties, including the unfortunate women.

I have tried to make two points. We already have a large number of laws, civil and personal, which have uniform application. And there are local practices by small religious groups, which are unbeknown to their national leaders, contrary to their religious laws.

A third and final point derives from the second. Just as the people who follow the little tradition can be and often are unaware of the great tradition, so are they of the statutory laws, or what the courts accept as the custom of their community. This is because these people — Hindu and Muslim, tribal and non-tribal — take their problems to their panchayat. The UCC will therefore not affect them, at least not for a long time. After all, Hindus, especially in the little tradition, continue to recognize bigamy and child marriage.

The immediate ineffectiveness of such legislation is, however, hardly a reason for not enacting it. If one has a law, one can expect it to become effective at some stage — just because a bonded labourer does not run away, is no reason to retain the legality of bondage. Hindu women are beginning to stretch their wings, and to use their rights.

Muslims have one very real fear; that in the guise of the UCC, Hindu personal law will be thrust upon them. Such a possibility should certainly be resisted. "Secular" or "uniform" should not be synonymous with "Hindu".

At the same time perhaps we should take a long look at the statutory personal laws which have applied to Hindus since 1955 and compare them to Shastric Hindu laws of old. It should then become quite clear that the two have hardly anything to do with each other. Marriage is no longer a sacrament, it is a contract. Divorce and widow remarriage are in. Child marriage is out. So is polygamy. No caste had prohibited polygamy though upper castes had forbidden divorce and remarriage. Daughters and wives inherit, just as do their brothers and sons.

Even adoption has undergone a sea change. Earlier a man adopted a son to give him and his ancestors water after death. If he died without adopting, his widow adopted in his name. Adoption was entirely for religious purposes. Under the Hindu Adoption and Maintenance Act a daughter can be adopted. Widows and unmarried women can adopt in their own right. Adoption has ceased to fulfil a religious need. It is entirely secular in its nature.

Except for a few reference to "sapinda" and "sagotra" and to customary rites, the statutory law has hardly anything to do with the shastras. All which prompted Dr J. Duncan Derrett, that eminent authority on Hindu law, to write a book called the *Death of the Hindu Law*. This is not to suggest that Hindu statutory law is perfect. Far from it, Hindu statutory law should also not be equated with secular or uniform law.

At any rate to ensure that the law of the majority is not imposed upon them lock, stock and barrel, the minorities must come up with constructive suggestions and the minorities must include, prominently, non-Muslims and tribals, otherwise they will be burdened with the laws of the two largest communities in the country. Merely to say ad nauseum: "This is against our religion", is no way to get a good UCC and it may not be the way, for very long, for stalling a uniform civil code.

Excerpt from *Mainstream*
6 July 1985

THE HINDU DEMAND FOR COMMON CIVIL CODE
Rajshekar V. T.

India's ruling class is a past master in sidetracking issues and diverting attention from the burning problems to mislead the people. As it controls the media, it can make and unmake things. It can convert a simple non-issue into an earth-shaking affair. This is what is happening today to the Muslim personal law (MPL). It began with the cry for emancipation of the Muslim women; the slogan was later amended to MPL. Finally the cry now is for the adoption of a common civil code (CCC).

The intention earlier was to annoy and harass the Muslims, the most uncompromising enemy of Brahminism, but now it appears that the intention is to adopt MPL for Hindus also. The upper castes have realized the hollowness of the Hindu law of marriage and inheritance and the usefulness of the MPL. This is evident from the fact that slowly and systematically the different changes that have been brought about in the Hindu law are an imitation of the progressive features of the MPL eg. divorce, right of inheritance for women, widow marriage etc. As the Hindu law is still in a transitory stage, the final destination of it is likely to be largely adoption of the MPL. But as it hurts the Hindu pride and arrogance to directly admit the superiority of the MPL, it is likely they have now adopted the safer device of a CCC, knowing full well that Muslims are not going to budge an inch from their law. And if ever they agree to a CCC, they will insist upon the total adoption of their own law. And the Hindus may intend to do so to show it as a gesture of goodwill to please the Muslims, but in reality to enjoy the fruits of the MPL. This is the secret which many Muslims also have not understood.

Such a conclusion is possible from the following facts:

1. When the Hindu Marriages Act was passed in 1955, and the Hindu Succession Act in 1956, there was already an Indian Succes-

sion Act. If the Hindu intention then was a CCC, they could have straight away called the Hindu Marriages Act as the "Indian" Marriages Act and the "Indian" Succession Act with suitable amendments if necessary. This would have taken care of all Indians. Still they passed the Hindu Marriages Act and the Hindu Succession Act exclusively for themselves. Where was their sense of "national integration" at that time and why did they not think abolishing the "communal laws" then? Does this it not expose the upper caste motive behind today's cry for CCC?

2. Previously there was no provision for divorce in the Hindu law. They hated and even now hate talaq, but still they provided divorce in the Hindu Marriage Act but made it so difficult that by the time an unwilling couple gets a decree of divorce their youth is lost. And after spoiling the lives of millions of unfortunate couples they came a little nearer to the Islamic law and introduced the provision of "divorce by mutual consent" after a year of marriage if both consent. But this provision is there for the Hindus only in the book. Some unwilling urban women use this chance, refuse to give their consent, and live separately claiming maintenance from their husbands. To avoid such a situation, some Hindu men have adopted two methods (a) they burn their wives to death destroying evidence of murder and project the crime as suicide. The so-called "dowry deaths" are in fact divorce deaths; (b) The other method is to marry another wife. Judicial decisions banning bigamy need such strict proof that it is virtually impossible to prove this second marriage, and if it is proved, it does not help either the first wife or the second wife. Both suffer because it leads to imprisonment of the husband under the Indian penal code. Hindu society is male-dominated and this has full religious sanction.

It is said a man tortured by his "unmanageable" wife feels it better to face an imaginary, unproven imprisonment than to get 10 years spoiled in protracted litigation and ruin his entire life. Many women's organizations are demanding that the strictness of the proof of second marriage should be diluted to book the bigamous husband. But if this is done and the second marriage is easily established, it will create a bigger problem of inheritance. The husband and the second wife also keep it a secret to avoid penal consequences. Thus a bigamous husband goes scotfree. Therefore, the only solution arrived at by the authorities on Hindu law is to simplify the law of evidence on second marriage and punish the bigamist and give, as a consequence, equal rights to the second wife and her children. The authorities feel that once this is done, it will be virtual adoption of the MPL minus the penalty for bigamy which they are ashamed to admit as it hurts the Hindu pride. The Hindu Marriage Act here has no solution and the minds of jurists are baffled.

3. A Hindu "suffering" at the hands of his wife due to her alleged adultery, callousness, sexual frigidity, arrogance, disease, and her higher social status under which she becomes a judge, officer, politician, social worker etc. which take away more of her time for these purposes than for her husband, or the man falling in love with another woman, like the actor, Dharmendra, and those who intend to take a second wife for any other reason (matrimonial matters being purely private affairs it is impossible to enumerate all reasons), resort to another method. They simply file an affidavit before a court that they have embraced Islam and thus get covered by the MPL and then take a second wife. Here the Hindus feel that the MPL rescues such people in distress and therefore, it must be destroyed. A Hindu keeps his conscience in cold-storage whenever he wants to take advantage of a thing, even if it is hostile to his religion. Talaq is one such thing.

4. The provision of divorce in MPL is preceded by many personal and social obligations like advice, sleeping separately for some period and persuasion by elders of both sides. Only after all these steps are exhausted, is talaq pronounced. The Hindu Marriages Act has also adopted these obligations — the difference being that the Hindu law wants these obligations to be performed by the judge. Efforts by the husband and wife and the elders are not recognized. The upper caste IAS-dominated bureaucrats, who are the *de facto* legislators of India, do not feel that the husbands, wives and elders are wise enough, and that they alone possess all the wisdom. After torturing millions of unwilling couples, they have now adopted the provision of divorce by mutual consent.

5. Every fifth house of an urban educated Hindu is a broken house. The initial infatuation being over, the office-going couple drift and estrangement creeps in. As the hold of religion is hardly there on the Hindus and ethics have no role to play in their life, soon the husband tries to imitate his polygamous and lecherous Aryan gods. And there the trouble begins. But middle-class morality prevents them from breaking the marriage because their religion helps neither the husband nor the wife. Such Hindus naturally like to take advantage of talaq.

6. A divorce of a Muslim couple gets a lot of publicity because the media is in the hands of Hindus. But the daily papers carry stories of innumerable broken Hindu houses. The husband and wife quarrel

and their going to the police and even leading to murder are a daily affair in India. But husband and wife discord is a rarity among Muslims because of the Muslim value system.

After analysing the rationale behind the Hindu mind in his latest cry for a CCC, we would like to throw some light on Muslim polygamy and talaq with reference to other laws to show the other side of the coin.

Muslim polygamy: despite living in a country where his sixth neighbour is a Muslim, the Hindu "intellectual" still wants to learn about Islam and Muslims from the books written by anti-Muslim European propagandists of the nineteenth century. After failing to wrench power from the Muslims, European authors have now started disproving all that they had once written. But the Hindu writer, journalist, judge, and bureaucrat still reads the same propaganda stuff and continues to say that every Muslim marries four women.

In UP schools, Hindu teachers tell young children in classes that "every Muslim eats during his lifetime 20 cows. And if we kill one Muslim, we can save 20 cows." Upper castes believe more in propaganda than facts. The Hindu collects statistics, conducts socio-economic surveys, mingles with Muslims and knows that not even one in the hundred Muslims he meets has more than one wife. A Hindu believes what he wants to believe. Still he goes on harping that every Muslim marries four women according to the MPL. The pity is that 95 per cent of the Muslims are so poor that they can't afford even one wife. But who is interested in facts? The Hindu refuses to think that just as the provision for divorce that he himself has introduced in the Hindu Marriage Act is applicable only in particular cases, so also the provision of Muslim polygamy applies only in particular cases.

The Hindu refuses to understand that marriage is not merely for sex, but also to meet other moral and social requirements like social security, economic guarantee in old age, mutual support, to protect war-widows, parentage, to help the disabled and cripled etc. Dowry has become a major problem in society partly because the number of girls far exceeds the population of marriageable boys. Since there are more girls than boys, parents of the boys can afford to be choosy. They search for younger, wealthier, and more beautiful girls and the older, poorer and not so beautiful girls may remain unmarried. That is why dowry demands exist and are paid.

These poor, older and not-so-good-looking girls are left to remain unmarried throughout their lives. They become housemaids, prostitutes, labourers and, in the advanced cities, call-girls, sales girls, and other white-collared employees etc. In medieval England, unmarried girls had adopted spinning as a means of livelihood and were called spinsters, which word even today is retained conveying the same meaning. Exploitative, male-dominated society, consisting of sex-starved journalists, politicians, bureaucrats and capitalists, make their surroundings glamorous employing these unfortunate, exploited women. So long as they are youthful they are wanted everywhere and, on attaining old age, they are left uncared for. To keep their future assured, the wise among these women run brothels and the unwise become housemaids, beggars or footpath vendors.

Pre-communist Shanghai had hundreds of such prostitutes. But the Chinese revolution ended male domination and with it prostitution became a thing of the past. To prostitutes their entire life is a life of misery. Somehow they exist but they never get their greatest natural desire fulfilled — the desire of motherhood — unless they are prepared to become unwed mothers. Who can solve their problem and give them a child and protection for their entire life?

Muslim scholars say it is to avoid the misery of such unfortunate women that the provision of polygamy is provided in Islam. (Sir M. Zafrullah Khan: *Islam — Its Meaning for Modern Man*; 1962). Is it not better for a woman to become someone's official second wife than to be a prostitute, keep or concubine, massager topless bearer, a call-girl and the like? The provision for polygamy in Islam, they say, is more in the interest of woman than in the interest of man. And we have every reason to believe that a woman is better treated among the Muslims than among the Hindus. Family life has a sanctity among Muslims. But to an upper caste Hindu, the woman is a doormat. Manu has said so.

The Hindu religion never took any interest in the woman's well being. The Brahmin considers everybody except himself and the cow to be Shudras (servants of Brahmins). Even a Brahmin woman is a Shudra. When 98 per cent of the non-Brahmin population (including 2 per cent Brahmin women) is Shudra, the Brahmin bureaucrat, jurist and journalist has no need to think from a rational angle; enough, if he has the media in his pocket. He is jealous that the MPL coupled with the high moral teachings of Islam, which every Muslim knows, has saved the Muslims from his clutches, and everyday scores of his slaves are freeing themselves from his clutches and embracing Islam. He desires that either this law is abolished so that Muslims also suffer like others or it is adopted for himself so that he may also enjoy the fruits of MPL. But Muslims are neither changing their law nor are they giving their law to the Hindu as CCC — notwithstanding threats of "Socialist Brahmins" like E.M.S. Namboodiripad.

The MPL is the only one which for the first time in the world recognized marriage not as a sacrament but as a contract; providing for divorce when such a contract, instead of helping the parties, causes hindrances. Islam is the only religion that for the first time gave the right of property to woman. All laws in the world today also consider marriage as a contract providing for divorce. Muslim social life has been highly moral more because of polygamy than because of marriage being a contract. Islam frowned upon adultery very severely.

Between the twentieth century and the seventh century, when the Mohammadan law was framed, millions of non-Muslim women have been drowned in water and burnt as witches in Europe. Since European laws did not provide for divorce and polygamy, husbands resorted to keeping mistresses, and to get rid of the unwanted wives, they accused them of "witchcraft".

The procedure adopted to prove witchcraft, which had the sanction of the church, state and the society, was to tie the hands and feet of the accused woman and throw her in water to be drowned, in which case the clergy absolved her of witchcraft and blessed her. If by chance she was not drowned, it was taken as a proof of her devilish power through which she was saved from drowning and she was condemned as a witch, the punishment for which was death by burning on a heap of wood. Either way, the moment a woman was accused of witchcraft she was sure to die. This was said to be the method adopted by European society to get rid of an unwanted wife. Instead of the words "I divorce you," the husband used to say: "My wife is a witch." This had a twofold object — to get rid of the existing wife and to get a second wife.

In India, women are exploited more than in any other country, because it has the sanction of Hindu religion and custom. God Rama's father, Dasarata, had many thousands of wives in addition to his three queens. Rama banished his wife Sita on suspicion of infidelity. Krishna's Radha was not his wife. Most of the Aryan gods were debauched and indulged in perverse sex. Thus polygamy, desertion, concubinage and adultery (rape) and even polyandry (Draupadi and the Pandavas) have religious sanction in Hinduism. Go to any temple and you see the proof of it carved on the temple walls. Rajneesh says Hinduism is the other word for free sex. The Hindu's obsession for sex is so great that he crystallized it into the worship of the male organ (linga) — a practice found in no other religion.

But the upper caste Hindus, who worship these very same Hindu

gods even today, consider the acts of his gods as a crime in the twentieth century if practised by a man. If Lord Macaulay while writing
the IPC had not taken the Mohammadan law of crime as the base,
adultery, rape, polygamy, gambling, obscenity, etc. would not have
been crimes in Hindu India. The widow of a Kshatriya had to die as
a sati; the widow of a Brahmin to live discarded with shaven head;
and widows of the Shudras had no restrictions of any kind. In common Hindi, or Hindustani, there is one word 'rand' for both prostitutes and widows. Thus, a Shudra widow was also a prostitute. De-
vadasi, a system of prostitution sanctioned by Hindu religion, is
practised even today and untouchable women are its main victims.
These women are enjoyed by the temple priests to whom woman
and money are not untouchable. Such a sex maniac is today trying
to give a lesson in morality to the Muslim!

History says in every time and place man has exploited the woman
for sex without any reciprocal responsibility upon himself, including
the responsibility to look after his own illegitimate children. Except
in socialist countries like China, Russia etc., a woman has a subor-
dinate place — even in USA, the world's richest country. Only the
official wife to take care of and be responsible for, and a variety of
women surrounding him (in the form of assistants, colleagues, sales
girls, call-girls, singers, dancers, artists, etc) is certainly the most
welcome thing for a rich, lecherous, lazy, easygoing man. Most of
the Aryan gods belong to this category. But Islam prohibits all this.
It provides for whipping a man for sex out of marriage, compels him
to have sex only after marriage, that too with the woman he loves.
He has to pay her the money demanded by her as mehr and binds
him to look after her and her children, entitling her children to inheritance even if she is divorced. He has to protect every woman
with whom he wants to have sex. This is the object of the MPL. Thus
Prophet Mohammad has come to help the women. MPL therefore
protects and honours woman. (Alfred Guillaume: *Islam*; Penguin
Books; 1954; p. 71). Apart from the Muslim men, the other party
who should feel aggrieved is the first wife. But to help build a healthy unexploitative society everybody has to suffer to some extent
and Mohammad's moral teachings have that much influence on his
female followers too, that they prefer their husbands to have a co-
wife than lead the life of a sinful debauch.

Muslims do not apply logic and dialectics to escape from the
rigours of the Islamic law, morals and prayers. Ramzan fasting without a single drop of water through the hot days of June for 15 to 18
hours a day, is one such example. Said Prophet Mohammad: "Of all

the permissible things the most hateful before God and me is talaq," and never resort to talaq.

The Hindu lawyers, jurists and "intellectuals" are, therefore, advised to read George Bernard Shaw's preface to his book, *On Getting Married*, and then come out with fresh arguments if they can find any.

Islamic polygamy has always been a distributor of wealth. Second and subsequent wives have always been from poorer families and their mehr have been higher, mostly in the form of solid immovables. This is one of the reasons that capitalism with all its evils has not developed in any Muslim country and the gap between the rich and poor is not so wide as in other non-communist countries.

No religion has assured full equality to women. It is only under socialism that the exploitation of women is prevented and sexual equality is assured. But our Hindu zealots are not interested in socialism but in Muslim-baiting. This shall not be allowed.

Extract from *The Dalit Voice*
16 August 1985

BEHIND DEMANDS FOR A UNIFORM CIVIL CODE
Javed Anand

With its decision to enact a new legislation, shifting the burden of maintenance of a divorced Muslim woman from her husband to her blood relations, the Union Government hopes to kill two birds with one stone. On the one hand, it seeks to silence the demand from several quarters that a Muslim woman be assured the guarantee of maintenance as any other woman of a different religious pursuasion. On the other hand, it expects to soothe the inflamed nerves of that vocal and organized section of the Muslim community according to whose interpretation of the shàriat and the Quran, the responsibility for the maintenance of a woman rests squarely with her blood relations and not with the husband once the period of iddat is over.

But this is unlikely to settle the storm raised in the wake of the Supreme Court judgement in the Shah Bano case either in the short or the long run. The Shah Bano case itself was concerned merely with the question of the right of a divorced Muslim woman to maintenance from her husband. But in the battle of demands and counter-demands that followed, the argument for a common/uniform civil code surfaced once again. A common or a uniform civil code is concerned not merely with the issue of maintenance, but a gamut of issues, pertaining to marriage, divorce, maintenance, custody of children, succession rights, and if you stretch the argument a bit further, even guardianship and adoption.

In the process, a political polarization of a most unusual kind has resulted, making nonsense of the traditional divides. Thus, we have, on the one hand, a large section of the left, many segments of the woman's movement and apparently, a sizable section of the Christian church, side by side with most communal Hindu organizations, arguing fervently in favour of a common civil code. On the other hand, are the fundamentalist Muslims who are vehemently opposed to any suggestion of changes in the Muslim personal law, leave alone tolerate talk of a common civil code. In an intermediate position between the two, lie a section of Muslim reformists and a section of the left and women's activists, whose arguments range from an immediate codification of Muslim personal law to a step-by-step progress towards a uniform, and ultimately, a common civil code.

While the demand for a uniform or a common civil code has been voiced with varying degrees of intensity at different points in post-Independence India, the fact remains that till today no draft of what a common civil code may look like exists. As of now, in matters concerning marriage, divorce, judicial separation, maintenance, custody of children, inheritance and adoption, Hindus, Muslims, Christians and other religious communities are governed by their separate personal laws. As an optional equalizer, exists the Special Marriages Act, 1954, which is open to a member from any religious community who opts for a civil marriage. Thus the secular statute has its own provision for divorce etc. Apparently, only Muslims are staunchly opposed to a common civil code. Does it mean then that a common civil code will be at great variance only with the Muslim personal law? Or does it mean that the other communities are more amenable to change than the Muslims?

To the knowledge of this correspondent, Prof. S.P. Sathe, the pro-vice-chancellor, Pune University, is the first one in the country to have recently taken upon himself the task of drafting a common civil code. In a telephone conversation, Prof. Sathe stated that, in the process of compiling all the provisions of the existing personal laws governing different religious communities, he has run into difficulty in extracting the religious from the non-religious components of these laws. "In some respects, even the recent changes in laws for Hindus have failed to fully secularize these laws," he maintained.

Citing an example, he pointed out that though, at the moment, law enables only a Hindu to adopt, he can only adopt a Hindu child. Moreover, he can adopt a child as a son only if he does not have a son, or adopt a girl if he does not have a daughter. This law is inspired by the Hindu's religious need for a male child to facilitate his heavenly journey after death and not to enable a person to give expression to love and affection to a child not his own, he pointed out. "The task now appears to be more difficult than I originally thought and all I can anticipate at the moment is that some plurality may have to be provided for, even in a uniform civil code," Prof. Sathe opined.

Pending the formulation, however rudimentary, of a draft, the most coherent touchstone being suggested for the drafting of a common civil code comes from women's rights activists and women lawyers with years of experience in dealing with the issue of women's rights. The simple demand of the women's movement is that a woman should have equal rights as a man and that no nation or religious community can take refuge in its cultural heritage, religious scriptures (divine or otherwise) or tradition to deny to women their present-day demands.

Writes Indira Jaising of the Lawyer's Collective in the latest edition of the newly-started *The Lawyers*, "The demand for reform (in personal laws in favour of a common civil code) must be a demand for sexual equality. It would be better to reformulate the demand so as to focus on the sex discrimination which is written into all personal laws. This will have the merit of not only emphasizing the secular nature of the demand but also its rationale, namely, the urgent need to make equality for women a reality under a Constitution that guarantees equality between sexes."

"I am convinced of the need for a common civil code here and now not so much because of general considerations about the desirable laws for a secular society etc., but because it will have a crucial bearing on the status of all Indian women who are discriminated to one extent or another by the existing laws," argued Ansuya Dutt, a noted lawyer with years of experience in dealing with matrimonial cases. In her opinion, Indian women remain divided and exploited, the more so on account of being divided along the frames set by the different personal laws. When brought under the purview of a single statute, women would more easily unite on a common platform and fight far more effectively for changes in their favour, she held.

What are the lacunas in the existing personal laws and how do women suffer as a result? The broad consensus on this issue is the following:

Hindu personal laws: The Hindu Marriage Act, 1955, which took its inspiration from the Special Marriages Act, rather than from Hindu scriptures or traditions, is commonly recognized as being the most progressive legislation from a woman's point of view. Amongst many other benefits, this enactment put to an end the centuries-old practice of polygamy and of keeping concubines amongst Hindu males. Besides, it transformed marriage from a sacrament into a contract, even making possible divorce by mutual consent between a Hindu couple. The Hindu Marriage Act is today virtually one and the same as the Special Marriages Act. One of the limitations of the Hindu Succession Act, 1956, is that while a woman is entitled to equal share of self-acquired property, she is denied any share in ancestral property.

Muslim personal law: The greatest discrimination against women in the still uncodified Muslim personal law in this country from a woman's point of view lies in the continued legal sanction to polygamy and the right to a Muslim man to divorce his wife by merely repeating talaq three times. A woman desirous of divorcing her husband under certain grounds, however, has to take recourse to a court of law under the provisions of the Dissolution of Muslim Marriages Act, 1939. As to the question of maintenance after divorce, that's what the Shah Bano controversy is all about. Besides, it is stated that while on the issue of custody of children the courts are guided primarily by the criteria of the welfare of the child in the case of all other personal laws, in case the Muslim personal law, the husband becomes the automatic custodian of the children, once the children attain a certain age.

Christian personal law: By common consent, the present Christian personal law is by far the most discriminatory against women. In the matter of divorce, for example, a Catholic can divorce his wife only on grounds of adultery and for no other reason. On the other hand, divorce sought by a woman on grounds of adultery is admissible only if this allegation is coupled with complaints of serious cruelty (of a nature which endangers her very life) or adultery coupled with desertion without reasonable cause for desertion for two years or more. If a Christian woman is proved guilty of adultery, the law provides that her entire property can be settled on her children and husband, a severe form of penalty that is not aimed at women from other communities. A Catholic couple seeking divorce must both obtain an annulment of the marriage certificate and a court decree before either party can contemplate remarriage.

The above are just some instances of discrimination against a woman vis-a-vis the man as per the provisions of the existing personal laws concerning the three major Indian communities. But, in the process of drawing up a common civil code, is there nothing in any one or more of the existing personal laws that are beneficial to women and could therefore be incorporated in a common civil code or to set them as one of the guidelines for a uniform civil code?

"Yes there are," opined Dutt. The provision for divorce by mutual consent as available in the Hindu Marriage Act or the Special Marriage Act, should be generalized. According to Dutt, one extremely relevant ground for divorce available to a Muslim woman alone today is the failure or neglect of her husband to maintain her for at least two years. She argued that in the socio-economic conditions prevailing in India today, this ground should be made available to all Indians. She is also strongly in favour of the mehr system amongst Muslims being generalized to all in addition to a guarantee of maintenance. A sum of money given by the husband to his wife at the time of marriage is one basic security for her, she argued. The Christian woman, it would appear, enjoys no advantages that could be sought to be extended to others.

If the progressive elements of the existing personal laws are synthesized, would that suffice? "No," say Jaising and Dutt, amongst many others. The totally new provisions proposed include — irretrievable breakdown of marriage as a ground for divorce, right of a divorced woman not merely for maintenance from the husband's income, but also a share in the husband's assets, and father and mother to be treated as joint natural guardians of children, against the present situation where only the father remains the natural guardian under all circumstances.

How do religious leaders from different communities respond to propositions of a common civil code or a uniform civil code as provided in the Directive Principles of the Constitution (as opposed to a common or uniform civil code that admits a plurality within the larger framework of the ethos of the state to which all the civil laws must conform as a minimum condition) whose guidelines may be handpicked from different personal laws or with new guidelines altogether?

"If complete equality between the sexes is the basic implication of a uniformity in all personal laws, then I am certain that it does not in any way violate the spirit or the normative aspect of the Quran," argues Muslim reformist leader, Asghar Ali Engineer. He contends that in the different socio-economic circumstances prevailing today, the formal aspect of law could be changed without jeopardizing the religious conviction of Muslims.

"History shows that whenever state laws and Hindu tradition have come in conflict, the Hindu samaj has come around to accepting modern laws," stated Vikram Savarkar, president, Akhil Bhartiya Hindu Mahasangh. He added that in his view an ideal civil code must be drafted by the coming together of top thinkers and legal pundits akin to the members of the Constituent Assembly. "Whatever they decide will be acceptable to Hindus and I am not worried about where all the individual elements of the code are taken from," he added. However, pending the finalizing and adoption of such an "ideal code", Savarkar demanded that the present Hindu Code Bill be made applicable to all Indians "since Hindus are well over 80 per cent of the total population".

Shiv Sena chief, Bal Thackeray, who declined to be drawn into commenting on elements or principles or sources of a common code, vociferously demanded that "one country must have only one rule of law and no concessions should be made at all to anyone in drawing up a draft". He argued that if Dr Ambedkar and others were not expected to consult all communities while drawing up the Constitution, there is no reason why things should be otherwise in drafting a common code.

After five years of ceaseless campaign for the repeal of the laws governing family matters of Christians and in favour of a common civil code, Kenneth A. Phillips, a believing Catholic, has no doubt that he has brought the Church hierarchy and a large percentage of the Christian community in favour of a common civil code. In support of his claim, Phillips points out that not only have numerous articles written by him in the mainstream national newspapers drawn favourable reactions from Christians, but his articles have even found place in religious magazines such as *The Examiner, The New Leader, The Herald* and *Home Life*.

The endorsement of Phillips' struggle for a common civil code comes from no less a person than Father Oswald Gracias, chancellor and Judge of the Ecclesiastical Court of the Archdiocese of Bombay. "It is my personal view that for the sake of national integration it would be a good thing that there be a common civil code for all Indians," Father Gracias told this correspondent in an interview. Stating that he failed to see why the civil law of any country should be called upon to reinforce religious laws, he added that, in his assessment, if the issue of a common civil code were to be officially brought on the agenda, the entire Church heirarchy would finally consent to it "in the interest of national integration". He admitted that the existing Christian divorce laws in India are discriminatory against women and that the sexes should be brought on par. Father Gracias, however, added that, instead of a common civil code being thrust on any community, it would be wise to first prepare a climate in its favour.

Extract from *The Sunday Observer*
23 February 1986

DOCUMENTATION

THE PERSONAL LAW FALLOUT

There have been, paradoxically, some benefits from the introduction of the Protection of Rights of Women Bill in Parliament, and perhaps the most important of these is that the liberal Muslim has suddenly discovered his voice. Moreover, it is a pleasant sound. A momentum that was growing in different parts of the country found a culmination in the resignation of Mr Arif Mohammad Khan from the Government. And it is this assertion of liberal Muslim opinion, rather than protests from anywhere else, which has put the Government on the defensive. But it is necessary to understand the compulsions which forced the Government to bring in this bill, and to appreciate when precisely the first and crucial round of this battle was lost.

When the Supreme Court judgement on the Shah Bano case was delivered, the response of the conservatives was hardly unpredictable. It was evident that they would oppose what they believed to be interference in the personal law of the Muslims; and it was equally obvious that their support on this issue would extend beyond simply the conservative pale. But even so, they could not build a public movement on this issue very easily. It was only after they put into effect a clever and well tried ruse that the response began to come from ordinary Muslims. What they did was simple: they shifted the issue involved in the Supreme Court judgement. The Supreme Court had ruled essentially on the rights of women in Muslim civil law. What the conservatives turned the battle into was the rights of Muslims in secular India. Instead of taking a position on whether women should be given protection from errant, aggressive and sometimes fickle husbands, the conservatives labelled the Supreme Court judgement the death warrant of Muslim identity in a Hindu-majority state. From pulpit and rostrum, in city street and village mosque, the maulvis spread the fear that this was the beginning of a fresh assault on the Muslim pattern of life. Full use was made of a few incidental — and unfortunate — remarks made in the course of the judgement which tended to disparage Islam. Today, they said, it was just the divorce law; tomorrow, the Supreme Court would begin to arbitrate on whether Muslims should be allowed to sound the azaan or pray in their mosques. (And a not-so-subtle use was made of the disputed monuments like the Babari mosque or the Ram Janam Bhoomi.) After Mr Arif Mohammad Khan, with the encouragement of the prime minister, put up his brilliant defence of the Supreme Court judgement in Parliament, the focus of the attack became Rajiv Gandhi, and the aim became political — the use of this confrontation to destroy the Muslim support base of the Congress. Moreover, an opportunity was beckoning — the by-elections of December 1985.

The tragedy is not that the conservatives played the game; after all, nothing else could have been expected. The truth is that the Opposition parties, with the commendable and praiseworthy exception of the Communists, participated fully in these dangerous communal politics. Leading the field in this was, unfortunately, the Janata Party: and we say unfortunately because there is a strong section of the party which watched helplessly as it moved into dangerous eddies. From the Janata platform during the by-elections the cry went up in front of Muslim audiences that Islam was once again in danger in India and it was time for the Muslims to show Delhi the extent of their power through the ballot box. It was, again, not only Syed Shahabuddin who made use of this strategy in his election from Kishanganj; the Muslim leaders who campaigned in Kendrapara in Orissa, as Chief Minister J.B. Patnaik ruefully complained, had the same message to offer. The strategy worked. And all the Congressmen who had kept their views to themselves suddenly popped up; after all, if there is one thing which a Congressman finds hard to swallow, it is defeat.

And Rajiv Gandhi too began to panic. He understood as much as anyone else that there was no way that the Congress could win an election without the support of the Muslims. The price that the leaders of the anti-Shah Bano case agitation demanded was an insurance policy — through a bill in Parliament. It is hardly surprising that the Janata still has not been able to make up its mind on how to vote on the bill. And Syed Shahabuddin, of course, is sitting pretty — for a while, he is a little more important than his colleagues. Cynicism has been the basis of decisions by everyone in this sordid business, and the trap has now securely tightened. The prime minister has told the Lok Sabha (to cheers from MPs) that the decision to bring in the bill was in continuation of the promise made at the time of framing the Constitution that the identity of every minority in India would be protected, implying that if this is the asking price then the Government has no option but to pay it.

The only parties to emerge with any credit are the Communists, and in particular the CPI(M) because the CPI(M) has to survive in two states with strong Muslim populations: West Bengal and Kerala. But the CPI(M) has been able to stick to its principled stand because it is a political party in the true sense, with a cadre which can go to the people and fight the battle against vested interests at the ground level. The Congress, which should have played a similar role, did not do so for the simple reason that the Congress party organization just does not exist; it is only a label which proves useful during elections rather than a political and ideological organization. It is this weakness which has proved so dangerously suicidal for the Congress in this crisis. It does not need much intelligence to guess what the implications of this are for the future.

Editorial, *The Telegraph*
7 March 1986

THE REAL GRIEVANCE

However retrograde and dangerous the proposed legislation on the rights of divorced Muslim women, the sad fact may have to be conceded that a majority of Muslims in India are opposed to any reform of what they believe to be shariat law. This is no argument against the Supreme Court judgement in the Shah Bano case, which merely upholds a divorced Muslim woman's right to claim maintenance under the law of the land without closing her option to be content with what is said to be provided under Muslim personal law. Nor is it an argument in favour of the Government's bill which seeks to deprive her of what she can claim for her husband under the relevant provisions of the Criminal Procedure Code, driving her to uncertain protection by others. The bill violates every canon of moral and social justice and is a shocking affront to human dignity; if the majority of India's Muslims do not find it repugnant to their individual and collective conscience, it is a depressing commentary on their sense of values and the level of their social awareness. But it will not do merely to deplore their outlook; it needs also to be examined why it persists. Clearly, more enlightened views can emerge only with a greater spread of education; but leaders of the community have not done nearly enough to promote education among the Muslim masses. Not merely the mullahs and other custodians of blind orthodoxy, but even many of the educated Muslim leaders seem to have a vested interest in the ignorance and social backwardness of the Muslim majority. Even this, however, is not the full explanation for the persistence of an obscurantist and separatist attitude.

If Muslims resist any attempt at reform in the name of their distinctive religious identity, it is at least partly because of a fear that any dilution of this identity would make them more vulnerable in a Hindu majority nation. Instead of realizing that reform, facilitating their integration in a non-sectarian national ethos, would enable them to compete with the majority community on common terms, they retreat further into a supposedly protective shell of isolation. This may be a perverse reaction, but others — which means mainly the Hindus — need also to consider whether they have done enough to demonstrate that Muslims stand to gain by a close identification with the national mainstream. In fact, the Hindus must ask themselves whether they have done much to help such integration; if social barriers persist, it is not merely because of Muslim orthodoxy. More important, the economic deprivation of a large number of Muslims cannot be explained entirely in terms of the community's social and educational backwardness; the laws and the rules may be entirely fair, but at least in some areas a suitable, and not always so subtle, discrimination does operate in practice in employment and other economic opportunities. This should be the community's real grievance, not any imaginary threat to their religious identity. This must in fact be a deeply felt grievance, but unfortunately it manifests itself not in demands for social and economic justice but in resistance to reform which is perceived as a threat to a distinctive identity. Justice is guaranteed by law, but the law cannot undo all the effects of instinct or conscious prejudice. The Muslims would be better able to fight injustice and safeguard their genuine interests if they were less obsessed with their separate tradition and culture, and their leaders less interested in perpetuating this obsession.

Editorial, *The Statesman*
10 March 1986

SCRAP THE BILL

Mr Arif Mohammad Khan has made history. He has demonstrated that some Congressmen still possess a conscience which stirs on certain issues; since the early sixties it is difficult to recall the last occasion when a Congress minister resigned on an issue of principle. Mr Khan's action is historic on two other counts. First, he is a Muslim, and let us face it, Muslim ministers must feel even more helpless than Hindu ministers in standing up to the prime minister. Secondly, he has resigned in protest against a bill which on any reckoning enjoys significant, if not majority, support in the Muslim community. There can be no question that the Muslim Women (Protection of Rights on Divorce) Bill is a wholly retrograde piece of legislation and that its introduction in the Lok Sabha represents a violation of the assurance the prime minister had given; he has not held the wide consultations he had promised and he has blatantly disregarded the opinion of educated Muslims. But the fact of support for it in the Muslim community cannot be denied. It is doubtless true that obscurantist mullahs and communalist Muslim leaders and organizations have used the Supreme Court's judgement in the Shah Bano case to whip up emotions and put pressure on the Government to exclude the Muslims from the purview of section 125 of the Criminal Procedure Code. But emotions have been stirred. So, in the act of resigning on this issue, Mr Khan has also taken up a battle against entrenched conservatism among the Muslims. All in all he has shown a kind of courage which has become rare in the Congress party, indeed in the country.

We have more than once expressed the view that change to bring the Muslims forward, though highly desirable in the interest of national integration, cannot be forced on them. But if there is a case for the Government's neutrality on the issue of a common civil code for all Indians which would do away with the Muslim personal law, there can be none for the Government's intervention in favour of retrogressive elements in the community. Mr Rajiv Gandhi has chosen to make precisely such an intervention. It is not possible for us to identify those in his entourage who have advised him and persuaded him to make such a humiliating surrender to the Muslim League and other forces of reaction. Perhaps not much persuasion was required; perhaps he was desperately keen to win back the Muslim vote which was supposed to have been alienated partly as a result of the Shah Bano affair. But whatever the factors at work behind the closed doors of the South Block, it is shocking beyond words that the prime minister, who had made "march into the twenty-first century" his battle-cry, should have endorsed a march into the seventh century for one eighth of the Indian people. The measure must be scrapped.

Mr Arif Mohammad Khan has not spelt out the reasons for his resignation. We know the main reason; we do not know the details. But as a Congressman he must find the acknowledgement by Mr Rajiv Gandhi of the Muslim League as the spokesman of the Muslim community galling. This recognition is implicit in the Government's decision to prepare the controversial legislation at the urging of the league and its desperate anxiety to introduce it. This must worry every Muslim in the Congress and in every other secular political party. Indeed, it must worry every nationalist Indian. The Muslim League is a fact and it certainly enjoys influence among the Muslims, especially in Kerala. But no prime minister has ever accepted or can ever accept it or any other communal organization as a spokesman of the community in question. Our parliamentary democracy is based on a joint electorate; the founding fathers deliberately rejected separate electorates which had led to partition in 1947 and would surely have produced another disaster in independent India. This means that a legislator represents the whole constituency and not a section of it. The concept of sovereignty of Parliament cannot rest on any other basis. If Mr Gandhi and his hand-picked aides are too young to have known the trauma of partition and to have drawn the necessary lesson, there are in the Congress party men old enough to have done so. Mr Khan has given them an opportunity to speak up; he has obliged the leadership to convene a meeting of the parliamentary party on Friday. They should use it to demand that a measure wholly offensive to the party's nationalist tradition be scrapped. The expedient of a reference to a select committee of both houses of Parliament can provide the necessary face-saver.

Editorial, *The Times of India*
28 February 1986

PROGRESSIVE MUSLIMS MUST ASSERT

The recent Supreme Court judgement about the applicability of section 125 of the Criminal Procedure Code pertaining to maintenance to a divorced wife has created a bitter controversy among the Muslims.

The fact that more than 100,000 could be mobilized in a massive procession in Bombay city on November 20, to protest against the Supreme Court order, demonstrates the intensity of the feelings that can be roused among the Muslim masses by the Ulama and communally oriented political leaders even on a social welfare measure safeguarding the rights of all Muslim women.

We have always defended the rights and privileges of the Muslim minority — in fact of all religious minorities, against the hegemonist tendency of the Hindu majority community. We also believe that the Muslims have been treated as second class citizens in India, as a sequel to the communal partition of the country and they deserve a fair deal to safeguard their identity in a secular set-up.

But the political leaders of the Muslim masses are doing a great disservice to themselves and to the entire community by building up a false campaign against a progressive decision of the Supreme Court which helps all sections of womanhood. Equality for women is a principle accepted by Muslims in several Muslim majority countries.

While it is the task of progressive sections of the Muslim intelligentsia to combat the influence of obscurantist political and religious leaders among them we quote here from a declaration adopted by a group of Muslim intellectuals, mostly Muslim women, on the Supreme Court order:

While the judgement has been welcomed by the progressive Muslims in general and Muslim women in particular, it has been strongly condemned as interference in the divine shariat and violation of Constitutional guarantees to profess and practice religion, by the Muslim leadership; religious as well as political.

Strong passions are sought to be generated and an all-India campaign has been launched. We would like to point out that the campaign against the Supreme Court judgement is politically rather than religiously motivated.

Islam not only gave high status to women, it also gave them concrete and well-defined rights in matters like divorce, marriage, maintenance; inheritance, etc. Very few religions in the world can boast of having accorded such elevated status and given such well-defined rights to women.

The Quran has also repeatedly exhorted men to be kind to women and treat them with ahsan — benevolence. It is unfortunate that what Allah gave to women in the Quran, the Ulama are trying to take away in the name of the shariat. We would like to point out that the shariat is also based on opinions of Muslim jurists and cannot be treated as only divine.

There are wide ranging differences among eminent Muslim jurists on various issues. For this reason a number of schools of the Islamic law have come into existence.

The Quran has not specifically mentioned period of maintenance, although the period of waiting for remarriage has been clearly mentioned. The Quran has meant to provide for divorced women on a reasonable scale in Verse 241 of Chapter 2. This provision on a reasonable scale could also mean a provision as long as the divorcee needs it, i.e. until she remarries, dies or can support herself. Whether she deserves maintenance beyond the period of iddat would be determined by a competent legal authority

The holy Quran commands human beings to be just and kind; in particular, kind to the weak. Kindness in certain circumstances can become obligatory. Allah exhorted us to be kind towards slaves and in modern times this kindness was made obligatory by legislating against slavery and all the Ulama accepted it in good grace although the right to own a place is recognized by the shariat. Why can't they then accept granting of maintenance to divorcees even after iddat in certain deserving cases? The kindness could be made obligatory in this case too.

In these difficult times of increasing inflationary pressures and rising needs it is almost impossible for middle class families to look after a divorced daughter. Even if they do, she will have to live under obligation rather than as a matter of right, subject to taunts and humiliation. Her personal dignity cannot be ensured.

The shariat is not final in as much as it is built on the interpretation of the Ulama and not on Allah's specific commandments. There are no clearly laid down injunctions by Allah that the divorcee shall not be given maintenance beyond the period of iddat.

We, therefore, welcome the Supreme Court judgement and urge the Government not to amend section 125 of the Criminal Procedure Code under pressure from a section of the Ulama and Muslim leaders. Their demand is not in conformity with the true spirit of the holy Quran.

The signatories to the declaration are well-known intellectuals: Kamila Tayabji, Asghar Ali Engineer, Shehnaaz, Shama Zaidi, A.J. Syed, Rukaiya Dosal, Shafiq Ahmed, Nasreen Fazalbhoy, Y.A. Fazalbhoy, Rafiq Sayyad, Salim Sheikh, Yasmeen Lukmani, Masooma Ranalvi, Ummul Ranalvi, Insheera Poonawala, Hasan Kutty. Irfan Engineer and S.R. Assur.

We broadly agree with these sentiments although we can state our case more vigorously. No doubt Muslim intellectuals are under social pressure not to express themselves freely on such delicate issues in the name of preserving the unity of Muslims as a minority.

There are already reports that the Bombay demonstration was organized with the blessings of powers that be with a tacit understanding that section 125 of Cr.P.C. would be amended in the name of respecting the sentiments of the Muslim minority.

We wish that the ruling party would not engage itself in such cheap gimmicks which can have a dangerous communal backlash in the peculiar conditions prevailing in India. It is for the forward-looking Muslim youth and intelligentsia to come forward and face the challenges of their obscurantist leaders. Let there be a national debate on the rights of women in general, irrespective of the religion they profess or practise.

Editorial, *Clarity*
24 November 1985

CONFUSING THE ISSUE

The minister of state for law, Mr H.R. Bhardwaj, is guilty of more than a minor political faux pas in telling newsmen at Indore that though the Directive Principles of the Constitution say that the state shall endeavour "to secure for the citizens a uniform civil code throughout the territory of India", the time is not ripe for it. "Nor can any deadline be fixed for legislation which will affect the Muslim minority in the country.'

What these remarks imply is a direct nexus between a common civil or family code and Muslim personal law, as though the introduction of the former is designed to cancel or even override the latter. To consider a uniform civil code as something aimed solely at Muslim personal law is to give a wholly mistaken twist to the argument. A common family law relating to marriage, divorce, maintenance, inheritance, adoption, guardianship, etc., would be no more anti-Muslim than is the prevailing Special Marriage Act. An optional uniform civil code or family laws act would merely give a choice to every individual to arrange his or her marital relations under a dispensation other than that of his or her personal law. It is a choice available as much to Muslims as to persons of any other religious community.

This point surprisingly has got lost in the long-drawn controversy over a uniform civil code. Muslims are not the only religious minority in India, nor the only community which has a personal law. Every community, and perhaps many of the sub-communities within almost every religious group have similar edicts. There is no reason therefore to view a common civil code as aimed at a particular community. The case for it rests simply on the need to provide an alternative to any and every Indian citizen, irrespective of religious or caste affiliations. Whether Muslim personal law needs urgent reform is something that Muslims can, and should, decide for themselves. It has nothing to do with the case for a common family law. A liberal and modern adoption law, which is most necessary has been thrice scuttled by religious objections although the application of such a law would be strictly optional. This illustrates the total irrationality that has distorted the debate.

Mr Bhardwaj also showed misplaced zeal in attacking the Supreme Court for pronouncing on the need for a uniform civil code in the course of the Shah Bano case. He was quite off the mark in declaring that the Supreme Court cannot tell the administration how to govern the country, or decide its fate. The judges did not set out to or in fact do so. If the minister's observations are to be taken seriously, they can only gratuitously pit the executive against the judiciary. The prime minister has tried bravely but not too wisely to defend Mr Bhardwaj and Mr Z.A. Ansari, minister for environment, for their statements in Parliament criticizing the judges of the Supreme Court. A re-reading of Article 121 might be useful.

Editorial, *Indian Express*
8 January 1986

UNDERSTAND THE PROBLEMS OF MUSLIMS
WITH AN OPEN HEART

Maulana Nadvi compared Mahatma Gandhi's approach (to religious problems) with that of the majority of countrymen today in the case of the Shah Bano and the Muslim divorcees' bill. He appealed to his fellow countrymen to try and understand the problems of Muslims and their approach with an open heart and think over them sympathetically and generously. Avoiding a polemical discussion he told those present what was the basis of approach of the Muslims in the matters pertaining to personal law. He said that in the *Shah Bano* v *Mohammad Ahmed Khan* case the Muslims disapproved of the Supreme Court judgement for the following reasons:

(1) This way the doors for interference in the Muslim personal law will open and the identity of Muslims and their individuality would be in danger.

(2) It is the opinion of the Muslims that the shariat provides more protection to a divorced women than the said suggestion of the Supreme Court. Will it not affect the self-respect of the poor divorcee if she has to beg for a few crumbs even after she has been separated from her husband who has driven her out of his house?

(3) Only those Ulama who have spent their lifetime in acquiring knowledge of religion and of the Arabic language are entitled to interpret the shariat.

He also expressed the fear that the way prices are going up and actual values falling, if the divorcing husband is compelled to pay maintenance until his divorced wife dies or marries again, it is quite likely that some misguided husbands might kill their wives slowly rather than divorce them. There are many examples of burning young women for bringing less dowry. It is also worth considering that very few divorces take place and no case has been reported wherein the divorced woman was compelled to beg from door to door or died of starvation.

He told his fellow countrymen for their information, delineating the basic principles of Islam, that Islam was different from other religions in this matter (he did not mean superiority of any religion). Its followers consider it a proclamation of God in which no change is possible. It is a code of life which encircles all its aspects completely. Its demands on its followers are much more strenuous in comparison with other religions. Perhaps it is this reason that other Indians cannot understand the Muslims' attitude on many problems and take them to be inflexible.

Muslims have a great regard and love for the holy Quran and the Prophet. They also intensely love the Urdu language as it is a confluence of Hindu and Muslim cultures and is the repository of their religious literature and traditions. The Muslim personal law, excepting a few things, is entirely based on the Quran and hadith and Muslims have been following it since the early Islamic period. Even then, leaving those matters which have been clearly dealt with in the hadith and Quran, the shariat has devised ways for facing the challenge of changing conditions.

The maulana remembered with reverence how Mahatma Gandhi had stood by the Muslims 66 years ago on the question of Khilafat. It was that movement which, for the first time, loosened the grip of British rule over India. Gandhiji adopted this approach in order to respect Muslim feelings. He thus won over Muslim hearts by supporting them on a problem which did not pertain to India (i.e. the Khilafat problem). What was its result? A great unity whose parallel cannot be found in our great country today. Gandhiji had said, "If Muslims are pained, Hindus also feel it." In order to explain his position the maulana quoted long excerpts from Gandhiji's biography and from *Young India*. The maulana also praised and admired Jawaharlal's wise and sympathetic approach in matters pertaining to Muslims.

Extract from the *Urdu Times*
23 May 1986

THIS IS TOMFOOLERY MISTER!

There is a wave, not for the first time. It was there many times before, mostly in Europe, on the gates of Asia, during the crusades, then at the time of the Turkish war, during the years of the Crimean and Balkan wars. Whenever the political temperature rises, wherever weapons for national freedom or social reform crackle and any Muslim power or Muslim population be a party to it, a trend to taunt Islam and Muslims and to tarnish their image arises.

This is not the nature of our country. This is the land which absorbs all religions.

All have the capacity to listen and tolerate. Here religious polemics have taken place right in the centre of the field. You tell us the qualities of your dharma, we shall describe the qualities of our religion. You learn something from us, we shall learn something from you. And we live together quarrelling and embracing.

This is the greatest quality of this piece of land which has digested thousands of years' old cultures. Here Islam too which came from four directions and in four forms has been an acceptable and respectable religion. And it (Islam) became moderate in its beliefs and customs due to the influence of this land; its bone got softened.

Sometimes in sheer obstinacy someone hungry for fame and outspoken, does something which makes denigrating each other's religion and society fashionable. But it is as transitory as the atmosphere of a cricket or hockey match: you see everyone involved and then you find the field deserted. But alas, for a year and half, in our own country, using different pretexts and platforms, the religion of Muslims, their way of life, their backwardness, are being so maligned that God save us from it . . . .

We are neither preachers of any dharma, nor are we counted among the pious servants of God. In fact, we ourselves do not know which religion, which belief and which *ism* has drenched our existence with its light . . . . Even then when we breathe from morning till evening in the atmosphere of news denigrating Islam and Islamic people which touches the limits of abuse — these days no day is free from this — the waves of anger arise within us. Muslim personal law is quite absurd, it should be abolished.

Let someone say how big it is! Civil and criminal laws are the same for all. A few lines from the book of law are there like an island in the sea which Indian Muslims have embraced, considering them as the sacred shariat, and they are happy with this much. If any person dressed in the best European dress is wearing a kada (iron bangle) or a mala (threaded beads) around his neck what is wrong with it! Let him be and his faith . . . .

Editorial after editorial is being written, statements in bold headlines are being published, ordinary journalists like Arun Shourie are playing with the details of the shariat in the name of research and are collecting heaps of latest knowledge on the subject. The common run-of-the-mill novelists like Guru Dutt do portray some knave, rapist "Abdul" as one of the dark characters. New liberal, enlightened, old tolerant people and well-experienced non-Muslim of high taste sees this puppet show and rubs his eyes in sheer wonder, and thinks, "Is this the way of prospering in the world?"

All this is going on but we felt great agony when we saw on the front page in *The Times of India*, a great representative of the national press, a small cartoon in which a hated oppressor and murderous goonda is pulling a small old woman tied with ropes. This lady is Shah Bano and it is obvious that the goonda is the symbol of that Indian Muslim who does not favour the common civil code.

Mr R.K. Laxman is a leading cartoonist of the country. He and Bal Thackeray have worked together on one table for years. We admire his art and appreciate it from the depth of our heart. It is a fact that in the turns and twists of his lines there is a sharper edge than in words. But what is this? Wherever this paper goes, on the tables on which it is kept, in the offices where its pages would spread, in the families in which it would be read — lakhs of children, women, our coming generation, the trustees of our culture who cast a glance over the cartoon would have the hated, terror-striking image of Indian Muslims. Would it not inject poison for years to come in their minds? . . . .

Even if we tolerate this, we would call it *pajipan* (tomfoolery).

Extract from Editorial, *Inquilab*
12 March 1986

LONG LIVE BALASAHEB DEORAS!

Looking to the India-wide protest by Indian Muslims on the issue of Muslim personal law the chief of the RSS, Balasaheb Deoras, has been flabbergasted and embarrassed. Embarrassment and fear is found in many other circles as well, and those differing on ideological and theoretical grounds are also included in them. Those claiming revivalism and are the torch bearers of the Hindu renaissance, Arya Samajis, are also seen among them. And, on the question of Muslim personal law the Muslims' insistence of their community's identity enrages the Arya Samajis too and they are seen holding a threat to the Muslims. They are inciting Hindus against Muslims and are engaged in inflaming communal passions but the embarrassment of Balasaheb Deoras is worth seeing. The poor Balasaheb is facing serious defeat in his destructive work. He has begun to feel that his precursor Guru Golwalkar's serious attempts throughout his life to pack off Muslims from India was in vain, though he spent crores of rupees on this work. He put lakhs and lakhs of his *swayam sevaks* on this front to massacre Muslims. The work of the country's division took place peacefully and peace would have prevailed even thereafter but Guru Golwalkar created such a situation that the larger part of north India became a vast field for looting and killing. Whatever the responsibility of other politicians for killing Muslims in Bharatpur, Alwar, Delhi, Punjab including Haryana, Rajasthan, Madhya Pradesh and Bengal, it was Guru Golwalkar who was seen on the battlefield everywhere. And while he lived he continued to cause the massacre of the remaining Indian Muslims and, in his own sense, continued to serve the Hindu religion. He continued to preach hatred against Muslims and also against Christians to some extent. He spread the fire of hatred everywhere in the country and tried to immerse it in the sea of fire and blood. How far his campaign for hatred succeeded even Golwalkar tired of estimating and departed from this world leaving behind another person to spit fire and blood. But even then Muslims in India survived and joyfully took an interest in national matters and continued to serve the country and earn their bread and butter.

Shri Golwalkar tried his best to destroy the economy of Muslims and restrict sources of their livlihood. But despite this Muslims are living today and insha Allah will continue to live....

When the Janata Government came to power, conditions changed somewhat and people thought that Balasaheb would also learn to respect human values but he steadfastly followed his profession of spreading poison and blood and fire. He equated cultivating hatred with the ideals of ancient Hindu religion and in order to promote his business he thought it necessary to support the ruling Congress from behind the scenes. As he wanted to hold aloft the hegemony of Brahminism and its pride, he found satisfaction of this passion in supporting Indira Gandhi's and Rajiv Gandhi's regimes. Thus, seeking refuge in their governments, he continued to make Muslims the target of oppression and tyranny.

But today he has again tried to awaken the Hindus using his method of communal incitement. He has started talking about protecting the Hindu sanskriti and Hindu culture and asked Hindus to come forward and make sacrifices for it and is also spitting venom against Muslims and Christians. Balasaheb complains that the Muslims do not become part of the Hindu mainstream. Why are they standing like a rock to maintain their separate existence and identity? In Balasaheb's view this behaviour of Muslims has endangered the greatness of Hindu religion and philosophy and therefore he is inciting Hindus against Muslims. But Balasaheb does not know that nature has created flexibility in the nature of the existing Muslims and the more they are suppressed the more they will rise though they have drifted far away from Islamic teachings and Islamic traditions. Balasaheb and his disciples are bent upon keeping them Muslims by beating them to pulp. Whatever the end result of Balasaheb's and the Arya Samajis' campaign of hatred, Muslims in this country are determined to survive. Whatever hue and cry they may raise, Muslims will march ahead to maintain their and their country's prestige and identity, they will not be defeated, insha Allah. Therefore we must say: long live Balasaheb!

Editorial, *Sangam Urdu Daily*
26 December 1985

SHARIAT AND REASON

A journalist, Yasin Dalal, has quoted from Mr A. A. Fyzee's book, *An Outline of Mohammadan Law*, a conversation like this:

The Prophet sent Muadh, one of his companions, as governor of one of the provinces. At the same time he was appointed as the qazi also. At that time no trained qazis were available. Therefore, the Prophet asked him, "On what basis will you judge?"

"According to divine injunctions," Muadh replied.

"If you don't get anything in it?"

"Then according to the practices (sunna) of the Messenger of God," Muadh said.

"If that is also not helpful?" the Prophet further tested his companion.

"Then I shall formulate the law according to my reason." The Prophet was satisfied with this reply.

In Islam there is place for reason (ijtehad).* The further example of this is found in the book of Mohammad Qutb, *Islam: the Misunderstood Religion*. The third† caliph Hazrat Umar bin Khattab was known for strictly following the injunctions of the shariat‡. He had suspended the sentence of amputation of hands during a famine, because it was possible that someone is compelled to steal due to hunger. One definite instance is like this. Some boys serving with Hatim bin Ali stole a she-bull from a person of the Muznah tribe. When Hazrat Umar questioned them they confessed to their crime. Umar ordered their hands to be amputated. But then he hesitated and said: "By God, had I not known that you make them starve despite their hard work (and for that reason even prohibited things permissible to them) I would have got their hands amputated." And then he took back the sentence of amputating the hands, and fined them.

Both these instances show that the Quranic injunctions must be followed and followed with reason. The holy Quran says, "Allah changes not the condition of a people, until they change their own condition." This and the above quoted are the instances that came to mind when our one lakh Muslim brothers took a morcha to Mantralaya. The Indian Constitution gives full freedom to every citizen to follow and

---

* *ijtehad* does not mean reason, it actually means to assert (to find truth). (Ed.)

† Hazrat Umar was the second, and not third caliph. (Ed.)

‡ In Hazrat Umar's time the word shariat was not current. This term came to be widely used in the 5th century of Islam. (Ed.)

practise one's own religion. Even then, how can one frame laws in a secular country which are not enforced even in a country where that religion is followed by an over-whelming majority? M. J. Akbar had arranged in his attractive TV programme *Newsline* a discussion on the shariat and Muslim women's rights between Mr Shahabuddin, the Janata party member of Parliament and the central minister Arif Mohammad Khan. Syed Shahabuddin, who upholds the orthodox view, could not reply to the arguments put forward by Arif Khan. The Muslim countries in the world do follow the shariat but they enforce laws from time to time in keeping with reason. Before Khomeini came to power the Muslims of Iran had achieved prosperity due to their liberal way of life[§].

In Pakistan Zia-ul-Haq talks of Islam in order to remain in power. Begum Liaqat had told a British journalist last year on the occasion of the 33rd death anniversary of her husband that "if our military rulers could do it they would make for us women a different path to walk on". Shahida Jamil, the Grey Inn Barrister in London, had told Mary Viver of *Sunday Times* about the case of Safia in Pakistan which shook the listener and the readers of the newspaper. The blind woman Safia was raped by the father and son of the household where she worked. According to law Safia ought to have produced four male witnesses and she should recognize, from the crowd, those who raped her. Where could a blind servant find witnesses from for what happened with her? She was sentenced to be flogged publicly and was awarded three years' imprisonment. Had Hazrat Umar been confronted with such a situation how would he have judged? With such practices of the shariat our Muslim brothers want to make society more religious-oriented and more humane!

If the insistence is on following the shariat then any Muslim who steals must have his hands amputated and if a person of another community steals he should be prose-cuted according to law. No Muslim can deal with banks as the Quran makes it very clear that "Allah will blot out usury, and He causes charity to prosper.... O you who believe, keep your duty to Allah and relinquish what remains (due) from usury, if you are believers". But there are Muslim cooperative banks in India and they are there in Muslim countries too. Using another word for 'interest' does not do away with interest....

About women, the Quran says thus: "Your women are a tilth for you (to cultivate) so go to your tilth as you will, and send (good deeds) before you for your soul, and fear Allah, and know that you will (one day) meet Him....

With these words the holy Quran shows the way of dealing with women. Today our Muslim brothers wish that their women should remain backward. Do they not want that like Indira Gandhi and Benazir Bhutto women should come forward? Do they want that the era of forceful women like Fatimah Jinnah and Begum Liaqat Ali should come to an end? Perhaps they do not wish that and if it is so and they show reason in not insisting on having a criminal code according to the shariat they should also insist on a common civil code and it would be quite welcome if, for that purpose, they take out a morcha like the one they took out on Wednesday.

Extract from Editorial, *Janmabhoomi Pravasi*
23 November 1985

§ This assertion is highly contentious. (Ed.)

THE TOUCHSTONE

In politics rarely does someone come to the fore sacrificing his position for the sake of policy and ideals. It is a matter of pleasure for us that the minister for energy, Mr Arif Khan, has set such a brilliant example. The fundamentalist Muslims have raised a hue and cry over the Supreme Court judgement that in the case of a divorced Muslim wife it is the duty of her divorcing husband to give maintenance to her according to the Indian Cr.P.C. 125. The Muslim mullahs and other Muslim leaders registered their protest against the judgement. The matter did not stop there. A central minister severely criticized Parliament, the Supreme Court and its Chief Justice.

But according to some Muslim reformists this judgement was given on the basis of social justice and it also embraces in its fold the high and progressive ideals of Islam. And according to them when the issue of weaker sections and women's rights is constantly being discussed in the country how can Muslim women be deprived of the benefits of the Supreme Court judgement?

Secondly, when Muslims accept all other sections of the Cr. P. C. how can they be exempted from this one section? From the social and familial point of view, the parents, it is generally thought, have fulfilled their duty by spending according to their capacity at the time of their daughter's marriage. But thereafter if the husband inhumanly and unilaterally divorces her why should the parents take the burden of the (divorced) woman and her children? The Central Government has set a bad example by introducing a bill in Parliament despite the reasonable opposition by all opposition political parties, and Muslim intellectuals, jurists, writers and religious scholars themselves. Not only this, it has given a setback to the country which is on the path of progress and has given strength to those who hold orthodox and reactionary views. If this argument is accepted, then different communities would keep on opposing any changes in the orthodox practices.

According to the Muslim reformists, the bill has been framed to please orthodox Muslims so that the Muslim vote-bank could be insured for the Congress-I party. The politicians have to play such games and have to change their policies also; but by going against fundamental principles, the Central Government has forfeited its claim to protect the rights of the weaker sections and of being reform-oriented.

In this respect, the courage and enthusiasm shown by Arif Mohammad Khan is really praiseworthy. After the Shah Bano case judgement, the atmosphere was very explosive and Shri Khan had to take a difficult decision. He submitted his resignation to the prime minister without any delay. According to a saying* it is on the touchstone that one can say whether it is gold or brass. Where other 'great people' prove to be brass on the touchstone, Shri Khan, by adhering to his principles, has renounced power for the sake of justice for the women of his community.

In doing this, Mr Khan is not alone; 125 prominent Muslims from different walks of life, men as well as women, have signed a memorandum to this effect and submitted it to the prime minister. Their demand is that no change should be made in Cr. P. C. 125 and the responsibility for maintaining the divorced Muslim woman should lie with her husband.

Extracts from Editorial, *Bombay Samacnar*
2 March 1986

* In Hindi (Ed.)

ALL INDIA MUSLIM PERSONAL LAW BOARD
(Poona Unit)

Date: 21.03.1986

Sir,

A large meeting of eminent Muslims of Pune City and District was held on 21.03.1986 at Osmania Masjid Hall, at 425, Kedari Road, Pune 411 001 at 9:00 p.m.

The said gathering extended its full support to the "Muslim Women (Protection of Rights on Divorce) Bill".

Following is the text of the resolution which was passed unanimously. You are requested to kindly publish the same in your esteemed journal.

Thanking you,

Sincerely yours,

Sd/-
(A.S. Chishti)
Convener

cc: President & Prime Minister of India,
    All Union & State Ministers.

Text of the Resolution

This gathering of distinguished Muslims from all over Pune City and District, hereby acknowledge the "Muslim Women (Protection of Rights on Divorce) Bill" as a right step in the right direction. It is in accordance with the Indian Constitution and duly regards all the democratic values and principles.

We unequivocally hail the bill. We are satisfied that our rightful demand has been found worthy of consideration by the Government.

We look towards the bill as a major step, which will close down the doors of intrusion in the shariat, which were made open by the Supreme Court's judgement.

We hope that our Hon. Prime Minister will stand undeterred, ignoring all the unnecessary hues and cries, din and bustle created by a few communalists and people having vested interests.

We strongly appeal to our Prime Minister to get the bill passed in the current session of Parliament.

We also appeal to our countrymen to rise to the occasion, setting aside all their differences. We appeal to them to take an unbiased and cursory (sic) view of the bill, which will prove that the provisions made in the bill are much broader, satisfactory and convincing than section 125 of the Criminal Procedure Code.

WHAT PROMINENT MUSLIMS SAY

It is no Crime for Muslim Women
to Raise Voice against Oppression

Maulana Ishaque Sanbhli

In a speech delivered in Malegaon on 27 January 1986, Maulana Ishaque Sanbhli, ex-M.P. and member, Jamiat-ul-Ulama, said that "it is no interference in religion to raise voice against oppression of women, Muslim or non-Muslim. If Muslim women raise their voice against oppression and for their rights we must support them. Their rights have been guaranteed in Section 125 of Cr.P.C. This section is applicable not only for Muslims but for followers of all religions and therefore we oppose any change in this section.

Extract from *Bebak Weekly*, Malegaon
3 January 1986

Maulana Abdul Hasain Nadvi

The problem of protection of the shariat today is the most important problem for the Muslims of India. Political and economic backwardness, deprivation of Government services, communal riots and dissemination of polytheistic beliefs in education and now an attempt is being made to prevent Muslims from practising in matters of nikah and talaq according to Muslim personal law. The Muslim feelings have been deeply hurt by the aggressive attacks from all sides on the Muslim personal law. The Government's vague and doubtful approach and the Supreme Court's recent judgement has made the future of Islam in this country dishonourable.

Extract from *Inquilab*
22 December 1985

Maulana Asad Madani

The Muslims want to lead life in their own way. India is the cradle of various religions and each religion enjoys equal freedom in this secular country and followers of every religion have been given the right to follow the principles of their religion. Muslims cannot tolerate any interference in shariat which is a divine law. If they are compelled in this respect, it can lead to undesirable consequences and the integrity of the country can be affected.

Extract from *Inquilab*
22 December 1985

CHARITY BEGINS AT HOME

Those women who sympathize with divorced Muslim women and who take out morchas and stage demonstrations against the oppression of Muslim women and who also
collect funds in order to help divorced Muslim women should look in their own
homes. They are well aware of the havoc the problem of dowry is causing in their own
society. Somewhere some married woman is compelled to commit suicide and at some
places her in-laws themselves finish her off. One such incident has taken place on 26
December in Vile Parle, a suburb of Bombay.

According to the news, 28-year-old Indira got married to Nitin on 21 May 1976. At
the time the parents of Indira gave ornaments of gold weighing 40 tolas and Rs 11,000
cash by way of dowry but despite this, Indira's in-laws began to harass her for obtaining more dowry from her parents. When the persecution continued inordinately, Indira's father Kapurchand lodged a complaint in Vile Parle police station first on 4 October 1980, a second time on 10 May, and for the third time on 20 May.

However, it is alleged that Indira, who is the mother of two children, was burnt to
death and in this horrible crime her husband is also alleged to be involved. It is alleged that he set fire to Indira's kerosene-soaked body. If Indira had not survived to
give her dying declaration this case perhaps would have been taken as that of
suicide . . . . According to the report of the Maharashtra Assembly, this year 120 cases
of burning to death on the question of dowry have taken place.

But from the many activities concerning Muslim personal law, it appears that for
many people in our country and for some political parties as well, the greatest problem of our era is to enforce a common civil code throughout the country and no trace
of Muslim personal law should remain. It is the duty of such great personalities and
committees for protection of women that they should turn their attention first to
women of their own community and try to save them first and give up worrying about
those Muslim women who have been well protected by the Islamic shariat which has
framed such laws that their rights can never be crushed; nor can they consider themselves inferior and status-less in their own society.

We would like to reiterate here that if some Muslim women who oppose Muslim
personal law in the name of the Shah Bano case or want changes in it, or if they desire
that a common civil code be imposed on the entire country then such women, though
their names be Muslim, should renounce Islam if they do not agree completely with
the Islamic shariat. Is it not hypocrisy to call oneself Muslim and at the same time not
to revere Islamic laws?

Extract from *The Urdu Times*
7 January 1986

IT WILL BE A BIG THING IF MUSLIMS AGREE
ON THE METHOD OF DIVORCE

Sir,
    There are many different methods of divorce among the Muslims. Those who fol-
low schools of jurisprudence pronounce talaq thrice and the wife becomes a divorcee at
once.

Among *ahl hadith* (people following the Prophet's sayings and doings) divorce is pronounced once every month and three divorces are given over three months and then the wife gets divorced.

Among *ahl Quran* (those who follow the holy Quran) the first divorce after *nikah* is the first and *only* one even if the word talaq is pronounced a hundred times. The period of iddat for divorce is three menstrual periods. Now if the couple after separation or without separation marries again and live a husband and wife and divorce again it would be a second divorce. Again after this second divorce if the couple gets married again with or without separation and get divorced again it would be the third divorce. Now the couple has no right to marry again without separation and until the woman marries another man and he divorces her or dies (See *Quran*, 2-230).

It would be a great achievement of the Muslim Personal Law Board if it succeeds in removing these differences spread over 1400 years and satisfies the ummah with any one method . . . .

Abdul Asrar Ramzi, Jodhpur.
(*Urdu Blitz*, 30-11-85)

SHAH BANO'S OPEN LETTER TO MUSLIMS

Brethren-in-Faith,
As-Salamu Alaikum

Maulana Mohammad Habib Yar Khan, Haji Abdul Ghaffar Saheb and other respectable gentlemen of Indore came to me and explained to me the Commands concerning nikah, divorce, dower and maintenance in the light of the Quran and hadith.

After listening to them and understanding what they said, I have come to the conclusion that the laws of Allah and the Prophet are everything for me and in them I have full faith and belief.

Since women were getting maintenance through law courts, I also filed a suit for the same in a court of law and was successful. It may be noted that till then I had no idea that it would amount to going against the shariat and no person had informed me about the shariat's view in this regard.

Now the Supreme Court has given the judgement on 23 April 1985 concerning maintenance of the divorced woman, which is apparently in my favour; but since this judgement is contrary to the Quran and the hadith and is an open interference in Muslim personal law, I, Shah Bano, being a Muslim, reject it and dissociate myself from every judgement which is contrary to the Islamic shariat.

I am aware of the agony and distress to which this judgement has subjected the Muslims of India today, and I demand of the Indian Government:

(1) To withdraw the said judgement of the Supreme Court immediately;
(2) That Muslim women be kept out of the purview of section 125 of the Criminal Procedure Code, or it should be amended;
(3) Article 44 of the Indian Constitution, in which there is a directive for enacting a uniform civil code for all, is quite contrary to the Quran and the hadith; Muslims be kept out of the purview of this article;
(4) Interference in Muslim personal law is against the Indian Constitution. Therefore, this interference be stopped, and a guarantee be given that no interference would be ever attempted in future.

In the end I thank Maulana Mohamed Habib Yar Khan and Haji Abdul Ghaffar Saheb of Indore who showed me the straight path and helped me follow the Truth and thus saved me in this world and in the hereafter.

Moreover, I also appeal to all the Ulama of India that they should establish a 'Safeguard for the Shariat Board' for the benefit of divorced women, through which they should be helped to get their shariat rights by settling the disputes concerning dower, divorce, maintenance, etc.

Was Salam.

(Thumb Impression of Shah Bano)
Dated: 2/11/1985

(Signature of four witnesses)

(Published in *Inquilab*, 13 November 1985, and translated into English by Mr A. Karim Shaikh.)

Extract from *Radiance*
24–30 November 1985

ISLAMIC SHARIAT BOARD (Regd.)
12/526 Kuttichira, Calicut 673001
Kerala

Before the Hon'ble Prime Minister of India, New Delhi

1.2.1986

Memorandum

Most Respected Sir,

Sub: Amendment of section 125 of Cr. P. C. — Bill before the Parliament to exclude Muslim divorcees from the ambit of law — Retention of the existing provision an imperative necessity — Plea for amendment unacceptable — Submissions regarding.

A strong public feeling is gaining ground among Muslims of India in support of the Supreme Court verdict in the Shah Bano case. The opposition to, and the hue and cry raised against the verdict of the Supreme Court by certain sections of the Muslim community are motivated by political and other considerations, rather than by a pious desire to uphold the sanctity of Muslim law. Most of these laws are inconsistent with and repugnant to the true shariat. The holy Quran and precepts of the Prophet ordain extraordinarily fair treatment to women and make it obligatory on the husband to make reasonable provision for the maintenance of his divorced wife.

2. The verdict of the Supreme Court in the Shah Bano case does not in any way contravene the injunctions of Islam on the subject. The views expressed by the commentators of the Quran and the eminent theologians, recognized by the Islamic world, corroborate the verdict of the Supreme Court. The considered

opinions of the authorities, ancient and modern, are given in the Annexure.

3. In view of these facts, we pray that the Government may be pleased to refrain from any action entailing the exclusion of divorced Muslim women from the purview of section 125 of the Cr. P. C.

With respectful regards,

Yours sincerely,

(P.V. SHOUKAT ALI)
Chairman,
Islamic Shariat Board.

Encl:
i. Annexure

Annexure

Opinions of Islamic Authorities on the Liability of the Husband to provide Maintenance for his Divorced Wife

1. Maulana Abul Kalam Azad, in his *Tarjumanul Quran* comments as follows: "Quran takes occasion to re-emphasize that proper consideration should be shown to the divorced woman in every circumstance. This repeated call for consideration to woman was for no other reason than that her position deserved due attention since she was comparatively weaker than man and her interests needed to be properly safeguarded" (*Tarjumanul Quran*; vol. 2, p. 109. Trans. and ed. by Syed Abdul Latif; Asia Publishing House; 1967).

2. Shah Waliullah Dahlavi, (born 1702) the well-known theologian of India in his commentary on the holy Quran gives the meaning of the verses 2:240 and 241, thus: "It is the obligation of those who ward off evil to give the divorced woman just and fair provision for life i.e. maintenance and accomodation. Allah explains thus His decrees, so that you may understand."

3. Shaikul Hind Allama Mahmood Hassan Deobandi, another eminent theologian of India, in his Urdu translation of the holy Quran, gives the meaning of verse 2:241 thus: "It is the obligation of those who ward off evil to pay maintenance to the divorced woman as per provisions of Law."

4. Muhammad Asad, a world renowned scholar and commentator of the holy Quran and of 'Sahihul Bukkari', states in his note on verse 2:241: "The amount of alimony — payable unless and until they remarry — has been left unspecified since it must depend on the husband's financial circumstances and on the social conditions of the times" (Muhammad Asad, *The Message of the Quran*; note 231; p.54; Darul Andulus; Gibraltar; 1984)

5. Muhammad Abdu and Rasheed Rida, the torch-bearers of Islamic renaissance in Egypt, in their widely accepted commentary on the holy Quran, *Al-Mahar*, records that the Prophet's grandson Imam Ḥasan gave 20,000 dirhams and a huge jar full of honey when he divorced his wife, and comment, "This was their practice" (vol. 2; p. 431).

6. Shaik Mustafa Assabai, a well-known theologian who delivered a series of lectures on Islam at Damascus University in 1961–62, expressed his opinion on the right of the divorced woman thus: "If the divorced woman is of marriage-

able age, maintenance should be paid till her remarriage; if she is old, it should be paid till her death"*(Al Mar athu-bynal-fiqhi-val-Qanum; p. 146). For reasons given in detail, he rejected the Government regulation that the payment of maintenance should be limited to a period of one year after iddat.

7. Imam Qurtubi, in his commentary on the holy Quran explains the reason for ordering payment of maintenance to the divorced woman thus: "Payment of maintenance is ordered for the reason that disrespect has been shown against the marital contract" (Imam Qurtubi, *Commentary on Quran*; vol. 3; p. 229).

8. Baidavi, in his widely-read commentary on the holy Quran further explains the reason for enjoining maintenance and holds the view that the quantum of maintenance is to be determined by the Government. "Maintenance is made obligatory so as to remove despair and grief caused to the woman by separation as a result of divorce. The quantum of maintenance is to be determined by the Government authority" (Baidavi, *Commentary on Holy Quran*; vol. 1, p. 110).

9. According to the author of *Thafseer Roohul Bayan*, maintenance is a recompense payable to the divorced woman: "Allah has ordered payment of maintenance as a recompense against the hardship imposed on the divorcee due to separation" (*Thasfeer Roohul Bayan*; vol. 1; p. 375).

10. Imam Hasan Basari and Atha ubn Abi Rabah were prominent disciples of the Prophet's immediate disciples (Thabi an). They were great theologians and commentators of the Quran. They lived 1200 years ago. Hasan Basari says: "There is no time limit regarding payment of maintenance. It should be paid according to one's capacity." (Ibn Hazam, *Muhalla*; vol. 10; p. 248; A.D 994-1064).

11. Athaubn Abi Rabah says: "I do not know that there is any fixed time limit for payment of maintenance." (*Ibid.* p. 248).

12. *Lisanul Arab* is the most prestigious Arabic lexicon written about 700 years back. This lexicon gives the meaning of mataa as below:

It has no time limit, for Allah has not fixed any time limit for the same. He has only enjoined the payment of maintenance.

All the above commentators of the holy Quran and the well-known authorities quoted above are unanimous that the husband is under an obligation to provide reasonable maintenance to a divorced wife till she is remarried. Therefore the provision under section 125 of Cr.P.C. making it obligatory on the husband to provide maintenance for his divorced wife who is unable to maintain herself does not in any way override the laws of Islamic shariat on the subject.

13. *Codification of Personal Laws in terms of Islamic Shariat.* The laws known as personal law of Muslims in India are merely based on case laws. The personal laws seriously depart from the basic concepts of the Islamic shariat. The holy Quran and precepts of the Prophet form the basic tenets of the shariat. Personal laws are mostly inconsistent with and often repugnant to the true tenets of Islam. Codification of the Islamic shariat in terms of the holy Quran and true precepts of the Prophet and enactment of the same is therefore an imperative necessity. The main objective of our Islamic Shariat Board is such a codification.

Chairman
Islamic Shariat Board

APPENDIX

STATEMENT BY LEADING FIGURES
IN MUSLIM INTELLIGENTSIA

We, the undersigned
DEMAND (1) that section 125 of the Cr.P.C. shall not be changed; (2) that the right of divorced Muslim women to claim maintenance from their husband or former husbands shall be preserved.
HOLD 1) that the exoneration of the husband from all responsibility for maintenance of divorced women is contrary to the provision and spirit of section 125 of the Cr.P.C. which is meant for indigent women and seeks to prevent destitution; 2) that the Government must ensure that rights guaranteed by the Constitution to women are upheld.

Signatories

1. Khwaja Ahmad Abbas (Writer & Film-maker)
2. Salim Ali (Biologist, Ornithologist, MP)
3. Moonis Raza (Vice Chancellor, Delhi University)
4. Abid Husain (Member, Planning Commission)
5. Obaid Siddiqui (Professor, TIFR)
6. Rais Ahmed (Educationist, Ex-Vice Chairman, UGC)
7. Shabana Azmi (Film Actress)
8. Javed Akthar (Filmscript Writer)
9. Sardar Jafri (Poet)
10. Saeed Mirza (Film-maker)
11. Rasheeduddin Khan (Professor, JNU)
12. Irfan Habib (Professor, AMU)
13. Bashir Husain Zaidi (former V.C., AMU)
14. M. A. Halim (Speaker, W. B. Assembly)
15. Badr-ud-din Tyabji (Ex-ICS)
16. E. Alkazi (Ex-Director, National School of Drama)
17. Zahoor Qasim (Secretary, Dept. of Ocean Development)
18. A. Rahman (Scientist)
19. Asghar Ali Engineer (Director of Institute of Islamic Studies)
20. Rashid Talib (Journalist)
21. Danial Latifi (Supreme Court Advocate)
22. Bashiruddin Ahmed (Senior Fellow, CSDS)

23. Shaharyar (Poet)
24. Ghulam Sheikh (Painter)
25. Kamila Tyabji (Chairman, Women's India Trust)
26. M. S. Agwani (Professor, JNU)
27. A. J. Kidwai (Director, Mass Communications)
28. Salman Haider (IAS)
29. Saeed Naqvi (Journalist)
30. Saleem Peeradina (Poet)
31. Seema Mustafa (Journalist)
32. Maqbool Ahmed (Professor, AMU)
33. Muzaffar Ali (Film-maker)
34. Mohibbul Hasan (Professor)
35. Anwar Azeem (Writer)
36. Najma Zaheer Baquir (Professor, JNU)
37. Anees Jung (Journalist)
38. Mushirul Hasan (Professor, Jamia Millia)
39. Feisal Alkazi (Theatre Director)
40. Zahida Zaidi (Professor, AMU)
41. Sajida Zaidi (Professor, AMU)
42. Iqtidar Alam Khan (Professor, AMU)
43. Shamshad Husain (Painter)
44. Hasan Suroor (Journalist)
45. Roshan Alkazi (Director, Art Gallery)
46. Moin Shakir (Professor, Marathwada University)
47. Amal Allana (Theatre Director)
48. Shaukat Kaifi (Film Actress)
49. Ali Baquir (Fellow, CSDS)
50. Jafar Zaheer (Aviation Consultant)
51. Aslam Qadeer (Professor, AMU)
52. Y. M. Adil (Film Writer)
53. Shafiq Naqvi (Writer)
54. Javed Alam (Reader, Himachal University)
55. Naseem Hasan (Social Scientist)
56. Salima Tyabji (Editor, OUP)
57. Muzammil Hussain (Artist)
58. Hasan Kutty (Documentary Film-maker)
59. Fatima Al Talib (Director, Advertising Agency)
60. Sameera Agha (Personnel Executive, TFAI)
61. Sahba Hussain (I. P. College, Delhi University)
62. Zoya Hasan (Reader, JNU)
63. Zakia Zaheer (Social worker)
64. Ghazala Ansari (Professor, AMU)
65. Ziaul Hasan (Journalist)
66. Ali Ashraf (Writer & Freedom Fighter)
67. Sadia Dehlvi (Editor, Shama)
68. Tahera Hasan (AIR Broadcaster)
69. Abida Samiuddin (Reader, AMU)
70. Shad Bano Ahmed (Professor, AMU)
71. Imrana Qadeer (Reader, JNU)
72. K. Azeem (Journalist)
73. Sughra Mehdi (Reader, Jamia Millia)
74. Azra Kidwai (Lecturer, Delhi University)
75. Sakina Hasan (Retd. Reader, Delhi University)
76. Syed Zaidi (Reader, Delhi University)
77. Amir Hasan (Professor, AMU)
78. Hindal Tyabji (IAS)
79. Saba Zaidi (TV Producer)
80. Shahla Haider
81. Askari Imam
82. S. A. Qayuum (Director, Arab Cultural Centre)
83. Laila Tyabji
84. Syeda Saiyadain (Writer)
85. Aijazuddin Ahmed (Professor, JNU)
86. Atiya Habib (Reader, JNU)
87. Habibur Rehman Kidwai (Reader, Jamia Millia)
88. Sayera Habib (Reader, AMU)
89. Kishwar Shabbir Khan (Professor, AMU)
90. Mehmood Reza
91. Maimoona Jafri (Reader, AMU)
92. Fauzia Mujeeb (Reader, AMU)
93. Q. M. Usmani (Reader, AMU)
94. Farhan Mujib (Reader, AMU)
95. Mehmood Haq (Professor, AMU)
96. Arif Rizvi (Reader, AMU)
97. Izhar Hussain (Professor, AMU)
98. S. S. Rizvi (Publishing)
99. Bilquees Musavi (Reader, AMU)
100. Shireen Moosvi (Reader, AMU)
101. S. Husain (Professor, AMU)
102. Tasneem Usmani (Librarian, American Centre)

103. Muzaffar Alam (Reader, AMU)
104. Rafat Zaheer (Social Worker)
105. Masooma Ali (Lecturer, Delhi University)
106. R. A. Khan (Reader, Jamia Millia)
107. Uzra Bilgrami
108. Asma Manzar (Civil Service)
109. Manzar Khan (Asst. Manager, Oxford University Press)
110. Rashida Siyar (Personnel Officer)
111. Latifa Nazir (Women's India Trust, Bombay)
112. Hamida Merchant (Women's India Trust, Bombay)
113. Akhtar Bano Sirajuddin
114. Mumtaz Begum
115. Ansari Shahraz
116. Birjees Kasim
117. S. S. Rizvi (Joint Secretary, Dept. of Agriculture)
118. Syed Zaidi (Oxford University Press)

Extract from *Mainstream*
8 March 1986

MEMORANDUM BY COMMITTEE FOR PROTECTION OF RIGHTS OF MUSLIM WOMEN

This memorandum was submitted to the prime minister on February 24, 1986. The signatories to the memorandum were: *Sahba Hussain* (Lecturer, I.P. College, Delhi); *Salima Tyabji* (Editor, Oxford University Press); *Imrana Quadeer* (Reader, JNU); *Azra Kidwai* (Lecturer, Delhi University); *A.J. Kidwai* (Former Vice Chancellor, Jamia Millia and present Director, Mass Communications Centre); *Irfan Habib* (Professor, AMU); *Zoya Hasan* (Reader, JNU); and *Danial Latifi* (Senior Advocate, Supreme Court of India.)

We consider it an important gain of our independence struggle that it led to the establishment of a secular state which contrasts with the situation prevailing in our neighbouring countries, as well as in most of the newly liberated countries of the third world.

Today, however, the secular fabric of our society is under severe pressure from various quarters. In our view the stable foundation of our secular polity can be strengthened not by offering concessions to communal/sectarian groups and interests with a view to achieving short-term political or electoral gains, but through positive and principled interventions which would preserve our secular identity. This course would best ensure the interests of all sections of our society, including the minorities. We view the specific question of the *right to maintenance of divorced Muslim women* in this perspective.

We believe that Muslim women have the right to maintenance — a right that they enjoy in several Muslim countries, through the rational and progressive interpretation of Islamic principles, as in Morocco, Iraq, Egypt, Turkey, Libya, Tunisia, Syria and Algeria. The interpretation being put forward by a section of the Muslim religious leadership in India, on the other hand, expresses a backward-looking perspective. We therefore specifically recommend the following, for a careful and comprehensive consideration of the Government of India.

1. We emphasize the necessity of safeguarding the interests of all sections of the minorities. That is why the demand to exclude Muslim women from the purview of section 125 of the Cr. P. C. (under which a divorced woman is entitled to take maintenance from her husband) would adversely affect both the rights and interests of Muslim women.

2. There is no provision in Muslim law which directly or indirectly prohibits a former husband from paying maintenance to his ex-wife after the iddat period. It is therefore erroneously argued that maintenance beyond the iddat period is contrary to the shariat.

3. Prior to the inclusion of section 125 of the Cr.P.C. which came into force in 1973, there was a provision for maintenance in section 488 in the old Cr. P. C. But there was no liability of payment to a divorced wife. Taking advantage of this lacuna many Muslim husbands divorced their wives when an application for maintenance was filed and thus escaped the liability to payment. To prevent this abuse and the hardship it caused to women, section 125 has rightly put the liability on the husband to pay maintenance even if he divorces his wife. However, it is given only in cases where husbands possess sufficient means to pay the maintenance allowance. The liability of the husband to pay maintenance, even if he divorces his wife, would act as an effective deterrent against hasty and irresponsible divorces. This is another reason why this provision should not be diluted.

4. The introduction of section 127 (3) (b) was a concession to the unreasonable demands of certain vested interests, who wanted to deny maintenance beyond the iddat period, on the plea that the mehr and maintenance during the iddat period would suffice. We consider this inimical to the interests of divorced Muslim women.

II

1. We feel that the right to maintenance beyond the period of iddat is an important and a positively helpful provision which provides security to a divorced woman. Evidence from different parts of the country indicates that a large number of Muslim women particularly belonging to poorer families are divorced and deserted. This can be corroborated by a survey of cases registered in rescue homes. This, in our view, reinforces the need for Muslim women particularly to have recourse to section 125.

2. Regardless of the rights and privileges that Islam may have conferred on Muslim women, they should not be denied the rights guaranteed by the Indian Constitution based on the recognition of equality, justice and fraternity of all citizens. It is imperative in a secular polity like ours to go beyond the rights conferred by various religions in order to evolve laws which would provide justice and succour to all women, irrespective of their religious beliefs.

III

1. Whereas criminal laws in their entirety apply to every community, it is really surprising that only one of its positive provisions — relating to women's rights — should be sought to be deleted on the dubious assumption that it is contrary to the Muslim

personal law. The Muslim personal law, for instance, stipulates specific punishments for crimes such as theft, robbery and rape which are rightly not accepted and are not applied. Likewise, the more humane civil and secular laws should be applied to all women regardless of their faith, and notwithstanding a conservative interpretation of personal laws by a section of their community.

2. Section 125 is a criminal law applicable to all citizens. Though the right to maintenance is a civil right, it forms a part of the criminal law so as to prevent a divorced woman from becoming a destitute. The provision of section 125 Cr. P. C seeks to prevent vagrancy which would occur in the case of poor Muslim women. Most women who seek maintenance have no means of livelihood. For them and for their children, maintenance is an absolute economic necessity.

3. Clearly section 125 is meant for indigent women as the maximum amount stipulated by this provision is only Rs 500.

IV

1. The judgement of the Supreme Court in the Shah Bano case has led to an intensive controversy particularly among Muslims. It is evident that those Muslims who have opposed the judgement have done so in the name of religion. They have used all the platforms available to them to reassert their weakening hold on Muslim public opinion, and have sought to exploit religion for sectional and communal political ends. They have taken advantage of the sense of insecurity among Muslims, caused by the persistence of communal riots and by discrimination in jobs and vocations. We feel that the growing influence of such exploitative communal elements should be effectively curbed, and they should be prevented from suppressing the rights of Muslim women under the cover of some religious decrees which are neither authentic nor consistent with the humanistic and rational spirit of Islam which lays considerable emphasis on the elevation of the status of women.

2. It is noteworthy that many important sections of Muslim public opinion, particularly among the educated and professional groups and segments have supported the right to maintenance. These include the intelligentsia, lawyers, teachers, social workers and even experts in the shariat law like Mirza Hamidullah Beg, the late Justice Murtuza Fazl Ali, Justice Khalid, former judge of the Supreme Court, Bahrul Islam, former chief justice of the Calcutta High Court, S. A. Masud, judge of the Ahmedabad High Court, Sattar Qureshy, Supreme Court advocate, Danial Latifi and A. G. Noorani. In the light of their views and judgement the Government would do well to consult a wider range of enlightened Muslim opinion, including competent jurists and legal experts in Islamic laws, before arriving at a decision on the matter.

3. Several articles and letters have appeared in the Urdu press, particularly in the *Quami Awaz* in which several women and men have strongly supported the right to maintenance under section 125 Cr. P.C. An attitude survey of Muslim women conducted by the Institute of Islamic Studies, Bombay, revealed that a large number of Muslim women also favour changes in rules relating to marriage, divorce and maintenance.

4. Equally, the experience of women's organizations working among Muslim women indicate that many amongst them have supported the right to maintenance. In our view, if avenues are open to them they would come forward to take advantage of this right, for at present the legal scales are heavily tilted against them. It is worth recording that an increasing number of cases for maintenance are being filed by Muslim women all over the country. In Calicut, for example, 200 such cases are filed every year. This

is an indication of both their support and need for maintenance. We believe that they should continue to receive state protection for the right to maintenance which is in accordance with the true spirit of Islam. In fact, experts have quoted extensively from the Quran to this effect. These include the learned commentaries and translations of the Quran made by Maulana Abul Kalam Azad, Allama Abdullah Yusuf Ali, Ahmed Reza Khan Barelvi and Fateh Muhammad Jullundhari. Reference should also be made to the Report of the Pakistan Government Commission on family laws.

V

1. It has been brought to our notice that the Government is sympathetic to the suggestions of a section of the Ulama and some Muslim leaders who have argued that the responsibility of maintenance after iddat should be shouldered by the father, or, in his absence, either by the brothers or the relatives, or alternatively, the responsibility is to be shared by the Muslim community as such. We understand that the Government is also examining the possibility of incorporating the provisions regarding maintenance (according to Muslim usage in India) into the Cr. P.C. through legislation. In support of such a move it is asserted that it would place Muslim women on a stronger footing and, in addition to their mehr, enable them to claim not only maintenance from their paternal/maternal family, but also enable them to have their claims legally enforced. Frankly we do not share such optimism. Indeed we consider such a move as retrogressive, and one which might well act as impetus to divorce amongst Muslims, particularly among the poorer sections.

2. The suggestion that Muslim women after divorce should have legal recourse only to her own family and not to her husband for maintenance is ludicrous. It would imply that a marriage contract for a Muslim woman involves only obligations and no rights which is totally contrary to the concept of nikah which essentially is a contract implying rights and obligations for both the parties. This means that after the woman has given the best of her life to her husband and raising his family she can be discarded and have no recourse to maintenance from her husband.

3. It seems extremely unlikely and unrealistic that a destitute woman would fight a legal battle against her own family for maintenance. The natural recourse of a woman in such circumstances is to fall back on her family for sustenance. If such support is not forthcoming it seems to us impractical that she be advised to file a suit against members of her own paternal/maternal family. With the breakup of the joint family system and the pressures of the economic crisis caused by galloping inflation, the woman may not like to add to the burden of her wider family. It is rarer still for the community to come forward to help her live with dignity. It is, however, possible that women who would not be welcomed in their father's and relatives' homes would find their position a little secure if a monthly allowance, even if it is a niggardly sum of Rs 200, was given to them.

4. In exonerating the husband from all responsibility of maintenance for a wife whom he had divorced for his own reasons is against the principles of social justice. The parents of the divorced woman cannot be expected to shoulder the responsibility and burden of their daughter who has been deserted/divorced for no fault of theirs.

5. Any attempt to change, alter or modify section 125 will hit the poor and the needy. The proposed law will violate Article 14 of the Indian Constitution which guarantees equal protection before the law; the State shall not deny to any persons equality before the law or the equal protection of the laws within the territory of India. Any law which violates Article 14 would be void.

VI

1. We understand the Government is considering the codification of Muslim personal law which, in its judgement, would protect women by making the payment of mehr commensurate with an increase in the husband's income. We do not believe this to be right. We fear that mehr will become a legal substitute for maintenance. Mehr, in most cases, is a paper transaction. Its fixation in the Indian subcontinent is more of a ritual and a formality rather than a realistic assessment of the genuine requirements in the event of a divorce. At any rate, the amount of the mehr is often most inadequate for anybody's lifelong maintenance. Given the status of most women, it is neither possible for the family to fix a reasonable amount of mehr nor desirable to insist on a larger mehr figure as the prospect of divorce is not taken into account at the time of the marriage. So, the question arises, can the divorced/deserted wife by debarred from further maintenance from her husband even if the amount paid to her is nominal.

2. We believe that mehr cannot absolve a husband of his liability to further maintain his divorced/deserted wife. Mehr is merely a consideration of money given at the time of marriage by the husband to the wife, as a token of his regard and responsibility. It can neither be a reasonable substitute for maintenance nor can it be treated as a final settlement in the event of divorce.

VII

1. Several Muslim countries have interpreted the Muslim personal law over the centuries in accordance with the spirit of Islam, and the specific requirements of their polity and society. It can be argued that this indeed is consistent with the ideas of justice, tolerance and compasion that the Quran enjoins on all Muslims. For instance, Syria, Iraq, Pakistan, Bangladesh and Sri Lanka, in particular, have modified Muslim family law and have set up arbitration councils to decide on its various aspects. India is among the few nations where the Muslim personal law continues to determine rules relating to polygamy, inheritance, and instant divorce. We are of the firm opinion that reforms in such areas, along with the right to maintenance, would enable Muslim women to acquire the rights and dignity they have been denied for so long.

We call upon the Government of India to ensure that the rights guaranteed by the Indian Constitution to women are upheld. We emphasize this in relation to the Muslim women particularly, who have been subjected to discrimination for so long. In our opinion, to deprive them of the rights granted by secular laws would be a retrograde measure. We therefore reiterate that under no circumstances should section 125 Cr. P. C. be repealed or any amendment introduced to exclude Muslim women from its beneficial purview.

Excerpt from the *Mainstream*
8 March 1986

Amendments Suggested in the Bill
All India Muslim Personal Law Conference, Bihar

(1) The bill provides for expenses during the iddat for all divorcees but no provision has been made for those divorcees who do not have an obligatory period of iddat (i.e. those who have been divorced before the consummation of marriage). Our Ulama have said that in such cases the divorcee be given, according to Islamic law, half of the mehr if fixed, or half of mehr mithl (i.e. ideal mehr) if not fixed.

(2) If the divorcee has a child, from her divorcing husband, the bill provides for its expenses only for two years whereas as per the Islamic law, following provisions should be made: (*a*) compensation for suckling the child; (*b*) compensation for looking after the child; and (*c*) the expenses for the child itself.

(3) There is no mention in the bill about who would be responsible for the child after two years. In the shariat the woman has been given the right to keep a son for five more years and a girl for seven more years, and charge the husband for looking after the child apart from the expenses incurred on the child.

(4) In the bill provision has been made for realization of mehr, if fixed, but the bill is silent about those cases where mehr has not been fixed. According to our amendment, in such cases she would be given mehr mithl (i.e. ideal mehr for her social status).

(5) The bill, puts the responsibility of maintaining a divorced woman (after the period of iddat) on those relatives who would inherit from her, without actually taking into account the Islamic principle. In Islamic law in some cases a non-inheriting person alone and in some cases he along with inheriting relatives is responsible for her maintenance. Moreover in the bill no distinction has been made between various categories and hierarchy of relatives. Therefore, the magistrate will have to face a lot of complications while applying this enactment. Also, many responsible relatives would go scot-free.

These amendments have been proposed by Mufti Muhammad Shariful Haq, Azamgarh, Maulana Mufti Ziaul Mustafa and seven other muftis.

Memorandum presented to the Prime Minister
Muslim Lawyers of Bombay High Court

Dear Prime Minister,

We, the members of Maharashtra Lawyers Forum, who practise in Bombay High Court, extend our fullest support to you through this memorandum for your just and secular stand in introducing the Muslim Women (Protection of Rights on Divorce) Bill 1986 in Parliament. We are pained to see that the communal and fascist elements in our country are showing with great enthusiasm their so-called sympathy with the Muslim divorced women. These communal forces have never had genuine concern for the welfare of Muslim women. The opposition parties, in collusion with communal forces, are giving political colour to this bill. They have ignored the secular and democratic values of our country and are sowing the seeds of hatred.

Sir, the Islamic intellectuals consider this bill as a great example of secularism and democracy which is reflected in our Constitution. We are watching with great interest the policies and programmes under your guidance and we are convinced that our country will keep on marching forward. It will become powerful in every field of life and peasants and common men will benefit.

It is time that the communal elements should stop worrying each other on the basis of caste, creed and religion and start living like the earlier citizens of India. It would be better if the national press does not waste its time on the Shah Bano versus Mohammad Ahmed controversy and spends more time on denouncing regionalism and caste and communal riots.

We pray to Allah for your longevity and for your successful service to this great nation.

Yours sincerely,

Jalaluddin (convenor),
A. Y. Qazi, vice chairman BRCC (I),
and 81 other lawyers.

AN OPEN LETTER TO THE MUSLIMS OF INDIA

Kamila Tyabji

So Shah Bano has been 'persuaded' *not* to accept the bare subsistence allowance from her husband that the Court had awarded her!

Pierre Crabites, a leading American judge in Cairo, has said of the founder of Islam: "The Prophet Mohammad was probably the greatest champion of women's rights the world has ever seen"; yet today his followers in India are unable to support the granting of Rs 179 per month as maintenance in spite of all the exhortations in the Quran itself that "to a divorced woman a reasonable maintenance is due".

And now it is suggested that we have shariat courts all over the country! In a community riddled by poverty and ignorance, instead of setting up technical schools and training centres and workshops we desperately need, money is to be poured into courts — when we are already paying for one judicial system.

Would it not be infinitely more worthwhile for Muslims to get together sensibly and decide what their law *is*, so that they could then insist that the courts enforce it?

During the last few days the Muslim community has shown a remarkable solidarity in expressing their love for the shariat and their own personal law. But what we love is what is laid down in the Quran, and what was further expounded by the Prophet Muhammad. Is this the law we are following?

For example, the Prophet himself had allowed a woman a divorce when she wanted one — but millions of Muslim women in India are denied such a right; and yet a man can obtain one (even though the Prophet had described divorce as 'hateful') by just saying "I divorce you; I divorce you; I divorce you," thrice even if he is drunk at the time! Is this the Muslim law?

The Islamic idea of dower (mehr) is a settlement on the *wife* by the husband at the time of marriage; but Muslim youths today ardently pursue an alien type of dowry, of which *they* and not their wives are the beneficiaries. Is this the Muslim law?

The Quran, whilst allowing that a man may marry more than one wife, expressly stated that he may do so only if he can treat them both equally; and added for good measure that, as he would never be able to treat them equally, it is better if he married only one. But today in India all thoughts of equality are forgotten, and one finds men abandoning their wives (or sending them back to their father's house) and marrying again with complete impunity. Should the first wife ask for a divorce, she not only forfeits her mehr but has to pay a heavy price for the privilege. One listens in vain for a whisper from our maulanas, saying that such second marriages are either void, or bigamous! What *is* the Muslim law?

What makes the situation tragic is that there are perfectly simple, and legitimate, ways *in the Muslim law itself* by which these wrongs could be righted — and which have been adopted by Muslims in almost all countries except ours. One effective way would be for bodies like the Jamaat-i-Islami, the Muslim Personal Law Board, etc., to declare that, in future, *at the time of all Muslim marriages certain clauses would be presumed in the nikahnama* (marriage contract). That marriage is a contract is indisputable in Muslim law — and innumerable women's meetings have voted for a standard nikahnama.

Some such action by Muslim leaders and maulanas would establish their sincerity and credibility, and bring our law into line with the advanced Muslim countries. Without that, it would appear that it is only we, and not they, who are seeking to preserve the nobility and purity of our religion — whilst they are clinging on to the accretions of centuries of male chauvinism. It is they, not us, who are bringing disrepute to the founder of Islam, and it is they who are throwing the Muslim law to the wolves.

GOA ROW OVER SHARIAT LAW

G R Singbal

Educated Goan Muslim youth have decided to start a door-to-door contact with their co-religionists in the renewed drive against extension of shariat laws to Goa.

The campaign to counter the propaganda by the supporters of shariat law within the community comes in the wake of fresh attempts to revive the demand for scrapping the old Portuguese family laws of Goa which forbid easy availability of divorce and remarriage.

The latest development follows a split within the newly formed Goa Muslim Personal Law Committee, set up recently to consider the question of desirability or otherwise of extending the shariat laws to Goa. The committee broke into two groups last week following a divergence of views.

In order to propagate its views, the pro-shariat group has announced the formation of the Goa Muslim Shariat Organization under Shaikh Haji Gaffar of Sanguem. The other faction is led by Sheikh Abdul Kadar, a prominent city businessman and mineowner.

Both sides have been questioning each other's motives, one group alleging that the opponents are too westernized and do not know their Quran, and the other decrying the pro-shariat group as being without any religious conviction, and opting for only easy divorce and remarriage.

The section favouring retention of the Portuguese law derives its strength from the support it has mustered to its cause from the educated Muslim youth and women. Unlike the shariat laws, the Portuguese family law has greater appeal for the Goan Muslim women because of the much-needed security its offers.

Sheikh Kadar proposes to educate co-religionists about the implications of the personal law. He asserts that there is nothing in the Portuguese law which goes against the basic tenets of Islam. Goan Muslims do perform nikah (religious marriage cere-mony) after the civil registration of their marriage, he points out.

One argument of the pro-shariat group is that the law is based on divine dictates and should, therefore, be accepted without question by devout Muslims. The group has announced plans to launch a similar door-to-door drive to bring home to Muslims the need to protect the shariat act.

Its activities will also include representing their demand for extension of the shariat act to both the local authorities and the Centre. To boost its campaign, the group also intends enlisting delegates of the All India Muslim Personal Law Board, consisting of legal luminaries and Ulamas.

The disturbing aspect of the current campaign is the regional lines on which it has effectively divided the Goan Muslim population. Of the total 43,000 Muslim popula-tion of Goa, the non-Goan component is estimated at about 15,000. The Shariat Law Committee claims the support of 22 jamats, but Sheikh Kadar avers that 98 per cent of the Goan Muslims favour retention of the Portuguese law.

He also alleges that foul methods are being used by the rival group to claim superiority of numbers. At a meeting called by the committee here on February 7, the pro-shariat group had successfully prevented participation of Goan Muslims by issuing fake an-nouncements in the local newspapers that the meeting had been cancelled. The next day they packed the venue with non-Goan Muslims brought from Vasco and Margao and passed a resolution ousting him from the committee presidentship.

The Kadar supporters resented it. However, what might have ended in clashes was averted after Sheikh Kadar hastily asked this supporters to withdraw from the scene.

The debate has tended to become acrimonious with both sides questioning each other's authority to be the sole custodians of Muslim interests in Goa. The Kadar Committee insists that implementation of the Muslim personal law in Goa is solely the concern of Goan Muslims and that the so-called shariat committee has no authority to spell out any opinion on the subject or take decisions.

In a public appeal through newspapers, the committee urged "all Goan Muslim brethren not to be carried away and get misguided by such acts of unscrupulous and frustrated elements who have infiltrated this peaceful territory and are aiming at vitiating the peaceful Goan atmosphere".

This brought an equally strong reaction from the other camp. Dismissing Sheikh Kadar as a "non-entity in the collective matters of religious jamats of Goa", the Gaffar group insisted that implementation of the personal law was very much the concern of Goan as well as non-Goan Muslims since the committee had invited suggestions from both. It also strongly objected to attempts to inject a 'Goan and non-Goan' element into the controversy.

Extract from the *Indian Express*
18 February 1986

PERSONAL LAW AND COMMON CODE

Sir, – I have recently had an exchange of correspondence with Syed Shahabuddin, Acting President of the All-India Muslim Majlis-e-Mushawrat, which is very thought-provoking and should be shared with a larger audience.

I have, on December 1, 1985, on behalf of Hindustani Andolan, sent out a circular on personal law and a common code, a copy of which reached Mr Shahabuddin. This reads as follows:

"Recently in Bombay a huge morcha was taken out by the Bombay Muslim Federation to protest against the Supreme Court judgement in the Shah Bano case. Among those who led the morcha was a Member of Parliament from Hyderabad. Several speakers present at the morcha used most abusive and intemperate language.

"The effigy of a Supreme Court judge was carried by some of those who participated in the morcha. They wanted to burn his effigy but ultimately they decided to tear it to pieces. All this has angered a large number of people belonging to various communities including Muslims . . . . .

"It is time we asked these so-called devout Muslim leaders a few questions. I have decided to do this as a very large but silent majority of Indians want these questions to be asked of these leaders. The following are the questions:

"Are they prepared to demand that the Criminal Procedure Code should be so amended that every Muslim can be awarded the punishment for any crime committed by him or her as laid down by the shariat? For example, any one of them found caught stealing should be prepared to let his hands be cut off or any one who commits adultery should be prepared to be stoned to death, etc.

"Are these leaders prepared to tell their fellow Muslims that they should stop selling, smuggling, distributing and consuming liquor and drugs as it is against the shariat and all those who flout this edict should be prepared to be flogged publicly?

"Are they prepared to tell their fellow Muslims not to deposit their money in any bank as banks charge interest from borrowers, which is against the shariat?

"Has any Muslim who has become a citizen of the US, Britain, Germany, Canada, etc. demanded that there should be a separate personal law for him? To the best of my knowledge, no nation will allow such a thing to happen.

"It is high time that we in India implemented the Directive Principles as laid down in the Indian Constitution that there should be one common civil code for all Indian citizens. It is time we once again mobilize support for our demand."

In response to this circular I received the following letter from Mr Shahabuddin in his capacity as Acting President of the Mushawrat in Delhi, dated December 24:

"If the Muslim community of India desires its freedom of conscience and freedom of religion to be respected, it is unjust of you to accuse them of fanaticism or acting against the unity and integrity of the country. They are not asking for the shariat to be applied to any other community and in the same way they do not want their family affairs to be regulated by imported or alien concepts. No external authority has the right or authority to decide whether or not personal or family affairs fall within the core area of their religion. May I add for your information that Islamic punishments can be awarded only by an Islamic state and under the Islamic law of evidence.

"You imply as if Muslims alone sell, smuggle, distribute and consume liquor and drugs. This, to say the least, is stupid. Is India to be governed by what any other country does or by what the Indian Constitution promises to people? As far as the Directive Principles are concerned, any objective mind would assert that the state must first implement the principles which touch common questions and purposes such as education, health, nutrition, livelihood, etc., rather than take up emotional and divisive issues.

"If the Hindustani Andolan has for any reason whatsoever come to the conclusion that its primary and immediate objective should be the introduction of a uniform civil code, I am afraid it has reduced itself to a Hindu Andolan with which no secular-minded person can have anything to do. I may caution you that through such activities you are weakening the fabric of national unity and it is time that you reconsider your priorities."

On receipt of this letter I replied to Mr Shahabuddin on December 30:

"My circular letter of December 1, 1985, is not regarding the agitation by the entire Muslim community (as you have made out) against the Supreme Court judgement, but against some bigoted and fundamentalist elements of the Muslim community. Many Muslim men and women have condemned the leaders of this morcha for using intemperate language against the Supreme Court judges and the Supreme Court judgement in the Shah Bano case. They have also expressed their unhappiness about the burning of the effigy of a Supreme Court judge.

"You do not like my use of the words 'fanatical elements'. How does one describe those who use most abusive language against the Supreme Court and about slogans like 'Supreme Court bandh karo', 'Supreme Court murdabad' and then proceed to burn the effigy of a Supreme Court judge using language which is unprintable? I hope you have not convinced yourself that the leaders of this morcha represented the sentiments of the entire Muslim community.

"I hope you will agree with me when I say that every religious group in our country has its share of fanatical elements who allow themselves to be exploited by petty and unscrupulous politicians. These politicians do not hesitate to say or do anything, even if it means gross misinterpretation of their religion and inciting hatred and violence in the name of God and religion. Don't you think people like you and me should work together and fight such elements instead of joining or encouraging those who raise slogans like Islam in danger or Hinduism in danger?

"You say that: 'No external authority has the right or authority to decide whether or not personal or family affairs fall within the core area of their religion.' Please spell out clearly what authority is acceptable to you. Your frank answer is very necessary in this regard as I do not know what precisely you have in mind when you talk of 'external authority'.

"It seems to me that you are not prepared to accept either the Government of India or the Parliament of India or the Supreme Court of India as the authority. This clearly reveals a 'take it or leave it' attitude. I must caution you against adopting this attitude as a vast majority of people of India are now getting sick and tired of those who go about flaunting this approach.

"I think the time has come for all sensible, moderate and truly secular minded Indians to work together in generating a climate for fruitful dialogue between members of different communities and religions on the subject of a common civil code. However, to begin with, let this dialogue be conducted between the Government and the enlightened religious leaders of the Muslim community.

"Care should be taken, however, that any conclusion or consensus arrived at cannot and should not be allowed to go against the national interest, thereby creating more ill will and mutual suspicion between different religious groups in the country and further weakening the fabric of national unity.

"When I say this, I have in mind the problem of population explosion in our country and the paramount need to control it through appropriate legislation governing marriage, divorce, etc., which can be applicable to every Indian. Politicians may go on postponing taking this decision on the pretext that this may endanger national unity but they forget that a vast majority of people in India want the decision to be taken without any further delay as they feel that it is not possible to achieve national unity with the help of empty slogans and the politics of appeasement motivated solely in consideration of votes.

"You have stated in your letter that I imply 'as if Muslims alone sell, smuggle, distribute and drink liquor and use drugs'. I do not know by what logic or understanding of the English language you have reached this conclusion.

"You have rightly asked 'Is India to be governed by what another country does or by what the Indian Constitution promises to the people?' In this context, I would like once again to raise the question, viz: 'Which other nation has a separate Muslim personal law for its Muslim citizens?' No nation will ever allow such a thing to happen. In India we have given to every Indian the freedom to follow his own religion, worship, etc. We are committed to 'Sarva Dharma Sama Bhava' (equal respect to all religions).

"The Hindustani Andolan is also committed to 'Sarva Dharma Sama Bhava', to national unity and integrity and, therefore, believes that the time has come for all patriotic Indians to work for a common civil code in consultation and cooperation with the leaders of all communities and religions in India.

"Finally if you believe that anyone who talks about a common civil code for all Indians must be described as a 'Hindu' communalist, you are at liberty to go ahead and put this 'dhobi mark' on Hindustani Andolan. We have nothing to fear."

Madhu Mehta
Hindustani Andolan
National Headquarters
84/A Nepean Sea Road
Bombay 400 006

Excerpt from the *Indian Express*
11 January 1986

UNIFORM CIVIL CODE

Sir, – I find that Mr Madhu Mehta has released my letter of December 24 on his circular of December 1 and his reply of December 30.

I replied to him on January 9 as follows:

"Please refer to your letter of December 30, 1985. I am happy to note that your letter was directed not entirely against the Muslim community which, in your view, deserves to be condemned. Even the facts on the basis of which you find them deserving of condemnation have been disputed but have you or your organization ever judged any other similar occurrence by equal standards? The democratic right of dissent can and does take ugly forms but so long as it does not threaten law and order or take the form of physical violence, we have to be somewhat tolerant.

"But coming to the substantive points you have raised, the word 'external authority' means any authority which is not competent to interpret the basic scriptures of the particular religion. I do not consider the Government of India, the Parliament of India or the Supreme Court of India as competent to interpret the scriptures which lay down the essentials of Islam, and this is not my view but the view of the Supreme Court itself.

"The Constitution never speaks of a common civil code, let me first correct you; it speaks of a uniform civil code, which implies plurality within the larger framework of the social ethos of the state to which all civil laws must confirm. I do not agree with you that the time has come for the introduction of a uniform civil code.

"I do not question your right to hold your opinion on the subject but I fail to see how a uniform civil code at this stage, imposed on the Muslim community against its will, will serve national interest or create goodwill or eliminate suspicion or strengthen the fabric of national unity. If at all, such an act would weaken national unity and slow down the process of national integration by aggravating unease and insecurity in the mind of the Muslim community.

"You seem to find a nexus between population control and personal law. A moment thought will reveal that in an endogamous society the marriage system has nothing to do with the rate of growth which is biologically determined and totally unrelated to whether one or more women are married to one man.

"I would request you to re-read and ponder over your own sentence about criminal activities and you will not fail to appreciate the in-built vilification of an entire community. Your question whether any other nation has a separate Muslim personal law for its Muslim citizens is to my mind totally irrelevant once you concede that our country is to be governed by our Constitution. I may, however, inform you, that, in Muslim countries, even in Egypt, non-Muslims are not governed by Muslim personal law and are subject to their own personal laws.

"Once again, you tend to think that religion is nothing more than ritual worship; once again you presume to decide what the essence of Islam would be to a Muslim; you have no such right. To a Muslim, Islam is a code of life and the Constitution of India does not only grant freedom of religion but freedom of conscience. A Muslim cannot pick and choose from among the injunctions of the Quran, as simplified by the traditions. Why must you force a Muslim Indian to be a good citizen and a bad Muslim or vice versa? Why cannot he be permitted to be a good Indian and a good Muslim at the same time?

"I am aware of the objects as well as of the activities of the Hindustani Andolan. Indeed I owe it to you to have been kept informed but I also recall that on a number of occasions I have responded to your circulars and this letter is the only time when you have responded.

"As far as the Janata party is concerned, it has not taken a stand either on the Shah Bano case or the uniform civil code. It has noted with interest the debate the Supreme Court judgement has generated within the Muslim community. The Muslim community must, in its view, be permitted to come to their own consensus without any pressure from outside. If Muslim society needs reform, the pace must be determined by themselves as well as the nature of change appropriate to their situation.

"The Janata party stands for non-interference with the personal law of any community or the imposition of any change in it against its will. The Janata party also stands for the protection of the religious rights of the religious minorities as enshrined in the Constitution, in letter and spirit.

"Today the cry for a uniform civil code has become the war-cry of those who are obsessed with effacing the religious identity of the Muslim community, with submerging them culturally, with forcing India into a common mould. In our history there has always been pressure for assimilation. To the extent that the Hindustani Andolan does not appreciate this historic and psychological reality, it falls into the trap of Hindu chauvinism.

"I request you to reconsider the position of the Hindustani Andolan on the question of the uniform civil code and I would like the Hindustani Andolan to dedicate itself to secure for all the people of India the realization of the other Directive Principles which are more concerned with their life, liberty, happiness and bread. In one word, your priorities must change in the national interest."

Syed Shahabuddin, MP
187 North Avenue
New Delhi 110 001

Excerpt from the *Indian Express*
21 January 1986

CONSTITUTION OF INDIA AND THE
UNIFORM CIVIL CODE

Dr N. Y. Dole

A heated debate has begun in our country on the issue of the common civil code since the judgement on Shah Bano case has been delivered.

The Supreme Court has decided to grant alimony to Shah Bano which must be given by her husband as per section 125 Cr. P. C.

But... why is there such an explosion of opinion on this issue this time, despite the fact that innumerable petitions on alimony are pending in the various courts?

One of the reasons is that Justice Chandrachud while delivering the judgement, has unnecessarily ventured to penetrate into the province of the Quran, shariat etc.; while attempting this, he has interpreted the Quran and explained it to defend his judgement. Had he restricted his scope of the judgement to the problem of alimony and to the issue of the protection of the rights of Muslim women, orthodox sections of Muslims would not have snatched the opportunity to fan the sentiments against the court's decision. Probably, the ambition of Justice Chandrachud to enroll his name as "the chief justice who delivered a historical judgement" might be a motive. Such a decision... let us not forget that Justice Chandrachud was also the Supreme Court Judge during the period of Emergency when it bowed down before the Government.

... The moment the judgement was delivered, orthodox Muslims sprung into action as the judgement mentioned "holy books" and also progressive Muslims, who were extremely weak... were activated. It was a section of progressive Muslims who demanded various rights (e.g. no more verbal talaq, implementation of uniform civil code etc.), first which made orthodox Muslims restless and enraged them.... But probably (the progressives) depended more on the "modern era" propagator, Rajiv Gandhi, for implementation... this brought about their strategic failure. In fact, Rajiv was pressurized by the onslaught of orthodox Muslims, and promised to reconsider the whole issue and, on the other hand, the fundamentalists forced Shah Bano to make a *volte face* (by withdrawing her petition) creating an extremely awkward situation for the progressives. Another example: Shahabuddin, the leader of the Janata party, contested the by-election to the Lok Sabha. He is a renowned orthodox Muslim and he won the election with a substantial margin.

It seems that those who gave undue importance to Justice Chandrachud's judgement became targets of mockery.

But the Supreme Court's decisions should not be treated as a "universal truth". How decisions are reversed overnight will become clear after studying the "Golaknath case".... For example, the issue of supremacy of the judiciary over Parliament was greatly debated in the above case. Socialists were upholding the supremacy of Parliament during that time. But when Emergency was declared, Indira Gandhi was upholding the supremacy of Parliament over the judiciary, and the same socialists reversed their stand and were opposing it tooth and nail....

Now orthodox Muslims are agitating for a change in the Constitution to invalidate the Supreme Court decision, whereas others are upholding it....

The saner view should be that the unexpected Supreme Court decision is a step forward for social progress. But it would be a myth to take it as a victory....

The whole confusion and inflamed passions (began) to develop when the propaganda was launched that all (civil) laws would be imposed upon the Muslims after the judgement (on alimony).

.... In fact, there was no need to bring in the issue of the common civil code at that time. But some Hindu fanatics (skilfully) kept aside (the issue of) Shah Bano and vehemently began to propagate for the implementation of a common civil code.

.... Today, one can see a clear picture. All Hindus are backing the so-called common civil code while Muslims are opposing it unanimously. But all sections of Hindus are not supporting the demand for a common civil code. The opposing sections of Hindus are: Sikhs, Buddhists, Jains, Virshaivas, scheduled castes and tribes, other castes, including R.S.S. ex-chief Golwalkar Guruji, who used to oppose the common civil code.

.... There is a common penal code for social customs which is applicable to all.The Cr. P. C. is also applicable to all .... But it is foolishness to demand a common code for marriage, divorce, inheritance, rites at the time of birth and death, for different religions, since the customs are different ... such a demand would be dogmatic.

Excerpt from *Sadhana*
20 February 1986

THE COMMON CIVIL CODE
(Seminar at Nanded)

The "Anjumane Nowjawanne" organization arranged an all-party seminar on the above subject under the chairmanship of Maulana Abdul Kayyum. Thousands of Muslim people attended the meeting held at the Pratibha Niketan.Natya Mandir.

.... Most Hindu speakers propounded that the common civil code should be accepted whereas Muslim leaders stated that laws should be implemented in all fields according to the shariat.

In the beginning, Principal M. S. Deshpande appealed to all Muslim brothers to change themselves according to the changing times. While following religious principles conscientiously in their private life, they must change themselves now. He gave various supporting statements from the books of M. R. A. Baig, secretary of the late barrister Jinnah.... He also said in his speech that those who have accepted Indian citizenship... must accept the common civil code.

.... Whereas, Advocate Abdul Rehman Siddiqui said vehemently that there is no need for Muslims to change themselves according to the times. The holy Quran is beyond time. For the well being of human beings, the Quran sharif has given commandments. But now the Supreme Court has interfered with the commandments of the Quran which will not be tolerated.... The Supreme Court, while delivering the judgement has substantiated its statements by quoting from Sir Zafrulla's book. But he belongs to the Ahmedi sect. The Muslims have no obligation to follow such judgements.

The Bharatiya Janata Party (former Jan Sangh) spokesman Advocate Maski supported the judgement and said that it is according to the shariat.

.... Maulana Abdul Kadar made a provocative speech saying that, "We will follow commandments of only Prophet Mohammed and no one else. If anyone prevents us from doing so, then we are ready to make the maximum sacrifice and then there will be bloodshed.... "

.... Immediately, Mr Sudhakar Doifode, editor of *Prajavani* got up and raised a strong objection to such a provocative speech. Ultimately, the chairman of the seminar, Maulana Abdul Kayyum, disallowed Maulana Abdul Kadar from continuing his speech.

Assistant superintendent of the Gurudwara Board, Advocate Paramjyot Singh, also supported the Supreme Court judgement and appealed to the Muslims to accept it in good spirit.

Mrs Sarfraz Begum also spoke, but not on the stage. She stood behind the curtain and delivered her speech. She supported all previous Muslim speakers. . . .

Sadashiv Patil, leader of the Janata party, said that all Indians must have religious freedom. But the issue of alimony is not at all connected with religion but is a social problem. . . . "While preparing a common civil code, Hindu laws will not be imposed on Muslims. We can select good parts from both the laws and prepare a common code." Adv. Godamgaohkar said that if Muslims are being adamant on the issue and if they expect support from the Muslim community all over the world, then the matter is serious. Islam is a liberal religion and Muslims must change themselves now.

Cong-I leader, Advocate Nurullakhan stated that, "we will welcome the implementation of all Quranic punishments, eg. cutting off hands for offences like theft, than punishment given under Indian penal laws," He also stated that there are smugglers and traitors like Kumar Narain in other religions.

Vishwa Hindu Parishad leader Dr K. M. Joshi expressed his views on behalf of all Hindus. He said that the Supreme Court has given a judgement based on humanity. But Muslim leaders want to consolidate their leadership on this issue for paltry political aspirations. They want to make the whole of India "green".

At the end, the chairman, Maulana Abdul Kayyum, stated that the commandments of the Quran are highest and no one, including the Government and the judiciary has any right to change them.

Excerpt from *Marathwada*
19 October 1985

VICTORY AND DEFEAT OF SHAH BANO

She won a right for talaq-affected women from the Supreme Court. She was a victorious woman. But she was defeated when she said, in a press conference, that the court's decision should be changed. Blind Muslim communalism and one-track-minded activists were victorious at that juncture.

. . . . But their victory is also not an easy one. . . . when the judgement was delivered, these selfish, fundamentalist leaders made a hue and cry about an attack on the (Muslim) religion. How can this (judgement) be treated as interference in the religion?. . . The Supreme Court has only interpreted on the question of how a divorced wife should be treated by her husband. Has it touched the religion? The Supreme Court has not at all hurt religious feelings. . . .

(On the private bill placed by Banatwala, Muslim League leader) Mrs Abida Begum and Zainul Bashir belonging to Cong.-I and, all other Muslim leaders belonging to other parties opposed the court's judgement on the ground of interference with Muslim religion. . . . Abida Begum is the widow of the late president Fakhruddin Ali Ahmed. . .

Banatwala wants that the right to decide alimony should be given to Muslim religious priests, he wants shariat-courts established in the country. . . now, Muslim progressives should come forward. Shah Bano's *volte-face* was due to pressure from such selfish leaders and fundamentalists.

. . . . Now these vested interests want to surround the Parliament to protest against the judgement. . . (we must remember) that there is an attempt to revive the fundamentalist religious movement all over the world, and these vested religious interests in

India are no exception to this. we must show them their real place... There are incitements (by these interested groups) to cut the hair of women, flogging them etc., in India. If these incidents continue, the rule of law in the country will not prevail... The *volte face* by Shah Bano will encourage the activities of these reactionaries. Unless progressive elements from the Muslim community come forward, the attempt to stop the wheel of history can be foiled by others.

Excerpt from *Kesari*
19 November 1985

CHALLENGE OF MULLAS-MAULAVIS

Last Wednesday was chosen by Muslim communal organizations in Bombay to protest against the Supreme Court judgement and a mammoth demonstration was organized by them.... The main purpose of the demonstration was a simple show of strength. From an observation of the huge demonstration, it would appear that, once again, communal Muslims in India had made preparations to recreate the climate that existed during the pre-partition period.

.... *The show of strength was directed mainly towards the progressive sections of the Muslims*. That is why the Muslim progressive elements and other non-Muslim sections must unite to oppose the fanatic Muslims, and must stand behind those who are attempting to amend the Muslim personal law.

.... The slogans and the speeches (in the demonstration) were outrageous and openly challenged the Government and the judiciary. Speakers said that no Government can remain in power if it interferes with Muslim personal law.... How can they speak in such offensive language? It is because the Congress party and all opposition parties have been habituated to wooing the votes of the fanatic Muslims .... It also shows that the Government has followed a policy of appeasement towards these fanatic Muslims....

Today, some of the Islamic nations are also changing the personal law as it exists in their country. Even during the period of Ayub Khan or Bhutto in Pakistan, certain changes were made in law. And all accepted these changes without a word. No Muslim from Pakistan thought to utter that Islam was in danger.... even mullas-maulavis had accepted the common Cr. P. C. in India. No one still says that it interferes with their religion....

We should not tolerate the demands of these fanatics. So far, in the name of secularism, *divisive* tendencies were thriving in the country. We have paid the price for it by accepting the partition and, after independence, we have also paid the price for "foreigners-problem in Assam".... If we do not want to repeat history, the challenging language of these communalists must be stopped right now.

Excerpt from *Loksatta*
30 November 1985

INTERVIEWS

Vikram Savarkar

Just because there are elections in Assam and Kerala, the Central Government is very much scared of Muslim voters. Therefore, Rajiv Gandhi gives more importance to the Muslims than to the Constitution — Rajiv has bowed down before the Muslim (community)....

... When asked about his reaction on Rajiv's stand on Muslim personal law, Mr Savarkar said that he was not surprised by Rajiv's *volte face*. Mr Savarkar bitterly said: "Rajiv's mother brought two Muslims as presidents of India. Even Nehru used to say that he became a Hindu accidentally.'

... He declared that he will shortly announce a practical programme (of protest) for implementation in which at least 5 per cent of the R.S.S. volunteers will join.

He said that he has filed a writ petition in the Supreme Court for implementation of the common civil code. But it has not yet come up for hearing (in the Supreme Court).

According to him, "No Muslim is patriotic since he believes only in the Quran." When asked whether he has read the Quran, he said that he has read it in English. He said that Muslims are pan-Islamic and have slogans like "Muslims of the world, unite."

Vikram Savarkar has already written a book — *Quran vs Constitution of India* which is proscribed by the Government and there is a case pending against him in the Dadar court. In the book, he has pointed out 36 places where the Quran totally differs from the Indian Constitution....

According to him, "Student's Islamic Movement of India held a conference in 1981 at Nagpur. In that conference, many resolutions were passed declaring that Muslims must break idols in India and must spread Islam throughout the country. It means that Muslims are creating a separate nation, now Hindus should not keep quiet."

Excerpt from *Loksatta*
6 December 1985

Domnique Gonsalves

After assuming power, Nehru should have begun to take steps towards implementation of a common civil code. He went on to woo the Muslim fanatics even after partition.... All leaders have taken an opportunistic position as they have an eye on the 11 crore Muslim votes. These bulk votes can tilt the balance of power in the country....

However, he said that the social and economic condition of Muslims have not changed even after Independence, e.g. in Bhiwandi 45 per cent of the population is Muslim, not more than 2 per cent of them figure in the unskilled category. How many Muslims are working as industrial workers? A very low percentage! They do not get jobs.

Bal Thackeray

Communal-minded Muslims, who have burnt the effigy of a Supreme Court judge and common civil code have no place in this country.... The issue is not of religion, but of poisonous seeds of treacherous tendencies. Can minorities in Pakistan take such an offensive stand? Those who do not accept our Constitution and laws, should quit the country and go to Karachi or Lahore.

He said that the Muslim demonstration in Bombay was very provocative. They were giving slogans like "We got Pakistan easily, now we will seize Hindustan in fighting". All these slogans remind us of pre-partition days. We have gulped the poison of partition, now we do not want any civil war in future. *There are large numbers of Muslims who are true to our country, Constitution and the laws, but the handful of communal Muslims should be prevented.* For this, we must have courage. All true patriotic Muslims must come forward to work for this. . . .

He also said that to protect the common civil code means protecting the sovereignty of our country. . . .

There might be many religions in the country, but there must be one constitution, and one common law applicable to all. . . .

"Are there different laws applicable to Muslims in Russia or America? And if not, can the Muslim community existing in those countries dare to show arrogance (as shown here)?". . . .

Excerpt from *Loksatta*.
2 December 1985

MEMORANDUM
The Joint Women's Programme

The Joint Women's Programme, a national women's organization, secular in nature (members belong to various religious and social backgrounds) organized several mass meetings and demonstrations throughout the country to create public awareness on the issue of Muslim personal law. Meetings were held in New Delhi, Kanpur, Allahabad, Calcutta and Bangalore where Muslim women from all walks of life debated on the Muslim Women (Protection of Rights on Divorce) Bill, which the Government proposes to introduce shortly.

Muslim women today are in a dilemma: should they succumb to the pressure of Muslim fundamentalists; or should they fight the discrimination? This controversy is related to the recent attempt to introduce the new Muslim Women (Protection of Rights on Divorce) Bill. The introduction of this bill would exclude Muslim women from the purview of section 125 Cr. P. C. If this new bill becomes a reality, no Muslim woman will have redressal from the courts — which she has hitherto been entitled to.

This bill is unconstitutional and is a retrogressive step in the sphere of women's development. At our meetings most women, particularly Muslim women, felt that the bill was a distortion of the shariat and violative of the rights guaranteed to women under the Quran and the sunnah. As it is, most of the time women are given a raw deal, and this bill is perhaps the unkindest cut of all. All women feel very strongly about this bill and pray that good sense will prevail, so that their Muslim sisters are not denied the advantage of seeking justice under section 125 Cr. P.C. Muslim participants urged the Government to focus on those points in the sunnah and the shariat which would help the community, instead of giving in to vested interests in the matter of the bill.

At the national level, the Joint Women's Programme joined hands with all the other national women's organizations in their appeal to the prime minister to withdraw the bill and uphold Article 14 of the Constitution that guarantees equal protection to all before law.

JWP cooperated with MARG in sending out telegrams to the prime minister against the bill. The Joint Women's Programme and all its centres throughout the country sent over a hundred such telegrams.

The outcome of our meetings and demonstrations at New Delhi, Kanpur, Bangalore, Allahabad and Calcutta brought forth the following recommendations:

1. The bill is a violation of the shariat. It goes against the shariat on many counts:

    (a) That it does not make any distinction between the different kinds of divorces; i.e. there is no difference between a divorce by the husband and the divorce sought by a wife (khula).

    (b) That the bill includes ghair mehrams (distant relations) to pay this maintenance.

    (c) That the religious provision of mataa is not defined in a separate section. (Mataa is the Quranic provision, in addition to mehr, which a husband has to make for a divorced wife. This could be a one-time, lump sum payment or, if the husband does not have enough capital, it could be paid, out of his income, in instalments.)

    (d) That the bill makes the wakf responsible for paying maintenance to a divorced Muslim woman. This is not possible unless the wakf is made so by the wakif for the purpose. No amount of money can be utilized out of a wakf unless the wakif has specified that it may be so used.

    (e) The question of maintenance of a divorced Muslim wife is directly related to the law of divorce, which is not properly codified in the shariat.

2. The bill is unconstitutional as it violates Article 14 of the constitution that guarantees equal protection to all before law.

3. The bill denies divorced Muslim women maintenance under section 125 Cr.P.C. It therefore separates Muslim women from women of other communities — who will continue to enjoy the privilege permitted by this section.

4. The bill is a setback to the goal of achieving a uniform civil code. It also retrogrades our endeavour towards national integration as it tends to discriminate between Muslim women and women from other communities and therefore the Muslim community from other communities. (The State shall endeavour to secure for the citizens a Uniform Civil Code throughout the territory of India — Directive Principle in Article 44).

POSTSCRIPT

Madhu Kishwar

The Muslim Women (Protection of Rights on Divorce) Bill was passed by Parliament in an atmosphere of total cynicism and spinelessness. The Congress (I) successfully drove a wedge between the two communities for narrow electoral purposes.

It is a pity that most Muslim leaders do not seem to realize that by pressing for this bill they have walked into a well-prepared trap. The bill has far more serious consequences than that of its going against the interests of Muslim women. It has become a potent weapon for spreading even more hatred and violence against Muslims. Most Hindus are being led to believe that this bill demonstrates the sinister designs of those Muslims who want to further 'break up the country'. For instance, a prominent Hindu politician is supposed to have remarked that this bill is proof that the mullahs and the Muslim League are running the country.

This is indeed a bizarre distortion of reality. The Muslim community may occasionally be given some token concesison because they represent an important vote bank.

However, in reality, they are in no position even to protect themselves from continued pogroms and riots. They are continually losing even the precarious foothold they once had in the country's political economy. Increasing and deliberate steps have been taken to reduce the Muslims to total dependence and immiseration, and yet these some Muslims are, paradoxically, being accused of hijacking the majority community and running the country. This is nothing but an attempt to justify further violence and discrimination against them, to make it appear as if the majority community is being forced to act in this inhuman way only in self defence.

Unfortunately, the Muslim leaders and large sections of the Muslim intelligentsia have bartered away the real interests of their community for a very dubious pittance. The ruling party has declared that it will soon be presenting a common civil code which any citizen will have the right to opt for. Given the political, intellectual, and moral bankruptcy of our parliamentarians, the task of evolving an egalitarian civil code that protects the human rights of all Indian's — including those forced into dependence and poverty — cannot be left to them or to the ruling party. Even if the rulers were to create a special constituent assembly for this purpose, they would, in all likelihood, fill it with forces which would unleash a further assault on human rights.

It is, therefore, imperative that the task of preparing this code be taken up by those groups who are committed to and have worked towards the human rights of all those oppressed in our society — people of disadvantaged minorities such as Muslims and tribals, as well as women in general.

Given the escalating scale of violence and injustice, we must immediately and urgently re-think and re-evaluate the very foundations of our society, using human rights as the touchstone rather than the misleading, manipulative and vague ritual-chant 'national unity and integrity' so favoured by our rulers.

10 May 1986

EVENTS

1. A letter sent to Prime Minister Rajiv Gandhi by more than 200 Muslim women from Madras on 13 October 1985, to strongly protest against the move to amend the Constitution to exempt Muslims from section 125 of the Cr. P.C.
2. Meeting held on 13 September 1985 in Chikhli organized by the Buldana Muslim Personal Law Committee to protest against the judgement.
3. The Bharatiya Janata Party organized the "Muslim Social Justice Conference" in Bombay on Monday, 30 September 1985 and resolved to extend all help to Muslim women in their struggle for justice.
4. 30–35 thousand Muslim women attended the conference in Malegaon (Maharashtra) and condemned, in a resolution, the Supreme Court judgement.
5. Conference organized by the Bhiwandi Muslim Personal Law Action Committee (Women) on 30 September to protest against the Supreme Court judgement.
6. Students of the Islamic Movement of India organized a conference for Muslim women on 5 October 1985 in Bombay at the Nagpada Neighbourhood House.
7. Complete strike in West Bengal on 5 October 1985 at the appeal of the All India Muslim Personal Law Board action committee; black flags were hoisted.
8. Meeting arranged by Press Asia International, New Delhi, on 9 October 1985 to discuss the rights of Muslim women and specially to discuss the problem of maintenance of divorced women.

9. Two day conference on 11 – 12 October 1985 organized by Jamiate-Ulema-e-Hind at Madani Hall, New Delhi. More than 600 maulanas, maulvis, writers and Islamic scholars participated from various states such as U.P., Bihar, Delhi, A.P., Maharashtra, Gujarat, M.P., Bengal, Assam, Haryana, H.P., Rajasthan, Karnataka, Tamil Nadu, Orissa, Tripura, Punjab and Jammu and Kashmir.

10. Meeting organized by the Maharashtra Action Committee (women's wing) of the All India Muslim Law Board, in Bombay on Sunday, 13 October 1985, to support Muslim personal law.

11. A case filed by the Hindu Mahasabha in the Supreme Court challenging Muslim personal law on 14 October 1985 in Hyderabad.

12. A huge morcha and conference organized by Anjumane Islahul Muslemin on 18 October 1985 in Indore. It seemed like a flood of mankind. All Muslim organizations, shops, mutton market, etc. were closed; even auto-rickshaws and thailas were off the road.

13. Conference organized at Siwan by the Idara-e-Shariyyah, Patna, Bihar, on 26–27 October 1985 to protest against the Supreme Court judgement in the Shah Bano case.

14. 'Struggle is the only way to solve the Muslim problem.' Seminars arranged by Jamia Millia Islamia on 31 October 1985.

15. Maulana Udaidulla Khan arrested and released on bail for giving provocative speeches in public meetings (Bombay, 2 November 1985).

16. Stone-throwing between two groups of Muslims in Parbhani on 8 November 1985. Lathiacharge by police at the time of morchas.

17. Shah Bano rejected by her letter of 11 November 1985, the judgement of the Supreme Court given on 23 April 1985.

18. 'Shariat courts to be established all over India.' Maulana Abdul Hasan Ali Nadvi, chairman of the All India Muslim Personal Law Board, told the press this in a conference in Calicut on 13 November 1985.

19. Police Commissioner of Bombay issued an order, on 15 November 1985, to Maulana Udaidulla to leave Bombay within twenty-four hours, in view of the law and order situation.

20. Shah Bano declared in Indore, on 15 November 1985, that her refusal to accept the Supreme Court judgement was not made under any pressure.

21. All India Muslim Personal Law Conference organized by the Madresa Anwarul Ulum at Muzaffarpur on 16 November 1985.

22. Conference organized by the All India Muslim Personal Law Committee, Muzaffarpur, on 16–17 November 1985.

23. A morcha organized in favour of Muslim personal law was stoned before it could march, by an opposing party, in Ahmednagar, on 18 November 1985.

24. More than 5 lakh Muslims of Bombay march to Mantrayala on 20 November 1985. Muslim business establishments closed from Colaba to Mulund, and Churchgate to Borivli to protest against the Supreme Court judgement. The rally was organized by the Bombay Muslim Federation.

25. Police fired a few rounds to quell a violent mob protesting against the Supreme Court judgement in Patna on 24 November 1985.

26. Lakhs of Muslims marched to the collectorate to give a memorandum in Gaya on 28 November 1985.

27. Procession organized by the Muslim Majlis in Lucknow on 30 November 1985.

28. Seminar organized by the Clarity Friends Circle, Bombay, on 30 November 1985 in support of the Supreme Court judgement.

29. One-day seminar in Akola, on 2 December 1985, organized by the Students Islamic Movement against the Supreme Court judgement.

30. Shri Kanayyalal Maharaj and Shri Jamna Singh pooh-poohed the alleged interference in Muslim personal law by the Supreme Court in a conference in Jamshedpur on 4 December 1985.

31. Conference organized by the All-India Momin Conference, Delhi, on 8 December 1985 to support Muslim personal law.

32. Seminar on the uniform civil code conducted in Cochin on Sunday, 8 December 1985 by the Bharatheeya Vichar Kendra. The topic was: 'Common Civil Code not anti-Islam'.

33. Rally by the Hindu Jagaran Manch, Bombay, on 9 December 1985 in favour of a common civil code.

34. A meeting of opposition leaders convened by Prime Minister Rajiv Gandhi on 17 December 1985 in New Delhi. The meeting decided to initiate a study on the modifications made in Muslim personal law in Islamic and other secular countries.

35. The Bharatiya Janata Party, Bombay, decided on 20 December 1985 to observe 1986 as the common civil code year. They also appealed to Mr Rajiv Gandhi to announce, in no uncertain terms, that the Government would not yield to the demand for separate laws for Muslims.

36. A high-power Muslim delegation comprising scholars, parliamentarians and others called on Prime Minister Rajiv Gandhi on 21 December 1985 in connection with the verdict in the Shah Bano case.

37. A meeting arranged by the Maharashtra Muslim Advocates Forum on 21 December 1985 to organize a convention of All India Muslim Advocates on 15–16 February 1986.

38. Babu Jagjivan Ram requested Mr Rajiv Gandhi to take concrete steps to protect Muslim personal law on 22 December 1985 in New Delhi.

39. The Institute of Islamic Studies Bombay held a workshop on 22 December 1985, in Bombay, on the 'Evolution of the Shariat'.

40. Conference organized by the Anjumane Falah-e-Millat, Banaras (Varanasi) during January 1986 to protest against the Supreme Court judgement.

41. More than 3 lakh Muslims marched, in Dhanbad, on 6 January 1986, to protest against the Supreme Court judgement.

42. The Jamat-I-Islami Hind organized a one-day seminar, on 11 January 1986, in Bombay, on the uniform civil code.

43. More than one thousand Muslim women held a dharna, at the office of the district magistrate, Darbhanga, Bihar, on 19 January 1986, in support of their 13 demands.

44. The Shariat Panchayat established in Akola on 21 January 1986.

45. Communal riots in Sangamner as reported, by Muslim Personal Law Committee, Maharashtra, on 23 January 1986.

46. Mr Danial Latifi told newsmen in Calcutta, on 29 January 1986, that the Supreme Court had not interfered with Muslim personal law in the Shah Bano case. The court has merely granted, to a woman, the rights guaranteed to her under law and under the Indian statutes.

47. The women's wing of the Rashtriya Ekjoot held a four-hour dharna in Bombay, on 30 January 1986, to demand a common civil code and to hail the Supreme Court judgement.

48. The All India Muslim Personal Law Board, New Delhi, decided, on 4 February 1986, to launch a country-wide agitation from 21 February 1986 in support of their demands which include the protection of Muslim personal law.

49. On 21 February 1986, major opposition parties in New Delhi frustrated the Government's attempts to immediately introduce a bill in Parliament. This bill,

seeking to protect the rights of divorced Muslim women, was a bid to pacify a section of Muslims agitating against the Supreme Court judgement.

50. Muslim women, who had suffered the rigours of divorce, members of the Muslim Satyashodhak Mandal of Pune, and other social organizations made an impassioned plea, on 22 February 1986, for a reconsideration of the proposed amendment. The amendment would deny divorced Muslim women the right to maintenance allowance – a right which existed under the civil laws.

51. The Muslim women bill was introduced in the Lok Sabha on 25 February 1986 amidst stiff opposition from the opposition members who described it as an affront to women.

52. The minister of state for energy, Mr Arif Mohammad Khan resigned, on 26 February 1986, protest against the controversial bill pertaining to divorced Muslim women's right to maintenance, introduced in the Lok Sabha.

53. Shah Bano went to court again claiming a mehr of three thousand silver coins from her former husband. She has filed a case in the lower court of Indore.

54. On 2 March 1986 morchas to the houses of several MPs were taken out by Rashtriya Ekjoot, Bombay, to press the demand for a common civil code and to protest against the 'retrograde' bill. Hundreds of women, representing about 15 women's organizations in New Delhi, also held a rally, on 6 March 1986, on the Boat Club lawns to protest against the Muslim women bill, which they described as a "direct attack on the fundamental rights of women".

55. Six organizations in Bombay held a joint morcha on 17 March 1986 at Churchgate station demanding retention of section 125 of the Cr. P. C. which ensures maintenance rights of divorced women irrespective of their religious background.

56. Morchas organized by the Women's Liberation Movement, in Bombay, on 21 March 1986. 35 women's organizations came together on a common platform to demand a new secular family code and the withdrawal of the proposed bill.

57. Public meeting organized by a women's body, Karmikar, on 22 March 1986, in New Delhi, urged people to unite and protest against the Muslim women bill as it was not only un-Islamic and unconstitutional, but also negated the very basic provisions of justice. The speakers included senior advocates.

58. The well-known social worker, Baba Amte, criticized the Muslim women bill before Parliament on 22 March 1986, in New Delhi. He warned that the bill would bring about "another ugly rift in the country".

59. Memorandum given on 27 March 1986 to Mr Rajiv Gandhi in New Delhi by the Muslim Women's Graduate Association, Bombay, favouring the Muslim women bill with a request that the said bill be passed.

60. The Muslim Personal Law Board, New Delhi, suggested a further amendment to the Muslim women bill which would give the children of divorced women maintenance provision for a longer period.

61. The Congress (I) MPs, who had reservations over the controversial Muslim women's bill were directed, on 10 April 1986, not to air their views on the bill or to unnecessarily link Muslim fundamentalism with it.

62. Supporters of the Muslim women bill disrupted the Indo-Pak mushairas held in Hyderabad, on 19 April 1986, under the chairmanship of the union commerce minister, P. Shiv Shankar. A large section of the 5,000-strong audience objected to the presence of three Urdu poets — who reportedly opposed the bill.

63. Meeting organized by the Jamia Islahul Banal in Bombay, on 20 April 1986, to support Muslim personal law.

64. A handful of progressive Muslims led by Mrs Saeeda Khan took out a morcha, on 23 April 1986, from Churchgate to Mantralaya in Bombay to protest against the Muslim women's bill.

Appendix

Union minister of state, Mr Z. A. Ansari, brought into focus the opposition to the Muslim women bill among a section of Congressmen in Trivandrum on 25 April 1986.

66. The BJP president, Mr L. K. Advani, made a last-minute appeal to the prime minister not to stand on prestige and to refer the Muslim women bill to the Supreme Court through the president (Bhopal, on 27 April 1986).

67. The prime minister, Mr Rajiv Gandhi, gave expression, on 30 April 1986, to his determination to see the bill through in the current session of Parliament. The bill would be considered by the Lok Sabha on 5–6 May 1986.

68. A memorandum, signed by over 6,000 people from all parts of the country, handed over to Mr A. K. Sen (law minister) in New Delhi on 1 May 1986, by the representatives of the Forum against Oppression of Women. The memorandum demanded the withdrawal of the Muslim women bill.

69. 15 Muslim members of the Janata Party resigned, on 1 May 1986, from the primary membership of the party, to protest against the resolution on the Muslim women bill adopted at the 4th national convention in Pune.

70. The former union minister, Mr Arif Mohammed Khan, reiterated, on 2 May 1986, in Cochin, that the Muslim women bill was anti-constitutional, anti-Islam and inhuman. He pointed out that, even if the bill was passed in the Lok Sabha, Parliament could amend its provisions later.

71. The opposition parties decided, on 3 May 1986, in New Delhi, to press for a division when the controversial Muslim women bill would be voted in the Loka Sabha after discussion.

72. The socialist leader, Mr Raj Narain, in New Delhi, on 3 May 1986, began a 72-hour hunger-strike to protest against the Muslim women bill which was to come up in Parliament.

73. Muslim lawyers and others plan to fight the Muslim women bill, if it is passed, in the Supreme Court and the bill would also be challenged in international forums. There are many educated Muslim women who would also challenge this bill.

74. In the Lok Sabha, on 5 May 1986, the Muslim bill was well on its way to being passed. The critics of the Muslim women bill, from the opposition benches, walked out of the Lok Sabha, when the house rejected their amendments for referring the bill.

75. Women's organizations in the capital protested against the introduction of the Muslim women bill in the Lok Sabha, by blocking the main entrance of the Parliament house with iron chains tied to their wrists and waists.

76. Over a hundred women courted arrest in front of Parliament, on 5 May 1986, in the afternoon, shouting "down with the black bill". The demonstrators shouted protest slogans against the bill and demanding the scrapping of the bill.

77. The bill on divorced Muslim women was strongly opposed at a symposium held on "Secular family laws and the rights of women" organized by the Indian School of Social Science, in Bombay, on 10 May 1986.

78. In Pune, on 13 May 1986, about 200 women, many of them Muslim divorcees, staged demonstrations in front of the Collector's office to register their strong protest against the Muslim women bill.

79. Representatives of 14 'progressive' Muslim organizations from all over India decided, on 16 May 1986, in New Delhi, to form a joint action committee in June, at Lucknow, to launch an agitation against communal forces, the passage of the Muslim women bill, and for the preparation of a compulsory common civil code.

80.   The president, Zail Singh, signed the bill on 20 May 1986, in New Delhi.
81.   The Muslim women's bill was challenged in the Supreme Court by the Anjuman-e-Taraqqi Pasand Muslim group, on 22 May 1986. The hearing will be on 29 May 1986, in the court of Justice S. C. Mukherjee.
82.   The first case in Kerala, seeking relief under the new Muslim Women Act, has been filed in the sessions court, at Trichur, by Mr Hamzai of Koorkencherry on 21 June 1986.